365
GREAT
MOMENTS IN
BIBLE
HISTORY

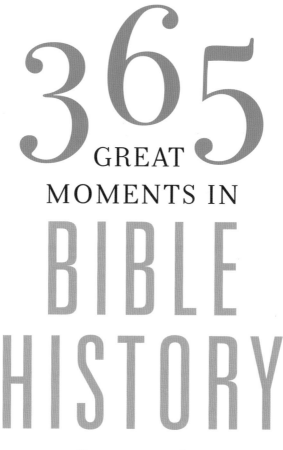

365

GREAT
MOMENTS IN

BIBLE
HISTORY

Key Events that
Affected Humanity's Future

ED STRAUSS

BARBOUR BOOKS
An Imprint of Barbour Publishing, Inc.

CONTENTS

INTRODUCTION

» Welcome to *365 Great Moments in Bible History*, the most pivotal, important stories in the Bible, arranged in chronological order. The events they describe are key moments in God's interactions with mankind. His continual interventions—both merciful deliverances and righteous judgments—reveal His great love, wisdom, and guiding hand. These, together with humanity's actions and responses, are the hinges upon which history hangs.

This book is ideal for you if you're new to the faith, and it will help you gain an understanding of what the Bible is all about. In addition, each story focuses on a clear lesson that you can benefit from. Taken together, these individual pieces of the puzzle make up God's Big Picture and reveal His overall purposes in history.

This book will also benefit you if you've been a Christian for many years and already know most of these stories. That's because it contains "treasures new and old" (see Matthew 13:52). It not only unearths scores of little-known Bible incidents; it also describes familiar episodes from fresh and fascinating perspectives and sets them in their historical context.

These 365 readings can be read one a day as a yearly devotional or studied several at a time to help you get a deeper perspective of the workings of God.

Note: The order of events in the Gospels is based largely upon the acclaimed 1978 volume *A Harmony of the Gospels*, by Robert L. Thomas and Stanley N. Gundry.

» Light isn't the first thing God created—"the heavens and the earth" predate it—but the Bible places light within the first day of Creation.

"Let there be light" are God's first recorded words, and they immediately brought definition to the primordial world. Until light appeared, the earth was "formless and empty" and "darkness was over the surface of the deep" (Genesis 1:1–3 NIV).

Suddenly, though, half of creation was bathed in a glowing energy that God called "day." Though darkness would remain (as "night"), everything that God would later bring into existence could now interact differently, more effectively, with the rest of Creation. That's undoubtedly why God "saw that the light was good" (Genesis 1:4 NIV).

Light travels at an incredible speed (more than 186,000 miles per second in the vacuum of space), and it takes sunlight between eight and nine minutes to reach the earth. But it's interesting to note that there was light *before* the sun existed—God made the sun on Creation's fourth day.

Light's importance is that it allows us to see and understand the physical world around us. Jesus, as "the light of the world" (John 9:5 NIV), illuminates the spiritual realm.

"Let there be light" are the Bible's first recorded words from God (Genesis 1:3).

» The Bible opens with these sweeping words: "In the beginning God created the heavens and the earth. The earth was formless and empty" (Genesis 1:1–2 NLT). Not only was the earth initially formless and empty, but the entire universe was a chaotic mass of unformed energy and matter. Even the stars hadn't coalesced yet!

We live in what is called "a fine-tuned universe." Even secular scientists are forced to admit that the laws of the universe seem deliberately designed to make life possible and are therefore proof of an intelligent Creator.

But at this early stage, only the raw stuff of creation existed—from which all of God's order and structure and beauty would spring. No place in the universe was yet fit for life. But God had a plan to create a habitable world for mankind.

"For the LORD is God, and he created the heavens and earth and put everything in place. He made the world to be lived in, not to be a place of empty chaos" (Isaiah 45:18 NLT).

Do you enjoy life? You ought to! God carefully designed everything to make life on earth possible.

3. CREATION OF PLANTS \\ GENESIS 1:11–13

» By the third morning of Creation, the earth was fully formed. That's when God caused the entire planet—from east to west, from the north pole to the south—to burst forth with a dizzying profusion of plant life.

Perhaps you've heard of the Cambrian explosion, when a plethora of life forms suddenly and inexplicably appeared in the fossil record. This was the Genesis explosion.

The Lord created all plants, from delicate orchids in the sun-dappled jungles to mighty redwoods towering along fog-shrouded coasts. You get the definite impression that Almighty God had a great deal of fun being creative. But He had immensely practical purposes in mind as well.

"The living God, who made the heavens and the earth. . .has shown kindness by giving you rain from heaven and crops in their seasons; he provides you with plenty of food and fills your hearts with joy" (Acts 14:15, 17 NIV). God created plants not only to awe us into silence with their beauty, but to serve as food. They nourish our bodies and give us energy.

But underlying this basic human need and woven throughout the fabric of God's plan was His desire to fill our hearts with joy.

4. CREATION OF ANIMALS \\ GENESIS 1:20–25

» On the fifth and sixth days of Creation, God designed every imaginable kind of animal—from colorful clownfish nestling among sea anemones to jaguars lurking in steaming rain forests; from pterodactyls soaring above windswept cliffs to monarch butterflies fluttering over delicate flowers; from thundering herds of shaggy bison to reclusive mountain gorillas.

Animals filled the rivers and the seas, the forests and the plains. In fact, every gram of soil on earth swarmed with millions of microscopic life forms. Even heat vents at the bottoms of the oceans and rocks far beneath the earth's surface were not forgotten. The entire planet Earth teemed with an astonishing variety of life.

God filled every crack and corner of the globe with living creatures, great and small. He had commanded, "Let the waters *abound* with an *abundance* of living creatures" (Genesis 1:20 NKJV, emphasis added). All the earth hastened to obey God's commands and filled with a bewildering abundance of fauna.

After God had created all these myriad species, He stamped every single one of them with His personal blessing—a blessing He intended to endure until the end of time: "And God blessed them, saying, 'Be fruitful and multiply'" (Genesis 1:22 NKJV).

5. CREATION OF MAN \\ GENESIS 1:26–28; 2:7

» Finally, God finished creating all animal life. The pale blue globe called Earth was overflowing with an unbelievably rich diversity of flora and fauna. The planet's entire interdependent ecosystem was up and running. Everything seemed complete. But it wasn't complete.

The triune God already enjoyed eternal communion. And God had created millions of angels before the first star came into being. When He "laid the earth's foundation. . .all the angels shouted for joy" (Job 38:4, 7 NIV). But even communion with angels wasn't enough. God longed for sentient physical beings to share His Creation with.

"God said, 'Let Us make man in Our image, according to Our likeness'. . .Then the LORD God formed man of dust from the ground, and breathed into his nostrils the breath of life; and man became a living being" (Genesis 1:26; 2:7 NASB).

Adam was created on the same day as the land animals, but though he had a physical body like them, he also had an eternal spirit. And this spirit was made in the image of God—literally designed for communion with the Father.

"For God is Spirit, so those who worship him must worship in spirit" (John 4:24 NLT).

Adam's eternal spirit was created in the image of God.

6. CREATION OF WOMAN \\ GENESIS 1:27; 2:18–24

» God created Adam and Eve on the sixth day, and like man, woman is also a spiritual being—made in the image of God. "So God created human beings in his own image. In the image of God he created them; male and female he created them" (Genesis 1:27 NLT).

However, Eve was created differently than any other living being. Every male and female animal was made from the earth. God said, "Let the land produce living creatures." And man was created "from the dust of the ground" (Genesis 1:24; 2:7 NIV). In contrast, the first woman was formed from a rib taken from the man's side.

Why did God create Eve in such a unique way? Because men and women are not simply animals, creatures of the earth, and God intended their relationship to be more than a physical union driven by sexual instincts.

Very likely, the female was taken from the male because human beings were created to have a relationship with—and spiritual union to—not only God (1 Corinthians 6:17), but each other. Men and women become "one flesh" (Genesis 2:24 KJV), but they are *also* to experience intimate spiritual union.

7. FALL OF SATAN \\ ISAIAH 14:12–15; EZEKIEL 28:11–17

» Angels, archangels, and other mighty heavenly beings called cherubim and seraphim were created before the physical universe came into existence—and they rejoiced at Creation. They worshipped God and gave Him great joy. But some of them weren't content with their places in His kingdom.

A highly exalted cherub named Lucifer ("Light bearer") had a position of great majesty and authority. But he was envious of God and aspired to be worshipped in His place.

Ezekiel describes his rebellion, saying, "You were the anointed cherub. . . . You were perfect in your ways from the day you were created, till iniquity was found in you. . . . Therefore I cast you as a profane thing out of the mountain of God" (Ezekiel 28:14–16 NKJV).

Isaiah declares, "How you are fallen from heaven, O Lucifer, son of the morning!" (Isaiah 14:12 NKJV).

Satan didn't rebel alone. And he didn't fall alone. He led one-third of the angels of heaven in his great rebellion, and they were cast out with him (Revelation 12:3–4, 7–9).

When Lucifer fell, he became known as the devil or Satan (the Accuser), and when his angels fell, they became known as evil spirits or demons.

» Adam and Eve lived in the Garden of Eden, a breathtakingly beautiful paradise. They simply picked their food off the trees. They should've been content—and they *were* until the serpent deceived them and made them dissatisfied.

The serpent convinced Adam and Eve to be dissatisfied with all they had in the Garden of Eden.

God had told Adam that he was free to eat the fruit of any tree in the garden, including the fruit of the Tree of Life. But they were not to eat the fruit of the Tree of the Knowledge of Good and Evil. Eve knew this command. She also knew that the punishment for disobeying was death.

But one day the serpent tricked Eve. He told her that God was withholding the best from them, that if she would eat the fruit of this tree, it would make her wise. She would know good and evil just like God. He convinced her to disbelieve God—she wouldn't *actually* die.

This serpent was none other than "that ancient serpent called the devil, or Satan, who leads the whole world astray" (Revelation 12:9 NIV).

Eve was deceived, and she not only ate the forbidden fruit herself, but gave some to Adam. And their disobedience brought physical and spiritual death upon humanity.

9. GOD CURSES THE EARTH \\ GENESIS 3:8-24

» Because Adam and Eve sinned, several curses overwhelmed the world. First, their once-perfect physical bodies became mortal. God informed Adam that he would "return to the ground. . .for you are dust, and to dust you shall return" (Genesis 3:19 NASB). This would fulfill God's warning that eating the forbidden fruit brought death.

Their disobedience also brought a curse upon the entire natural world. God said, "Cursed is the ground. . .thorns and thistles it shall bring forth for you" (Genesis 3:17–18 NKJV). Paul tells us that as a result, all creation came under "bondage to decay" (Romans 8:21 NIV).

Up till then, they'd had an easy life. But God now told Eve that she would only give birth by "painful labor," and He now told Adam that he would only produce food by "painful toil" (Genesis 3:16–17 NIV).

Amazingly, a promise of redemption was made when God cursed the serpent. God told the devil that there would be war between him and a descendant of the woman—the Messiah: "You will strike his heel [seek to kill Jesus]" but "he will crush your head [deliver a mortal blow]" (Genesis 3:15 NIV). (See also 1 John 3:8.)

10. CAIN AND ABEL GIVE OFFERINGS \\ GENESIS 4:1–7

» Adam and Eve had two sons, whom they named Cain and Abel. Cain worked the soil and grew vegetables, fruit, and grain. Abel spent his days watching the family's sheep.

When it came time to make an offering, Cain offered some of his produce. God was still speaking to humanity (Genesis 4:6, 9) but didn't acknowledge Cain's offering. However, Abel "brought of the firstborn of his flock" (Genesis 4:4 NKJV), and "God spoke well of his offerings" (Hebrews 11:4 NIV).

Why? Though God would later command animal offerings, as Abel provided here, Cain apparently made his offering from inappropriate motives.

"It was by faith that Abel brought a more acceptable offering to God than Cain did. Abel's offering gave evidence that he was a righteous man" (Hebrews 11:4 NLT).

Why did Abel obey God and Cain disobey? Because that's what they were in the *habit* of doing. "Cain had been doing what was evil, and his brother had been doing what was righteous" (1 John 3:12 NLT). May we, like Abel, continually obey God.

» When God refused to accept his offering, "Cain was very angry" (Genesis 4:5 NIV). He was seething with indignation.

Knowing where such anger could lead, God warned him: "If you do what is right, will you not be accepted? But if you do not do what is right, sin is crouching at your door; it desires to have you, but you must rule over it" (Genesis 4:6–7 NIV).

Cain committed the world's first murder by killing his brother.

Peter warned that "your adversary the devil walks about like a roaring lion, seeking whom he may devour" (1 Peter 5:8 NKJV). In Cain's case, the devil was no longer prowling around. He had *found* someone to devour. Thoughts of violence were even now crouching at the door of Cain's heart.

Rage desired to overcome him. The solution was to exercise self-control. This Cain failed to do. The result was the world's first crime. Cain murdered his brother then buried him to cover his evil deed. But God had seen everything.

Cain was banished from the very thing that had given him his sense of worth. From then on, he would no longer till the soil, but be a restless wanderer. "There is no peace. . .for the wicked" (Isaiah 48:22 NKJV).

12. WICKEDNESS INCREASES ON EARTH \\ GENESIS 6:1-13

» In the second generation from Adam, "people first began to worship the LORD by name" (Genesis 4:26 NLT). Life was difficult, and mankind was painfully aware of what they'd lost. So some began seeking God's presence and His favor.

A few generations later, Enoch walked so closely with God that He literally took him from the world (Genesis 5:23–24). But Enoch was the exception.

As human beings began to multiply, they increasingly followed their *own* selfish desires. By Noah's day, society had become thoroughly corrupt.

"The LORD saw how great the wickedness of the human race had become on the earth, and that every inclination of the thoughts of the human heart was only evil all the time" (Genesis 6:5 NIV). In fact, "the earth had become corrupt and was filled with violence. . .for everyone on earth was corrupt" (Genesis 6:11–12 NLT).

Finally, people became *so* depraved that, so it appears, they broke the most basic rules of God's natural order and began having intercourse with fallen angels (Genesis 6:1–4). The result was giant offspring called Nephilim. God had blessed man and woman and told them to have children—but *these* actions brought a curse.

13. GOD CALLS NOAH \\ GENESIS 5:28–29; 6:6-10

» The world was so wicked that God regretted that He'd even made mankind. So He determined to destroy all life on earth with a colossal flood.

But hidden in a corner of this corrupt world was one righteous man. Noah had been raised in a family who'd had a rough time of it. When Noah was born, his father said, "May he bring us relief from our work and the painful labor of farming this ground that the LORD has cursed" (Genesis 5:29 NLT).

But despite Noah's hard upbringing—or perhaps because of it—he sought God.

"Noah was a righteous man, blameless among the people of his time, and he walked faithfully with God." Because he obeyed God and communed with Him daily, "Noah found favor in the eyes of the LORD" (Genesis 6:8–9 NIV).

Noah chose God, so God chose Noah—and decided to spare him and his family and thus preserve a remnant of mankind.

In a world that seems to have gone crazy, don't think that God ever overlooks or forgets about you. "The eyes of the LORD are in every place, keeping watch on the evil *and the good*" (Proverbs 15:3 NKJV, emphasis added).

14. NOAH BUILDS THE ARK \\ GENESIS 6:13–22; 7:1–9

» God told Noah to construct a ship "450 feet long, 75 feet wide, and 45 feet high" (Genesis 6:15 NLT). It needed to be that huge to hold pairs of every land animal on earth, as well as food to last for over a year.

Noah was likely living beside a forest, because such an ambitious project required untold tons of cypress wood.

Many people believe it took 120 years to build the ark because Genesis 6:3 (NASB) says that mankind's "days shall be one hundred and twenty years." Finally, the day came when Noah was finished, so he took the animals on board. Then he and his family boarded.

Since Noah was the only human being moved with godly fear, he and his family were the only ones saved on the ark.

"By faith Noah, being divinely warned of things not yet seen, moved with godly fear, prepared an ark for the saving of his household, by which he condemned the world and became heir of the righteousness which is according to faith" (Hebrews 11:7 NKJV).

How did Noah's actions condemn the world? Because not one other person on earth was moved with godly fear, so no one helped him prepare the ark—and no one got on board.

Today, Jesus is our ark, saving us from a doomed world.

15. THE FLOOD STRIKES // GENESIS 7:10–24; 8:1–19

❯❯ The ark was built. The food was loaded. The animals were on board. Then Noah and his family sat inside the ship for seven days, waiting for the end. Their unbelieving neighbors must have had a good time mocking them.

Suddenly, powerful quakes ruptured the crust of the earth and vast subterranean oceans burst out with tremendous force, shooting water thousands of feet into the air. A monstrous rainstorm engulfed the entire planet for forty days.

The floodwaters rose swiftly, sweeping away everything in their path. Those who survived the initial cataclysm sought refuge on hilltops—but these too were soon engulfed by the churning, rising waters.

"Everything that breathed and lived on dry land died. God wiped out every living thing on the earth. . . . All were destroyed. The only people who survived were Noah and those with him" (Genesis 7:22–23 NLT).

The waters finally receded, and the ark came to rest on the mountains of Ararat. Then Noah and every living creature on the ark stepped forth into a new world. Humanity had been given a second chance.

16. BUILDING THE TOWER OF BABEL \\ GENESIS 11:1–9

❯❯ After Noah's family emerged from the ark, the population of the earth increased rapidly. At that time, all people lived together and spoke the same language. They all traveled to what is now southern Iraq, at the junction of the Tigris and Euphrates Rivers. There they found a warm climate and fertile land, so they settled down.

Noah's descendants tried to build a great tower rather than scatter around the world (Genesis 11:4).

Now, God's first command to mankind had been, "Be fruitful and increase in number; fill the earth"

(Genesis 1:28 NIV). This command was still in force. They were to populate the *entire* earth.

But Noah's descendants decided to stay together and build a great city with a tower that stood high over the plains. They reasoned that this focal point "will. . .keep us from being scattered all over the world" (Genesis 11:4 NLT). So they began to build the tower.

When God saw what they were doing, He caused them to speak different languages. One group of people couldn't understand what the next group was saying. Unable to work together or even to live together, they scattered throughout the earth.

When people set their hearts to disobey God's commands, He doesn't hesitate to bring their plans to nothing.

17. GOD CALLS ABRAM \\ GENESIS 11:31–32; 12:1–5

» Terah and his family lived in Ur, in southern Mesopotamia. One day, he took Abram (Abraham), Sarai, and Lot and traveled north to Haran. There they lived many years and prospered. But after Terah's death, God called Abram to leave this comfortable life.

God told him, "Get out of your country, from your family and from your father's house, to a land that I will show you. I will make you a great nation; I will bless you" (Genesis 12:1–2 NKJV). Abram obeyed. He packed up and headed south to Canaan.

This was not the first time God had spoken to him. "The God of glory appeared to our father Abraham when he was in Mesopotamia, before he dwelt in Haran, and said to him, 'Get out of your country and from your relatives, and come to a land that I will show you'" (Acts 7:2–3 NKJV).

Terah had apparently moved north at his son's request, but when they got as far as Haran, decided to settle there.

Going to Canaan was Abram's call, not Terah's. That's why Abram had to step out from his father's shadow to fulfill his *own* destiny. We must do the same.

18. ABRAM LETS LOT CHOOSE \\ GENESIS 13:5–17

» The land of Canaan had a dry climate with slight rains and at the moment was recovering from a prolonged drought. There wasn't enough grazing land to sustain all Abram's and Lot's flocks and herds. Rather than quarrel over pasture, Abram decided it was best to separate.

He and Lot climbed to the top of a hill and surveyed the land below. Abram gave his nephew first choice. "Let's part company," he said. "If you go to the left, I'll go to the right; if you go to the right, I'll go to the left" (Genesis 13:9 NIV).

Instead of saying, "No, Uncle, you choose first," Lot glanced at the dry hills of Canaan. Then he gazed upon the well-watered plain of the Jordan. It was like the Garden of Eden. Lot chose the lush valley.

After he left, God told Abram to look to the north, to the south, to the east, and to the west. He told him that every bit of land he could see was his—including the portion Lot had just chosen to settle in.

When you possess such great promises—as we *do* (Romans 8:32)— you can afford to be generous.

19. SHEPHERDS BATTLE KINGS \\ GENESIS 14:1–24

» When Abram lived in Canaan, the lands east of the Jordan River, from Bashan to the plains south of the Dead Sea, were paying tribute to Kedorlaomer and other foreign kings. But after Lot settled in Sodom, the kings of these cities revolted against their foreign oppressors.

Within a year, Kedorlaomer arrived with a coalition of five armies on a punitive raid. They sacked city after city and, in a final battle, crushed the armies of Sodom, Gomorrah, Admah, Zeboiim, and Zoar. Kedorlaomer then took all their riches and headed home.

It wasn't Abram's fight. He was peacefully tending sheep in Canaan, west of the Jordan. But they had taken his nephew Lot, and that made it Abram's concern. Hastily assembling his 318 shepherds and his Amorite allies, Abram raced in pursuit.

He overtook Kedorlaomer's armies to the north and struck them in a surprise night attack. He recovered everything they'd stolen— including Lot and all his possessions.

How could a coalition of shepherds defeat five armies of professional soldiers? Melchizedek summed it up when he said, "Blessed be Abram by God Most High. . .who has defeated your enemies for you" (Genesis 14:19–20 NLT).

God still fights for His people today.

20. GOD PROMISES ABRAHAM A SON \\ GENESIS 15:1–7

» The sun had set, and darkness settled over Canaan. Abram was in his tent, unable to sleep. He was troubled by the fact that he was now old but still had no son. God had promised him Canaan, but Abram had no children to inherit the land. Suddenly God spoke: "Do not be afraid, Abram. I am your shield, your exceedingly great reward" (Genesis 15:1 NKJV).

Three mysterious visitors told Abram that he would have a son (Genesis 18).

It was wonderful that God was a shield always protecting him. It was deeply rewarding knowing God personally. But Abram was concerned that he had no children. When he died, his servant Eliezer would inherit everything.

God informed Abram that this wasn't so. His own descendants would inherit this promise.

God led Abram out of his tent. He told him to look up at the immense vault of heaven and to count all the stars—if indeed he could count them. Then God informed him that this was how many descendants he would have.

"Abram believed the Lord, and he credited it to him as righteousness" (Genesis 15:6 NIV).

God began by talking about their relationship and ended by describing Abram's standing with Him. The promise of descendants came from this close relationship.

21. CONCEIVING ISHMAEL \\ GENESIS 16:1–16

» Years passed after God's promise to Abram. But Sarai his wife failed to become pregnant. She felt intense pressure to produce a child but was incapable of doing so.

Then Sarai had a thought: God had promised Abram that a child from his body would be his heir—but He hadn't specified that *she* must bear that child. According to the customs of that day, if a wife gave her slave to her husband, any child the slave bore counted as a child of the wife. So Sarai told Abram to sleep with Hagar.

Hagar promptly became pregnant. This was supposed to be good news, but Hagar also began to despise barren Sarai. As a result, Sarai mistreated Hagar to the point where she fled into the desert to escape.

Fortunately, the angel of God intervened and stopped Hagar. He told her, "Go back to your mistress and submit to her" (Genesis 16:9 NIV). In other words, serve her with a humble attitude. And Hagar obeyed.

Like Sarai and Hagar, we can make a huge mess of relationships when we follow our own ideas and emotions. But all is not lost. God is able to restore even badly broken relationships.

22. DESTRUCTION OF SODOM AND GOMORRAH
\\ GENESIS 18:1–2, 16–22; 19:1–28

» One day three visitors—God and two angels in human form—visited Abram (now called Abraham). God warned Abraham that Sodom and Gomorrah were in imminent danger of being destroyed.

Later, the angels entered Sodom, where Lot took them into his home. That evening, however, a mob surrounded Lot's house and demanded that he bring the strangers out so they could violate them. In blazing power, the angels blinded them.

Just after sunrise, the angels led Lot and his family out the city gates and warned them, "Flee for your lives! Don't look back. . . ! Flee to the mountains or you will be swept away!" (Genesis 19:17 NIV).

No sooner had they reached the city of Zoar than a burning mixture rained down on Sodom and Gomorrah, utterly covering them. Perhaps God had caused the valley's vast bitumen deposits to erupt in a tremendous explosion, sending sulphur and salt over the cities. . .or perhaps He simply dropped His fire from the sky.

Lot and his daughters retreated behind the city walls, but Lot's wife stopped and gave a last longing look at her home—and became a "pillar of salt" (Genesis 19:26).

Her unwillingness to forsake a corrupt life became a warning to all generations. Jesus said, "Remember Lot's wife" (Luke 17:32 KJV).

23. BIRTH OF ISAAC \\ GENESIS 18:1–15; 21:1–7

» When God had visited Abraham, He'd shared some astonishing news: within a year his wife would bear a son. This was no small miracle. Sarah (formerly Sarai) was nearly ninety.

Abraham believed God. Being strong in faith, he overlooked the fact that he and Sarah were now old. "He did not waver at the promise of God through unbelief, but was. . .fully convinced that what He had promised He was also able to perform" (Romans 4:20–21 NKJV).

When Sarah heard the news, however, she could barely keep from laughing out loud—so God asked, "Why did Sarah laugh and say, 'Will I really have a child, now that I am old?' Is anything too hard for the LORD?" But Sarah lied, "I did not laugh." God replied, "Yes, you did laugh" (Genesis 18:13–15 NIV).

Sure enough, the following year Sarah gave birth to a son and called him Isaac, which means "laughter." The amazing miracle constantly made her laugh with joy, and everyone who heard about it couldn't keep from laughing as well (Genesis 21:6).

Everyone indeed! God made Sarah laugh, but *He* had the last laugh. "He who sits in the heavens laughs" (Psalm 2:4 NASB).

24. ISAAC IS NEARLY SACRIFICED \\ GENESIS 22:1–19

❯❯ One day God called, "Abraham!" He replied, "Here I am" (Genesis 22:1 NIV). By that he meant, "Here I am, ready to do whatever You ask."

God then shocked him by telling him to take his son Isaac—who was to inherit the promises God had given Abraham—and to sacrifice him on Mount Moriah. Abraham was stunned. But early the next morning he set out.

Abraham left his servants a distance away, promising, "We will worship and then we will come back to you" (Genesis 22:5 NIV). Then he and Isaac continued on. Once on the mount, Abraham built an altar, bound Isaac, laid him on the altar, and raised the knife.

Suddenly God called, "Abraham! Abraham!" Again

Abraham had faith that God would fulfill His promise even if he sacrificed his son Isaac.

Abraham answered, "Here I am" (Genesis 22:11 NIV). God then told him *not* to sacrifice Isaac—stating that because he had been willing to sacrifice his beloved son, God would bless him beyond measure.

How could Abraham say, "*We* will come back to you?" How could he believe that God's promises would be fulfilled if he sacrificed Isaac? The Bible explains: "Abraham reasoned that if Isaac died, God was able to bring him back to life again" (Hebrews 11:19 NLT).

25. FINDING A WIFE FOR ISAAC \\ GENESIS 23:1-2; 24:1-67; 25:20

» Isaac was forty years old and unmarried, but he was in no hurry. Then his mother, Sarah, died. Despite mourning himself, Abraham realized that Isaac was suffering intense grief. He decided that it was time for his son to get married.

The local Canaanite women wouldn't do. So Abraham sent his servant Eliezer far to the north to find a wife from his own kinspeople. Eliezer made the trek and eventually arrived at the well outside the town of Nahor.

He didn't want to pick just any woman as Isaac's wife. He wanted God's choice. So before the women came to get water, Eliezer prayed that the one God had chosen would volunteer to draw water for him and his men—*and* all their camels.

Rebekah did just that. Eliezer was so overjoyed that he made the marriage arrangements the same day, and not long after, Rebekah arrived in Abraham's camp and met Isaac. "Then. . .she became his wife, and he loved her. So Isaac was comforted after his mother's death" (Genesis 24:67 NKJV).

When we're facing a hard choice and ask God to lead us, He will. It may just take a little time.

26. ESAU SELLS HIS BIRTHRIGHT \\ GENESIS 25:19-34

» When Rebecca was pregnant with Jacob and Esau, God told her, "Two nations are in your womb. . .and the older will serve the younger" (Genesis 25:23 NIV). At least, that was the most *likely* interpretation.

The Hebrew words could also mean, "The greater one will serve the lesser one." That may have been how Isaac understood it. In other words, although Jacob was greater, he had to serve his brother simply because Esau had been born first.

To Jacob, however, it was obvious that he was destined to rule over his brother. For that, however, he needed the birthright. Fortunately, it was clear that Esau put little value on inheriting most of their father's possessions.

One day when Esau returned from an exhausting hunt, Jacob had just cooked a delicious, steaming lentil stew. When Esau demanded some, Jacob replied, "First sell me your birthright" (Genesis 25:31 NIV). Instead of laughing, "No way!" and continuing on to the tent to grab some cold food, Esau thoughtlessly agreed.

The Bible warns, "Make sure that no one is immoral or godless like Esau, who traded his birthright as the firstborn son for a single meal" (Hebrews 12:16 NLT).

27. JACOB ACQUIRES ESAU'S BLESSING \\ GENESIS 27:1–37

» Esau was so thoughtless that he probably never considered that God would hold him to his word. As far as he was concerned, "selling his birthright" was just a joke. And to Isaac's understanding, Esau—although immoral and godless—was still his heir.

Thus, one day when Isaac felt low and thought he'd soon die, he sent Esau out hunting for game. He told him to cook it the way he liked it and promised that after he'd eaten, he'd pronounce the oldest son's blessing upon him.

Jacob deceived his father in order to receive the blessing that was meant for Esau.

However, Rebekah overheard and quickly had two young goats butchered, flavored, and cooked. She then sent Jacob into blind Isaac's tent pretending to be Esau. By imitating Esau's voice and wearing goatskins on his arms—to feel like his hairy brother—Jacob convinced his father that he was Esau.

After he had eaten, Isaac blessed Jacob, and although there was deception involved, Isaac (unlike Esau) understood that when he gave his word, it was final. As he explained, "I blessed him—and indeed he will be blessed!" (Genesis 27:33 NIV).

Isaac had an "Aha!" moment and soon understood that God had chosen *Jacob* to inherit His promises (Genesis 28:1–4).

>> Esau was furious and plotted to kill Jacob, so Jacob was forced to leave Canaan. He fled to Haran in the far north under the pretext of looking for a wife—and there lived in exile.

Jacob's uncle Laban welcomed him into his home, and Jacob promptly fell in love with Laban's daughter Rachel. Since Jacob lacked a bride price, he agreed to work for seven years in exchange for her.

The morning after their wedding night, however, Jacob discovered that Laban had slipped him Rachel's older sister, Leah. Jacob had no choice but to agree to work *another* seven years for Rachel. When all was said and done, he ended up with four wives.

Afterward, Jacob worked to acquire flocks and herds. Again, Laban continually attempted to defraud him. As Jacob said, "Yes, for twenty years I slaved in your house! . . . And you changed my wages ten times!" (Genesis 31:41 NLT).

All this treachery and adversity must have seemed like a curse to Jacob, but God used it to give him riches and a large family that would be the foundation of an entire nation. God also often uses adversity to teach *us* valuable lessons.

29. JACOB WRESTLES WITH GOD \\ GENESIS 32:3–32

Jacob wrestled with the Angel of the Lord.

>> Jacob now returned to Canaan. God had blessed him, but he knew that he'd now have to face Esau—and he was fearful. What if his brother still wanted to kill him?

Jacob sent his family and flocks on ahead, and stayed behind to pray. But as he was alone, desperately seeking God and battling his fears, a man rushed from the gathering gloom and attacked him.

Jacob was in top physical shape from years of hard work, so for hours he and the stranger battled. At some point,

Jacob realized that his opponent was no mere man, but was a divine being. This was a test! So Jacob absolutely refused to stop fighting.

Suddenly the man dislocated Jacob's hip. Unable to continue wrestling, Jacob simply locked his arms around the stranger and held on. The man said, "Let Me go, for the day breaks." Jacob answered, "I will not let You go unless You bless me!" (Genesis 32:26 NKJV).

So the Lord blessed him, and added, "You have struggled with God and with men, and have prevailed" (Genesis 32:28 NKJV.) Often, like Jacob, we too simply have to hold on to God until He blesses us.

30. FIERCE REVENGE ON SHECHEM \\ GENESIS 33:18–20; 34:1–31

» After an emotional reunion with Esau, Jacob and his family and all their flocks traveled south until they came to Shechem. There Jacob bought a plot of land, set up his tents, and dug a well (John 4:11–12). It seemed as good a place as any to settle down.

Dinah, one of Jacob's daughters, went out to visit the local women. But when the prince saw her, he seized her and raped her. After violating her, he fell in love with her and implored Jacob to let him marry her.

Jacob's sons were furious. They insisted that they would only allow Dinah to marry him if all the men of Shechem were circumcised. The citizens agreed. But while they were recovering, Simeon and Levi walked boldly into Shechem and killed every male. The other brothers then pillaged the city. As a result, Jacob's family had to quickly leave.

The brothers were right to be angry, but Simeon and Levi's rage was insane. In his final blessings to his sons, Jacob said of these two, "A curse on their anger, for it is fierce; a curse on their wrath, for it is cruel" (Genesis 49:7 NLT).

31. JOSEPH IS SOLD AS A SLAVE \\ GENESIS 37:1–36

» Jacob had a son by his beloved wife, Rachel, and named him Joseph. Jacob loved him more than his other sons and showered him with favors. One day he gave him "a tunic of many colors" (Genesis 37:3 NKJV), but apparently gave nothing to his other sons.

Joseph, in turn, was loyal to his father, and whenever his older brothers did something wrong, "he brought their father a bad report about them" (Genesis 37:2 NIV).

All of this was already enough to make Joseph's older brothers hate him. But then Joseph started having vivid dreams. He dreamed that all his brothers bowed down to him. These dreams were from God, but Joseph's mistake was to boast about them to his brothers. This infuriated them even more.

Joseph had to be humbled by God before he could do the things that God had planned for him.

One day when Joseph was checking up on them, far from their father's camp, his older brothers ripped his colorful tunic from him, threw him into an empty water pit, then sold him to some Midianite merchants. The merchants took Joseph to Egypt, where he became a slave.

God had planned great things for Joseph, but He couldn't use Joseph until He had worked the pride out of him.

32. POTIPHAR'S WIFE TEMPTS JOSEPH \\ GENESIS 39:1–23

» Potiphar, the captain of Pharaoh's guard, bought Joseph and set him to work with the slaves in his household. The years slowly passed.

God was with Joseph, and his conscientious, diligent work habits served him well. When Potiphar realized that his household was prospering and everything was running smoothly because of Joseph, he put him in charge of his entire palatial estate.

Meanwhile, Potiphar was often away at work, and his bored wife was used to having whatever she wanted. "Joseph was a very handsome and well-built young man, and Potiphar's wife soon began to look at him lustfully. 'Come and sleep with me,' she demanded'" (Genesis 39:7 NLT).

He refused, but she kept attempting to seduce Joseph day after day. Finally, she ripped his outer robe from him. Then when Potiphar came home, she accused Joseph of trying to rape her. Potiphar was outraged and threw him in prison.

Joseph lost his position and his reputation, but he didn't lose his integrity and the presence of God. "And the LORD was with Joseph in the prison and showed him his faithful love" (Genesis 39:21 NLT).

God still gives us strength today to resist temptation (1 Corinthians 10:13).

33. JOSEPH INTERPRETS PHARAOH'S DREAMS
\\ GENESIS 40:1–23; 41:1–43

» When Joseph arrived in prison, "they bruised his feet with shackles, his neck was put in irons" (Psalm 105:18 NIV). But God favored him, and soon Joseph was running the entire prison.

One night, two of Pharaoh's prisoners had dreams, and Joseph correctly interpreted them. Just as Joseph said, one man was restored to his position as royal cupbearer.

Then one night Pharaoh had troubling dreams. Seven starving cows came out of the Nile River and devoured seven well-fed cattle. Then seven shriveled, scorched heads of grain consumed seven full heads of grain.

Pharaoh asked his wise men and magicians to interpret his dreams, but they couldn't. Then the cupbearer remembered Joseph. Quickly he was brought from prison. When asked if he could interpret the dreams, Joseph replied, "I cannot do it, but God will give Pharaoh the answer he desires" (Genesis 41:16 NIV).

God gave Joseph the interpretation: seven years of abundant harvests would be followed by seven years of unprecedented famine. Pharaoh promptly placed Joseph in charge of Egypt to prepare for the coming disaster.

Joseph had learned true humility and dependence upon God—and was ready to be used greatly by Him.

34. JOSEPH FORGIVES HIS BROTHERS
\\ GENESIS 42:1–24; 43:15–16; 45:1–15

» The seven years of bountiful harvests came, and Joseph stored up vast quantities of grain. Then the famine began, devastating not only Egypt, but Canaan.

One day Joseph's brothers came to Egypt to buy grain. Joseph was now grown, so they didn't recognize him—but he knew them. Joseph decided to test them. He accused them of being spies, threw Simeon in prison, and said that he'd only release him if they brought their youngest brother, Benjamin, to Egypt.

Joseph's brothers began talking together in Hebrew, lamenting that God had brought this trouble upon them because of what they'd done to Joseph. Joseph understood their words and was moved to tears.

Sometime later the brothers returned with Benjamin. When Joseph accused Benjamin of stealing and announced that he'd keep him as a slave, Judah made an impassioned plea that losing this son would kill their aged father, Jacob. As a result, Joseph revealed to them that he was their long-lost brother.

Joseph then forgave his brothers. "Then he threw his arms around his brother Benjamin and wept, and. . .he kissed all his brothers and wept over them" (Genesis 45:14–15 NIV).

God's way is always love and forgiveness (Colossians 3:13).

35. THE ISRAELITES MOVE TO EGYPT \\ GENESIS 45:16–28; 46:26–30

»When news reached Pharaoh's palace that Joseph's brothers had come, Pharaoh and all his officials were pleased. Pharaoh told Joseph, "Tell your brothers, 'Do this. . .get your father and come. Never mind about your belongings, because the best of all Egypt will be yours'" (Genesis 45:19–20 NIV).

When the eleven brothers informed their father that Joseph was not only alive but was governor of the kingdom of Egypt, Jacob couldn't believe them. But after they told him all the details, and he saw the carts full of costly goods Joseph had sent, he was convinced.

So Jacob and all his extended family—his sons, daughters, and grandchildren— left droughttricken Canaan behind and trekked to Egypt. And true to his word, Pharaoh gave them the well-watered, fertile land of Goshen, in the eastern Nile delta, to dwell in.

Jacob and his family left Canaan, moving to Egypt's most fertile regions to be with Joseph.

When he heard that they had arrived, Joseph mounted his chariot and went to meet them. "As soon as Joseph appeared before him, he threw his arms around his father and wept for a long time" (Genesis 46:29 NIV).

However much fame and fortune you amass, don't ever forget: family is important. Truly love your family.

36. JACOB BLESSES HIS SONS \\ GENESIS 48:1–22; 49:1–33

» When Joseph heard that Jacob was dying, he took Manasseh and Ephraim to him. Joseph was ruler of Egypt, but when he brought his sons to his father to receive God's blessing, "he bowed himself with his face to the earth" (Genesis 48:12 KJV). Joseph had dreamed that his father would bow before him (Genesis 37:9–11), but now it was Joseph's turn to bow.

Jacob then pronounced a blessing on his two grandsons, giving them an inheritance among his own sons.

Afterward, Jacob called his other eleven sons and pronounced blessings and prophetic words over them. One beautiful prophecy stands out above them all. After declaring that Judah would be ruler over all his descendants (Genesis 49:8), Jacob prophesied: "The scepter will not depart from Judah, nor the ruler's staff from between his feet, until he to whom it belongs [the Messiah] shall come and the obedience of the nations shall be his" (Genesis 49:10 NIV).

Jacob was a frail old man, but the Spirit of God was upon him. The words he spoke were invested with the power of the Almighty. Small wonder that Joseph bowed when he came into his presence.

37. THE ISRAELITES INCREASE IN NUMBERS \\ EXODUS 1:1-7

» Apart from escaping the drought, there were other reasons why God moved the Hebrews to Egypt—and kept them there for 430 years.

In Canaan, Jacob's sons and daughters were getting caught up in idol worship (Genesis 35:2–4). In addition, they were intermarrying with Canaanites and thought nothing of having sex with shrine prostitutes (Genesis 38:1–2, 13–21 NIV). They were in danger of being assimilated and disappearing as a distinct people.

And then there was the matter of the prophecies—that God would give their descendants the entire land of Canaan. If the impetuous, misguided Hebrews had attempted to fulfill those promises prematurely, they would have been wiped out (Genesis 34:25–30).

God therefore moved the children of Israel to Egypt where they had four centuries to peacefully increase in numbers. Safe in the Nile delta, "their descendants, the Israelites, had many children and grandchildren. In fact, they multiplied so greatly that they became extremely powerful and filled the land" (Exodus 1:7 NLT). Only then were they ready to return to Canaan.

God sometimes gives us long-term promises. We shouldn't be impatient if they're not fulfilled immediately. His delays are not necessarily denials.

38. SATAN ATTACKS JOB \\ JOB 1:1-22; 2:1-8

» Shortly after Jacob and his family moved to Egypt, an amazing story took place in the land of Uz, to the southeast of Canaan.

There was a man there named Job. He was the wealthiest of all the men of the East, and he believed in the God of Abraham. His closest friends came from Edom and were descended from Esau.

Job was a righteous man and constantly communed with God. As a result, God put a hedge of protection around Job and everything that he owned.

The devil appeared before God one day and asked, "Does Job fear God for nothing?" He challenged God, "But now, stretch out Your hand and touch all that he has, and he will surely curse You to Your face!" (Job 1:9, 11 NKJV).

God allowed Satan to take away all of Job's material possessions— even to kill his sons and daughters—but still Job worshipped God. Then Satan received permission to strike Job with disgusting, painful boils from head to toe, but still Job refused to curse God. Job's sufferings lasted for literal months (Job 7:3–5).

May we too find the strength, despite our tests and afflictions, to praise God.

39. JOB ENDURES ENDLESS ACCUSATIONS
\\ JOB 4:7–8; 11:6, 10–17; 15:1–6

» When Job's friends heard about his troubles, they came to comfort him. And at first they did. When they saw how great his grief was, they sat for seven days saying nothing (Job 2:11–13).

At first, they encouraged him that because he *was* righteous, he simply needed to persevere, and God would again bless him (Job 4:3–7; 8:6, 21).

Eventually, his friend named Zophar became convinced that Job was guilty of secret sins—in fact, God wasn't even judging him as much as he deserved (11:6). Zophar urged Job to repent. From then on, Job continued to protest his innocence, and his three friends continued insisting that he must be guilty.

When they saw his suffering, Job's friends tried to convince him that he was being punished for his sins. Even Job's wife suggested he "curse God and die" (Job 2:9).

They argued from every possible angle that God always judges wickedness—and even though they couldn't think of any sin Job had committed, they were convinced that he *must* have sinned. Why? Because he was suffering.

In the end, God rebuked Job's friends and restored his fortunes. "You have heard of the endurance of Job and have seen the outcome of the Lord's dealings, that the Lord is full of compassion and is merciful" (James 5:11 NASB).

40. EGYPTIANS OPPRESS THE ISRAELITES \\ EXODUS 1:8–22

» At first, the Egyptians treated the Hebrews royally, but after they began to increase in number, the Egyptians worried that they'd rise up and take over. So they stripped the Hebrews of all their land and wealth and reduced them to slavery.

"They made their lives bitter with harsh labor in brick and mortar and with all kinds of work in the fields; in all their harsh labor the Egyptians worked them ruthlessly" (Exodus 1:14 NIV). For centuries afterward, the Hebrews remembered life in Egypt as being in "the midst of the iron furnace" (1 Kings 8:51 NASB).

The Hebrews didn't build the pyramids, but they did build treasure cities for Pharaoh—or as some translations put it, military store cities.

Soon the oppression became so bad that Pharaoh commanded the Israelites to kill their newborn males and to let only the females live. In the face of such cruelty, "the Israelites groaned in their slavery and cried out" (Exodus 2:23 NIV).

God used their suffering to make the Israelites willing to leave the lush Nile River valley. They had become very settled and complacent in Egypt and had lost all interest in moving on to the promised land.

41. ABANDONED BABY ADOPTED \\ EXODUS 2:1–10

❯❯ A young Hebrew couple named Amram and Jochabed already had a daughter and a son (Numbers 26:59) when the order came to throw all male Hebrew newborns into the Nile River. But when their second son was born, they just couldn't do it.

"Moses' parents hid him for three months when he was born. They saw that God had given them an unusual child, and they were not afraid to disobey the king's command" (Hebrews 11:23 NLT).

When Jochabed could no longer hide him, she placed her baby in a papyrus basket and nestled it among the reeds at the water's edge. She had technically obeyed the command, but was clearly hoping that some Egyptian woman would take pity on her son.

By serendipitous chance, Pharaoh's daughter came to bathe in the river, saw the basket, and had one of her slave girls bring it to her. When she saw the beautiful child and heard him cry, her heart went out to him, and she adopted him. She named him *Moses,* which means "drawn from the water."

And so it was that the son of slaves was raised as a prince in the courts of Pharaoh.

42. MOSES FLEES AS A FUGITIVE \\ EXODUS 2:11–15

❯❯ "Moses was learned in all the wisdom of the Egyptians" (Acts 7:22 NKJV), and when he discovered that he himself was Hebrew, he studied their wisdom too. He came across an ancient prophecy that Abraham's descendants would spend four hundred years in Egypt before leaving (Genesis 15:13–14), and it had been *almost* four hundred years!

"But when the time of the promise drew near which God had sworn to Abraham. . .he supposed that his brethren would have understood that God would deliver them by his hand" (Acts 7:17, 25 NKJV).

Convinced that he was the mighty deliverer, Moses set about to fulfill his destiny. But in one rash act, he killed an Egyptian taskmaster. Instead of setting all the slaves free, he was forced to flee Egypt. . .alone.

He spent the next forty years in exile, learning patience and dependence upon God. When God was ready, He *did* use Moses to deliver His people—but it took 430 years (Exodus 12:40–41). It turns out that "four hundred years" had been a general time frame, not a precise figure.

We also do well to avoid insisting that end-time prophecies will be fulfilled in the time and manner in which we believe they must happen.

43. ENCOUNTER AT THE BURNING BUSH \\ EXODUS 3:1–17; 4:10–15

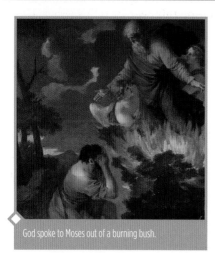

God spoke to Moses out of a burning bush.

» Moses spent forty years as a shepherd, and one day when he was watching flocks near Mount Horeb, he saw a strange sight: a bush was aflame, but it wasn't consumed. Curious, he went for a closer look.

That's when God spoke out of the burning bush and told Moses that He was the God of his forefathers and that He was sending him to Egypt to deliver His people.

Moses had once prided himself in his training and abilities, but now he asked, "Who am I that I should go to Pharaoh and bring the Israelites out of Egypt?" (Exodus 3:11 NIV). God told Moses not to worry: He would go with him. God then gave him miraculous signs to perform.

However, Moses had lost self-confidence to the point where he didn't believe God could use him. He begged, "Please send someone else" (Exodus 4:13 NIV). God actually got mad then but informed Moses that He was sending his brother, Aaron, to help him.

We might marvel at Moses for arguing with God's holy presence, but we too often talk back to God, even when He clearly speaks to us from His Word.

44. MOSES CONFRONTS PHARAOH \\ EXODUS 5:1–23; 7:1–13

» Moses was already suffering a lack of confidence. What happened after he arrived in Egypt tested him severely. When he asked Pharaoh to let the Israelites go into the wilderness to worship God, Pharaoh increased their workload instead. From then on, they had to gather their own straw to make bricks.

The Israelites became angry with Moses, so he complained, "Why, LORD, why have you brought trouble on this people? Is this why you sent me? Ever since I went to Pharaoh to speak in your name. . .you have not rescued your people at all" (Exodus 5:22–23 NIV).

God sent Moses back to Pharaoh to do a miracle. But God warned Moses that even this wouldn't change his mind. Aaron threw down Moses' staff, and right before Pharaoh's eyes, it morphed into a snake.

Pharaoh summoned his magicians and they cast down their staffs—which also changed into snakes. The fact that Moses' serpent consumed theirs didn't impress Pharaoh. He hardened his heart and refused to let the Israelites go.

When God has promised to do something, we often expect it to work out quickly and easily. This isn't always the case—and God has His reasons.

45. TEN PLAGUES DEVASTATE EGYPT \\ EXODUS 7:14–10:29

» God then began to do astonishing wonders. He sent a plague of blood upon the Nile River. But Pharaoh still refused to relent. This was followed by a grotesque plague of frogs, a plague of gnats, and a plague of flies. Still Pharaoh resisted. So far, the plagues had merely caused discomfort.

God then sent a plague that killed all the Egyptians' livestock. This was followed by a plague of painful boils that afflicted both man and beast. Still Pharaoh resisted.

God then sent an unprecedented hailstorm that flattened all the Egyptians' crops, stripped trees bare, and killed anyone out in the open. Pharaoh persisted in stubbornly resisting God.

Then as new crops began springing up, God sent the largest locust swarm in Egypt's history to devour every plant in sight. This was followed by three days of utter darkness.

A plague of blood in the Nile River was the first of ten disasters God sent upon Egypt.

Bible scholars explain how each of these plagues may have been natural yearly occurrences in Egypt, albeit greatly amplified by God. And *that* could have been why Pharaoh refused to believe that they were divine miracles.

When we make up our minds not to believe, miracles can happen all around us, and we still won't be persuaded.

46. THE LORD PASSES OVER \\ EXODUS 11:1–12:31

» God was about to bring one final plague. Moses told Pharaoh, "Thus says the LORD: 'About midnight I will go out into the midst of Egypt; and all the firstborn in the land of Egypt shall die'" (Exodus 11:4–5 NKJV).

God instructed the Israelites to kill a lamb and to smear its blood on their doorposts. He promised, "When I see the blood I will pass over you, and no plague will befall you to destroy you" (Exodus 12:13 NASB). This is where the term *Passover* originates.

While the plague was striking the land, the Israelites were eating the lambs they'd killed. And they were dressed and ready to leave.

Then at midnight the Lord struck the firstborn of every family in Egypt—from the firstborn of Pharaoh to the firstborn of the prisoner in the dungeon.

This final mighty plague shook Pharaoh to his core. He sent for Moses and Aaron during the night and ordered, "Get out! Leave my people—and take the rest of the Israelites with you!" (Exodus 12:31 NLT).

Jesus was the ultimate Passover lamb, slain for us during the Jewish Passover feast (1 Corinthians 5:7). His blood covers our sins.

47. THE ISRAELITES LEAVE EGYPT \\ EXODUS 12:31–41; 13:20–22

» All Egypt was in an uproar, wailing over their dead. No one was sleeping. The terrified Egyptians urged the Hebrews to leave immediately. Otherwise, they believed, they would *all* die (Exodus 12:33).

Moses had instructed the Hebrew slaves to ask their masters for articles of silver and gold and for fine clothing—and the Egyptians were so desperate for them to depart that they gave them whatever they asked for. So in the end, the Egyptians *did* pay them for all their slave labor.

God thought of every detail, including how the Israelites would be able to see the way when they left Egypt in the middle of the night. God suddenly appeared in their midst in a pillar of fire, giving light to them. He then moved ahead and led them out of Egypt.

The Hebrews couldn't understand why God had allowed them to suffer for so many centuries. And when He finally did send the deliverer, nothing seemed to work. Pharaoh said "no" at every step. But God was executing His plan the entire time.

God is still at work in our lives today, though we may not always see evidence of that.

48. GOD PARTS THE SEA \\ EXODUS 14:1–31

» When the Israelites came to the Red Sea, they learned that Pharaoh had changed his mind and had sent his chariots after them. They were trapped!

Then God did an astonishing miracle and parted the waters before them. "The floods stood upright like a heap; the depths congealed in the heart of the sea" (Exodus 15:8 NKJV). "Congealed" means "hardened," so it appears that God performed a completely supernatural miracle.

The parting of the Red Sea is often referred to as one of God's greatest miracles.

God could *also* have amplified natural means. Genesis 14:21 (KJV) specifies, "The LORD caused the sea to go back by a strong east wind all that night... and the waters were divided." Even today, a phenomenon called "wind setdown" (sustained east-west winds) at the Bitter Lakes, north of the Red Sea, pushes the waters aside, exposing the bottom.

God then stopped the wind abruptly, causing the waters to rush back with punishing force, drowning Pharaoh's chariots.

However God did the miracle, He did it. The Israelites escaped slavery and Egypt's chariot armies were destroyed. And for centuries, *this* miracle was referred to as the greatest of God's wonders of old—the defining event in the Hebrews' history.

What pivotal, life-changing miracle has God done in *your* life?

49. MANNA DESCENDS FROM HEAVEN \\ EXODUS 16:1-35

» Soon after the Israelites headed into the Sinai desert, they ran out of food. They then complained that Moses had brought them out into the wilderness to starve them to death.

That, of course, was not the plan—but they *were* in a barren desert. So God said, "I will rain down bread from heaven for you" (Exodus 16:4 NIV). And He did! The next morning thin flakes like frost covered the desert floor for miles around. The Israelites asked, "Manna?" which is Hebrew for "What is it?"

"The manna looked like small coriander seeds, and it was pale yellow like gum resin. The people. . .boiled it in a pot and made it into flat cakes. These cakes tasted like pastries baked with olive oil" (Numbers 11:7–8 NLT).

The Bible calls manna "the bread of heaven" and "angels' food" (Psalm 78:24–25 NKJV). And the Israelites had a miraculous supply of it the entire forty years they were in the desert.

One day some Jews told Jesus that God had given their ancestors bread from heaven and asked what *He* would do for them. Jesus replied, "I am the bread of life" (John 6:35 NKJV).

50. WATER FROM THE ROCK \\ EXODUS 17:1–7

>> The pillar of cloud and fire led the Israelites in all their travels (Exodus 13:21–22; 40:36–37). Now it guided them southward and finally stopped at a place called Rephidim, near Mount Sinai. There was a problem, however. There was no water there.

In plain view of the cloud of God's presence, some Israelites demanded, "Is the LORD among us or not?" Others whined to Moses, "Why did you bring us up out of Egypt to make us. . .die of thirst?" Others demanded, "Give us water to drink" (Exodus 17:2, 3, 7 NIV).

Still others were so mad that they began plotting to stone Moses to death.

When Moses hit a rock with his staff, water gushed from it.

Moses cried out to God, "What should I do with these people? They are ready to stone me!" The Lord answered, "Walk out in front of the people." Yes, walk straight up to the angry, growing mob.

The Lord added, "Take your staff. . .I will stand before you on the rock at Mount Sinai. Strike the rock, and water will come gushing out" (Exodus 17:4–6 NLT). So Moses believed God, struck the rock, and water flowed out.

Sometimes God lets you be tested severely before He does a miracle.

51. THE AMALEKITES ATTACK \\ EXODUS 17:8–16

» Fierce Amalekite raiders had inhabited the harsh Sinai desert for hundreds of years, and the desert was now crawling with them. They'd been watching the Israelite camp for weeks and had finally gathered enough tribes to mount an attack.

Moses commanded Joshua, "Choose some men to go out and fight the army of Amalek for us. Tomorrow, I will stand at the top of the hill, holding the staff of God in my hand" (Exodus 17:9 NLT). Why was *that* necessary? The staff was a visible reminder of God's power.

The next morning, Joshua prepared to do battle. Meanwhile, Moses, Aaron, and Hur climbed a nearby hill. As long as Moses held the staff up, the Israelites were winning. But whenever he became tired and lowered his hands, the Amalekites began winning.

After a while, Moses became too exhausted to hold his arms up at all. So he sat on a stone, and Aaron and Hur stood at his sides, holding up his hands until sunset. And Joshua's fighters completely defeated the Amalekites.

We too need to be reminded that we can't gain victories in our own strength. We need to depend on God at all times.

52. MEETING GOD AT MOUNT SINAI \\ EXODUS 19:1–25; 20:18–21

» When God had spoken from the burning bush, He told Moses, "When you have brought the people out of Egypt, you will worship God on this mountain" (Exodus 3:12 NIV).

As the people watched from the base of the mountain, God came down in all His holy power and "there was thunder and lightning, with a thick cloud over the mountain." Everyone trembled with fear.

Then Moses led the people out of the camp to meet God. And the Lord descended on the mountain in fire. "The smoke billowed up from it like smoke from a furnace, and the whole mountain trembled violently" (Exodus 19:16–18 NIV).

The astonished people were commanded to stop at the mountain's foot. God didn't want the curious to touch it and warned them that they'd die if they did (Exodus 19:12).

In their first meeting, God had even warned Moses, "Do not draw near this place. . . . For the place where you stand is holy ground" (Exodus 3:5 NKJV). We must respect God. We can't simply tramp into His presence.

Only Jesus' death for our sins allows us to enter God's presence now—but even so, we must do so with reverence.

53. RECEIVING THE TEN COMMANDMENTS \\ EXODUS 20:1–17; 34:1–2, 2

❯❯ Then the Lord called Moses to the top of the mountain and for the next forty days gave Moses laws to govern His people.

"And when He had made an end of speaking with him on Mount Sinai, He gave Moses two . . .tablets of stone, written with the finger of God" (Exodus 31:18 NKJV). These tablets contained the Ten Commandments. Moses then carried them down the mountain.

But when he saw the people dancing around the golden calf, "Moses' anger burned, and he threw the tablets from his hands and shattered them at the foot of the mountain" (Exodus 32:19 NASB).

God gave Moses two tablets that were inscribed with the Ten Commandments, but Moses broke them out of anger.

Then God told Moses, "Chisel out two stone tablets like the first ones. I will write on them the same words that were on the tablets you smashed" (Exodus 34:1 NLT). The first time, God Himself had carved the stone tablets. This time Moses had to carve them. And he had to carry them to the top of the mountain. And spend *another* forty days there (Exodus 34:4, 28).

When God gives you something priceless, value and cherish it. If you don't, replacing it—if that's even possible—can take a lot of time and effort.

54. THE GOLDEN CALF \\ EXODUS 32:1-35

» The first time Moses went up the mountain, after he was gone many days, the people became restless. They told Aaron. "Come on, make us some gods who can lead us. We don't know what happened to this fellow Moses" (Exodus 32:1 NLT).

First of all, *God* had led them to this mountain and was on it with Moses right now—and they weren't to go anywhere until He said so.

Second, they didn't actually want to be led anywhere. They just wanted to have a wild party.

Third, Aaron was their human leader while Moses was absent. But he wasn't up to the task, so he yielded to their pressure and made an idol of a golden calf. "Moses saw that the people were running wild and that Aaron had let them get out of control" (Exodus 32:25 NIV).

God was prepared to wipe out everyone for revolting against Him, but Moses pleaded with God, so He spared them. Nevertheless, three thousand of the worst offenders died.

When Moses returned to the mountain and spent another forty days away, there wasn't a repeat incident. They had learned their lesson. May we learn from our past mistakes as well.

55. MAKING THE ARK AND THE TABERNACLE
\\ EXODUS 35:4–35; 39:32–43

» God gave Moses detailed instructions for how to make the Tent of Meeting—His worship tent, the tabernacle—as well as the ark of the covenant, altars, and other articles of worship.

When the Israelites had left Egypt, their masters had given them treasure—gold, silver, bronze, onyx stones, and other gems, as well as fine linen, purple and scarlet yarn, leather, olive oil, spices, and more.

Moses therefore said, "From what you have, take an offering for the Lord. Everyone who is willing is to bring to the Lord an offering" (Exodus 35:5 NIV). And the people *were* willing and gave generously.

Moses also said, "All who are skilled among you are to come and make everything the Lord has commanded" (Exodus 35:10 NIV). Skilled artisans stepped forward. God then chose two men, Bezalel and Oholiab, to lead the work.

After some months, everything was complete. God then instructed them to set up His worship tent, and when they had done so, "the glory of the Lord filled the tabernacle" (Exodus 40:34 NASB).

We are asked to give God of our finances and time. He in turn blesses us with His holy presence.

The Lord commanded the Israelites to build the Tent of Meeting, and He blessed them with His presence.

56. TWELVE SPIES REPORT ON CANAAN \\ NUMBERS 13:1–33; 14:1–10

» Finally the Israelites left Mount Sinai and traveled until they came to the oasis of Kadesh, just south of Canaan. From there Moses sent twelve men to spy out the land.

After forty days, the spies returned. Ten of them conceded that it was a good land, but focused on the negatives: the people living there were strong, and their cities were large and fortified. There were even giants!

When the Israelites heard this, they were greatly discouraged. But a spy named Caleb shouted, "Let's go at once to take the land. We can certainly conquer it!"

The other spies argued, "We can't go up against them! They are stronger than we are!" (Numbers 13:30–31 NLT). For emphasis they added, "There we saw the giants. . .we were like grasshoppers in our own sight, and so we were in their sight" (Numbers 13:33 NKJV).

Caleb argued that they didn't need to fear giants or any Canaanites, because their strength would crumble. God was for Israel. But the people were too discouraged to trust God.

Their unbelief caused them years of needless privation and hardship. We too must believe God's promises if we wish to avoid failing.

57. WANDERING FORTY YEARS \\ NUMBERS 14:11–38; DEUTERONOMY 2:14–15

» From the day they left Egypt, it took the Israelites two years to reach Kadesh. Their spies then spent forty days spying in Canaan.

But when the spies brought back a negative report, the people wept and wailed, "If only we had died in Egypt! Or in this wilderness! Why is the LORD bringing us to this land only to let us fall by the sword?" (Numbers 14:2–3 NIV).

God told them that He would give them exactly what they requested: the entire older generation who refused to enter the promised land would die in the wilderness. They would wander a year for each of the forty days. They had already spent two years in the desert; there were thirty-eight more years to go.

The older generation had complained that if they attempted an invasion, the Canaanites would kill them and enslave their children. God said the opposite would happen: their children would go in and *conquer* the Canaanites. (When that entire older generation of doubters finally died, God told Moses that it was time to take the younger generation into Canaan.)

Be careful what you ask for. God might give you what you request.

58. KORAH AND COHORTS REBEL \\ NUMBERS 16:1–35

>> One day Korah, Dathan, Abiram, and 250 Israelite rulers confronted Moses and Aaron, saying, "The whole community is holy, every one of them, and the LORD is with them. Why then do you set yourselves above the LORD's assembly?" (Numbers 16:3 NIV).

They were accusing Moses of exalting himself. But he had never wanted to be God's spokesperson. And Aaron? Both he and Moses were only doing their jobs because God had called them to.

The rulers were disguising *their* own lust for more power under the pretext that "the whole community is holy," so Moses declared, "In the morning the LORD will show who belongs to him and who is holy" (Numbers 16:5 NIV).

Moses told the 250 rulers to take their censers, put burning coals and incense in them, and appear before the Lord. So they did.

God judged Korah and his followers when they accused Moses and Aaron of exalting themselves.

Korah, Dathan, and Abiram were standing with their families beside their tents when suddenly the ground literally opened beneath them and swallowed them up. The next instant, fire consumed the 250 rulers offering incense.

Christ has cleansed us, so we *are* all holy—but we still have to respect those whom God has appointed as leaders (Hebrews 13:7, 17).

» One day the Israelites arrived at the Desert of Zin near Kadesh. There was no water there, yet God had led them there. But the people grumbled to Moses: "Why did you bring [us] into this wilderness, that we and our livestock should die here?" (Numbers 20:4 NIV).

Moses had had enough! After all the miracles God had done, the Israelites still doubted that the Lord was leading them. Nevertheless, God had mercy, telling Moses to take his staff and merely *speak* to a rock. If he did that, water would gush out.

Moses walked up to the rock. "Listen, you rebels!" he shouted. "Must we bring you water from this rock?" (Numbers 20:10 NLT). He then *whacked* the rock with his staff. . .twice.

Because of this outburst, God told Moses that he wouldn't be able to lead the Israelites into Canaan. "Trouble came to Moses because of them; for they rebelled against the Spirit of God, and rash words came from Moses' lips" (Psalm 106:32–33 NIV).

The Israelites had provoked Moses, to be sure, but God still expected him to control his temper and obey His instructions. And He expects the same of us today.

» The younger Israelites finally headed to Canaan. They traveled around the land of Edom through the desolate, stifling-hot depression of the Arabah—"and the soul of the people became very discouraged on the way" (Numbers 21:4 NKJV).

In the midst of this desolation, however, God still faithfully sent manna.

The people complained to Moses: "Why have you brought us out of Egypt to die here in the wilderness? There is nothing to eat here and nothing to drink. And we hate this horrible manna!" (Numbers 21:5 NLT).

As a result, God sent serpents that bit them, and many died. Desperate, the people repented, confessing that they'd sinned by speaking against the Lord and against Moses.

God heard and told Moses to make a bronze serpent and attach it to a pole. He promised that anyone who had been bitten would live if they simply looked at it. Moses told the people, and they looked and were healed.

Centuries later, Jesus promised, "As Moses lifted up the serpent in the wilderness, even so must the Son of Man be lifted up, that whoever believes in Him should not perish but have eternal life" (John 3:14–15 NKJV).

Michaelangelo's painting of the bronze snake.

61. THE AMORITES PROVOKE WAR \\ NUMBERS 21:21–35; DEUTERONOMY 2:26–3:11

» Strictly speaking, the land of Canaan—which God had promised the Israelites—consisted of the kingdoms of Canaanites and Amorites living *west* of the Jordan River. The two Amorite kingdoms that occupied the plains east of the river weren't originally included.

Therefore, the Israelites sent messengers to Sihon, king of the Amorites of Bashan. They asked permission to simply pass through his land on their way to Canaan. Sihon foolishly refused and gathered his army to come out against Israel.

The Israelites swiftly defeated Sihon and took possession of his entire kingdom.

Og, king of the northern Amorites, was a giant. He ruled over a vast kingdom, and now he marshaled *his* army to fight Israel. But God told Moses, "Do not fear him, for I have delivered him into your hand, with all his people and his land" (Numbers 21:34 NKJV).

The Israelites defeated the northern Amorites as well. Like Sihon, Og had brought destruction upon his kingdom. This also greatly increased the amount of land that the Israelites owned—so the Amorites' animosity actually worked in their favor.

God still allows opposition and adversity to work out for our good.

62. BALAAM GETS GREEDY \\ NUMBERS 22:1–35

» The Israelites camped just north of the land of Moab, and Balak, king of Moab, "was sick with dread" (Numbers 22:3 NKJV). He couldn't defeat the Israelites. But he knew of a seer named Balaam who cursed people and they were defeated. So he sent messengers to Balaam, urging him to come curse the Israelites.

But God instructed Balaam, "You shall not go with them; you shall not curse the people, for they are blessed" (Numbers 22:12 NIV).

Balak sent more messengers, offering Balaam huge rewards. Now Balaam was tempted. He told them to wait while he checked again if God had anything new to say. He was therefore delighted that *this* time God gave him permission to go.

God warned Balaam to speak only what He commanded, but He saw covetousness filling his heart and thus sent an angel to kill him. Balaam was only spared because his donkey saw the angel and avoided it three times. Then, miraculously, the donkey "spoke with a human voice and restrained the prophet's madness" (2 Peter 2:16 NIV).

God has given each of us gifts, but selfish motivations can totally derail our usefulness if we're not very careful.

63. THE MIDIANITES SEDUCE ISRAEL \\ NUMBERS 25:1–15; 31:16; JOSHUA 13:22

» Balaam was so badly shaken up over nearly being slain by the angel that when he arrived in Moab, he refused to speak a curse against the Israelites. Instead, he gave several powerful prophecies blessing them.

However, afterward, Balaam once again lusted for Balak's promised rewards and finally came up with a plan: he advised Balak on how to tempt the Israelites to sin— so that God *Himself* would curse them. As a result, Midianite and Moabite women seduced the men of Israel, engaging in sex with them and leading them to worship Baal.

So God sent a plague among the Israelites and twenty-four thousand people died. "These women caused the chil-

Moses ordered the people into war against the Midianites after they led the Israelite men to sin against God.

dren of Israel, through the counsel of Balaam, to trespass against the LORD. . .and there was a plague among the congregation of the LORD" (Numbers 31:16 NKJV).

Moses ordered the Israelites to wage war against the Midianites because they had lured them into lascivious idolatry, and "the children of Israel also killed with the sword Balaam. . .the soothsayer" (Joshua 13:22 NKJV).

Balaam "wandered off the right road and. . .loved to earn money by doing wrong" (2 Peter 2:15 NLT). May we never follow his covetous example, even in small ways.

64. JOSHUA BECOMES LEADER \\ DEUTERONOMY 31:1–8; 34:9; JOSHUA 1:1–11

» Joshua had been commander of Israel's armies ever since they left Egypt (Exodus 17:9) and had repeatedly proved himself to be a godly, courageous leader. He had also been Moses' personal aide for years (Exodus 24:13). So when Moses' time came to die, God told him to commission Joshua as the new leader.

After Moses died, God told Joshua, "As I was with Moses, so I will be with you; I will never leave you nor forsake you. Be strong and courageous, because you will lead these people to inherit the land" (Joshua 1:5–6 NIV).

God told him two more times, "Be strong and courageous." He would *need* to be. He had a huge, dangerous job ahead of him.

God then gave Joshua the secret to ongoing power and success, saying, "This book of the law shall not depart from your mouth, but you shall meditate on it day and night. . . .for then you will make your way prosperous, and then you will have success" (Joshua 1:8 NASB).

Like Joshua, we today face many challenges, and the secret to our success is the same—to faithfully study the Word of God and obey it.

65. CROSSING THE JORDAN RIVER \\ JOSHUA 3:1–17; 4:1–18

» The Israelites prepared to cross the Jordan River into Canaan. Normally, the Jordan isn't very wide, but it was springtime and the river was swollen with rain and melted snow. It overflowed its banks onto the flood plains.

But the instant the priests stepped into the river carrying the ark, the water dropped and the riverbed emptied. Only after *all* the Israelites crossed did the river flow again. The Canaanites' "hearts melted in fear and they no longer had the courage to face the Israelites" (Joshua 5:1 NIV).

How did God do this? Joshua 3:16 (NIV) tells us that "the water . . .piled up. . . a great distance away, at a town called Adam." The river gorge is narrow at that spot and in 1927 the cliffs collapsed there and dammed the Jordan for twenty hours.

Perhaps God caused a similar landslide in Joshua's day. Psalm 114:3–7 indicates that He once used an earthquake to "drive back" the Jordan.

God emptied the Jordan River so that the Israelites could enter the promised land.

Even though God may have used natural means, the *exact timing* of the river drying up was a huge miracle! Speaking of timing, the instant the last priest walked out of the riverbed, the Jordan flooded back again.

God *still* uses miracles of divine timing to accomplish His will today.

66. RAHAB SPARES THE SPIES \\ JOSHUA 2:1–24; 6:22–25

» Joshua sent two men out as spies, and they entered Jericho and rented a room from a harlot named Rahab. But someone became suspicious and reported them.

When Rahab realized this, she quickly led the men up to her flat roof, where she had laid out stalks of flax to dry. She declared that the Lord God of the Hebrews was the true God and that she knew that He had given them the land of Canaan.

Then she told them: "Now therefore, I beg you, swear to me by the Lord, since I have shown you kindness, that you also will. . .deliver our lives from death" (Joshua 2:12–13 NKJV). They promised, so she concealed them under the flax.

Soldiers arrived and searched her house, but Rahab said that the spies had already slipped out the gates, so the soldiers rushed off. Rahab then let the spies down the city wall on a rope.

When Jericho was taken, Joshua spared Rahab and her family because she believed in God and had acted on her faith! "By faith the prostitute Rahab, because she welcomed the spies, was not killed with those who were disobedient" (Hebrews 11:31 NIV).

67. JERICHO'S WALLS COLLAPSE \\ JOSHUA 6:1–21

» Jericho was the gateway to Canaan, just across the Jordan River. It had high, thick walls and was virtually impregnable. And now that the Israelites surrounded them, they barred their gates and settled in for a long siege. They had plenty of food.

God then gave Joshua odd instructions: for six days his army was to escort the ark of the covenant around Jericho, once a day. On the seventh day, they were to circle the city seven times. When the priests sounded a long blast on the trumpets, the army was to shout.

Then the city walls would simply. . .collapse.

It took tremendous faith to believe such a tactic would work—but Joshua believed. So they obeyed God's instructions to the letter, and the mighty walls of Jericho came crashing down. The Israelites then conquered the defenseless city.

We don't know how God did this miracle. Maybe He sent an earthquake at the exact second the army shouted. However He did it, the surrounding Canaanites heard of Jericho's fall and were absolutely terrified.

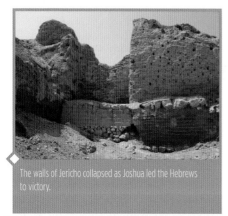
The walls of Jericho collapsed as Joshua led the Hebrews to victory.

God still puts us in situations where we have to do odd things to accomplish His will. May we have the faith to obey.

68. DISASTER AT AI \\ JOSHUA 7:1–8:29

» The Israelites came to Ai. *Ai* means "ruins," and it was little more than a community of Canaanites living inside the ruined walls of a former town.

But when the Israelites attacked, the men of Ai charged. The Israelites fled, and thirty-six were killed. Joshua was stunned. Why had God allowed this defeat? Now all the Canaanites would hear of it, be emboldened to attack in one massive battle, and wipe Israel out.

God then told Joshua that Israel had disobeyed Him. He had warned them not to take any plunder from Jericho, but an Israelite named Achan had secretly taken a wedge of gold and some other treasure and buried them under his tent.

The Lord said, "For they have even taken some of the accursed things, and have both stolen and deceived" (Joshua 7:11 NKJV). Disobeying God was so serious that He had allowed the entire nation to suffer defeat.

After they had dealt with Achan, God told Joshua to attack Ai again. This time the Israelites did things God's way and were successful.

"Whoever conceals their sins does not prosper" (Proverbs 28:13 NIV). Make sure that no hidden sin hinders your walk with God.

69. THE GIBEONITES DECEIVE ISRAEL \\ JOSHUA 9:1–27

» God had commanded the Israelites not to make a peace treaty with any Canaanites, but to fight them, drive them out, and possess their cities and lands.

One day, weary travelers from Gibeon arrived at the Israelite camp. They claimed to be ambassadors from a distant country who had been sent to make a peace treaty.

Their clothes were worn and patched, their wineskins were cracked and mended, and their leftover bread was dry and moldy, so the Israelites "did not inquire of the LORD. Then Joshua made a treaty of peace with them. . .and the leaders of the assembly ratified it by oath" (Joshua 9:14–15 NIV).

Three days later, however, they found out that Gibeon was a great Amorite city in Canaan, the capitol of three other cities. The Israelites were upset, but they'd sworn an oath to God and thus couldn't battle the Gibeonites and possess their land.

Remembering to pray is very important, but there's another lesson here: many people lightly give their word then break it, but God expected the Israelites to honor their oath in perpetuity. He judged all Israel with a three-year famine after Saul broke this treaty (2 Samuel 21:1–6).

70. GOD STRETCHES OUT DAYLIGHT \\ JOSHUA 10:1–15

» The Israelites were dismayed by Gibeon's deceptive treaty, but the other Amorites were outraged. They decided to annihilate them for making peace with the enemy. Soon the armies of five Amorite kings were besieging Gibeon.

Gibeon begged Israel to come to their defense, and Joshua's response was swift. After an all-night march, the Israelites struck the Amorite armies at dawn. The fighting was fierce and lasted all day. It continued to rage even as the sun was setting in the west.

God made the sun stand still until the Israelites had defeated their enemies.

Joshua needed to finish the battle, so he prayed, "'Let the sun stand still over Gibeon, and the moon over the valley of Aijalon.' So the sun stood still and the moon stayed in place until the nation of Israel had defeated its enemies" (Joshua 10:12–13 NLT).

As this bizarre day simply refused to end, the Amorites finally broke ranks and fled— but the Lord destroyed them with a terrific hailstorm that pounded them until they reached the city of Azekah. The hail killed more men than the Israelites had.

When God wants to do miracles to show His great power, He is well able to bend the laws of nature and make them serve His purposes.

71. THE GREAT NORTHERN BATTLE \\ JOSHUA 11:1–15

» After the battle of Gibeon, the Israelites continued attacking enemy cities and rapidly conquered much of south Canaan in a single protracted campaign (Joshua 10:28–43).

These stunning victories alarmed the Canaanites in the north, and the king of Hazor quickly assembled a coalition of many kings. The plan was to marshal their armies at the waters of Merom, then march south together and crush Israel. Soon a vast horde of fighting men and chariots covered the landscape.

When he heard about this development, Joshua prayed, and God told him, "Do not be afraid of them. By this time tomorrow I will hand all of them over to Israel as dead men" (Joshua 11:6 NLT).

By this time tomorrow? Joshua was in the south of Canaan. He knew what he had to do. Without hesitation he marched his entire army north and boldly attacked. And the Lord gave Israel a tremendous victory. They completely routed their enemies, fighting until not one Canaanite soldier remained alive.

In just two huge campaigns, the Israelites conquered most of northern and southern Canaan. When we obey God boldly and instantly, He can use us to do great things.

72. CONQUERING AND SETTLING THE LAND \\ JOSHUA 11:16–23

» The Israelites conquered much of Canaan in a few months. "So Joshua took this entire land: the hill country, all the Negev. . .the western foothills, the Arabah and the mountains of Israel." But the Bible *also* informs us that "Joshua waged war. . .for a long time" (Joshua 11:16, 18 NIV).

How long? Well, Caleb was forty when, after two years in the desert, the spies explored Canaan. Then the Israelites wandered for thirty-eight years. At the *end* of the wars of Canaan, Caleb conquered Hebron at age eighty-five (Joshua 14:6–13). So the wars lasted seven years.

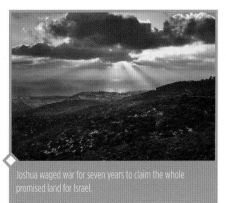

Joshua waged war for seven years to claim the whole promised land for Israel.

"Joshua took the whole land. . .and Joshua gave it as an inheritance to Israel according to their divisions by their tribes. Then the land rested from war" (Joshua 11:23 NKJV).

Some years later, God told Joshua that although he was now too old to fight, much land remained to be conquered. It would, however, be the job of individual tribes to conquer the remaining territory allotted to them. They began to do this after Joshua's death (Joshua 13:1; Judges 1:1–26).

God helps us gain great victories, but sometimes the battles never completely end. There will often be ongoing mopping up to do.

73. LANDLESS DANITES HEAD NORTH \\ JUDGES 1:34; 18:1–31

» Some of the tribes of Israel were successful in their continuing conquests. Others were not. "As for the tribe of Dan, the Amorites forced them back into the hill country and would not let them come down into the plains" (Judges 1:34 NLT).

A common complaint the Israelites gave was that the Canaanites had iron chariots. When the men of Ephraim and Manasseh told this to Joshua, he assured them that they would "drive out the Canaanites, though they have iron chariots and are strong" (Joshua 17:18 NKJV). But the men of Dan didn't have this kind of faith.

So they chose five men and sent them far to the north to find someplace easier to conquer. The spies came to the city of Laish and saw that the Canaanites were wealthy because their land was fertile. And, very importantly, they had no allies living nearby.

So six hundred men from the tribe of Dan, armed with weapons of war, marched north. They attacked and conquered Laish. Then they brought their families north and settled there.

God hadn't allotted the land in the north to Dan. That was their *own* idea. God allowed it to work, but it wasn't His highest or best will.

74. ISRAEL IS REPEATEDLY OPPRESSED \\ JUDGES 1:27–36; 2:1–23; 3:1–6

» The Danites weren't the only ones who had trouble conquering Canaanites. Other tribes had the same problem. They couldn't drive them out because "the Canaanites were determined to stay in that region" (Judges 1:27 NLT). Apparently more determined than the Israelites.

God's people either didn't believe that He would help them or didn't desire God's promises enough. And they compromised. "When the Israelites grew stronger, they forced the Canaanites to work as slaves, but they never did drive them completely out" (Judges 1:28 NLT). After all, it was beneficial keeping the Canaanites as slaves.

The result was predictable: "The Israelites lived among the Canaanites. . . . They took their daughters in marriage and gave their own daughters to their sons, and served their gods" (Judges 3:5–6 NIV).

God's reaction was also predictable: just as He had warned, He judged His people. He sent invaders and raiders "whom they were no longer able to resist" (Judges 2:14 NIV) into their land to oppress them.

When the Israelites cried out to God, He was faithful to raise up warriors to deliver them. But it was a constant, vicious cycle. May we not be guilty of compromise and disobedience.

75. WAR WITH THE BENJAMITES \\ JUDGES 19:1–20:48

» When the Israelites were still newly settled in Canaan, a Levite and his concubine were traveling home and stopped in a town in Benjamin. There, a mob violated the woman all night, causing her death.

The armies of Israel gathered at Mizpeh and sent a message to Benjamin, telling them to hand over those who had committed the crime. Instead of complying, the Benjamites marshaled their warriors. They were superb fighting men and knew it.

The Israelites approached the ark of the covenant and asked God if they should attack the Benjaminites (Judges 20:26–28).

In the first battle, the Benjamites slew thousands of Israelites. Shaken, the Israelites asked God, "Should we fight against our relatives from Benjamin again?" God answered, "Go out and fight against them" (Judges 20:23 NLT).

The next day, the Israelites launched another attack. Once again, the Benjamites killed thousands. That evening, the Israelites prayed desperately, "Should we fight. . .again, or should we stop?" The Lord answered, "Go! Tomorrow I will hand them over to you" (Judges 20:28 NLT).

It took great faith for the Israelites to persist. But they did, and the third time they won. Sometimes when you attempt something and fail repeatedly, you wonder if you should go on. Often the answer is yes. You just need to be courageous and persist.

76. OTHNIEL THROWS OFF FOREIGN INVADERS
\\ JOSHUA 15:13–19; JUDGES 3:7–11

» During Joshua's initial wars of conquest, Caleb promised, "I will give my daughter Aksah in marriage to the man who attacks and captures Kiriath Sepher" (Joshua 15:16 NIV).

Aksah was beautiful, so young Othniel was highly motivated and led an army to attack and conquer this city. He then married Aksah. With her came a large farm with two springs of water. So Othniel enjoyed many years of farming, loving his wife, and raising a family.

But when he was old, his courage and leadership skills were once again needed. Israel disobeyed, so God allowed a foreign king, Cushan-Rishathaim, to invade and oppress them.

The Israelites endured this occupation for eight years. Finally, Othniel had enough. "The Spirit of the LORD came on him, so that he became Israel's judge and went to war" (Judges 3:10 NIV). He rose up, rallied the Israelites, and drove out the foreigners.

Then he went back to farming, loving his beautiful wife, and enjoying his family. He also was busy judging Israel for the next forty years.

Don't think God is through with you once you're old. He may call upon you to accomplish even greater things for Him.

77. EHUD ASSASSINATES A DESPOT \\ JUDGES 3:12–30

» During the Israelite civil war, the tribe of Benjamin had almost been wiped out. It's a good thing they weren't, because God raised up a deliverer from among them.

Now, the Israelites had sinned against God, so "the LORD strengthened Eglon the king of Moab against Israel" (Judges 3:12 NASB). Eglon conquered Israel and made them pay tribute for eighteen years. A left-handed Benjamite named Ehud was tasked with delivering their payments.

Now, Ehud hand-crafted a dagger eighteen inches long and fastened it beneath his robe on the right-hand side. No one suspected anything, because in a nation of right-handed warriors, such a weapon would have invariably been fastened on the left side.

After Ehud delivered the tribute, he told Eglon, "I have a secret message for you, O king." Eglon ordered, "Keep silence!" He sent his attendants from the room and closed the doors (Judges 3:19 NKJV). Ehud then whipped out the dagger and killed the despot.

Ehud escaped by the porch, rallied the Israelites, and drove out the Moabites. His plan succeeded because he prepared its details meticulously, acted boldly, and—most of all—was inspired by God. The lessons for us are clear.

78. DEBORAH GOES TO BATTLE \\ JUDGES 4:1–24

» Remember the Canaanites with iron chariots whom Israel couldn't drive out? A Canaanite king named Jabin reoccupied Hazor, built an army of nine hundred chariots, then conquered all the Israelites of the north. He oppressed them for twenty years.

Now, God raised up a woman named Deborah to judge Israel. One day she summoned the warrior Barak. She told him that if he gathered an army on Mount Tabor near the Kishon River, God would lure the Canaanites and deliver them into his hands.

Barak knew that God's presence was with Deborah, so he said, "If you go with me, I will go; but if you don't go with me, I won't go" (Judges 4:8 NIV). So Deborah went.

Deborah led the Israelites to defeat Jabin, king of the Canaanites. The battle was won when another woman, Jael, killed the enemy commander with a tent peg.

Apparently, God sent a sudden, heavy downpour, causing the Kishon River to overflow its banks, and most of the nine hundred chariots were swept away (Judges 5:4, 21). Barak then attacked those who survived.

This battle broke the back of the Canaanite army. "And from that time on Israel became stronger and stronger against King Jabin until they finally destroyed him" (Judges 4:24 NLT). Often we need just one decisive win to start us down the road to total victory.

79. GIDEON ROUTS THE MIDIANITES \\ JUDGES 6:1–7:25

» For seven years, whenever it was harvesttime, hordes of Midianites swept in from the desert, and their massive flocks and herds devoured the Israelites' crops.

One day an angel appeared to Gideon saying, "Mighty hero, the LORD is with you!" Gideon replied, "Sir, if the LORD is with us. . .where are all the miracles our ancestors told us about?" (Judges 6:12–13 NLT). Gideon would *get* his answer.

Gideon had faltering faith and had to be reassured repeatedly—but in the end, he gathered an army of thirty-two thousand men. Then God said, "If I let all of you fight the Midianites, the Israelites will boast to me that they saved themselves by their own strength" (Judges 7:2 NLT).

So He had Gideon send everyone home except for three hundred men.

God had him position these men on the hills around the vast enemy camp by night. Then every man smashed a clay pot, held up a torch, and blew on a trumpet. The Midianites panicked, began killing one another, and fled. Then all Israel helped defeat them.

Yes, God often uses our strength and skills, but there are times when He wants to defy logic and do a miracle.

80. THE RISE AND FALL OF ABIMELECH \\ JUDGES 9:1–57

» "No sooner had Gideon died than the Israelites. . .set up Baal-Berith as their god" (Judges 8:33 NIV). Gideon's son Abimelech worshipped this god. The temple to Baal-Berith was in Shechem, his mother's city.

Now, Abimelech wanted to be king of Shechem. To eliminate all competition, he plotted against his seventy brothers. The men of Shechem agreed and gave him silver from the temple of Baal-Berith. With this money, Abimelech hired lowlifes to massacre his brothers.

Only Gideon's youngest son, Jotham, escaped. And he prophesied that because of the evil they had done, Abimelech and the men of Shechem would destroy one another.

Abimelech did become king, but he ruled only three years. Then "God stirred up animosity between Abimelek and the citizens of Shechem" (Judges 9:23 NIV). Abimelech attacked the city. When one thousand citizens locked themselves in the temple of Baal-Berith, he set it on fire, killing them all.

Abimelech then besieged the tower in the neighboring city of Thebez, but there a woman dropped a millstone on his head, killing him.

"Do not be deceived, God is not mocked; for whatever a man sows, that he will also reap" (Galatians 6:7 NKJV).

81. JEPHTHAH'S WAR AND FOOLISH VOW \\ JUDGES 11:1–40

» Jephthah's father was a famous Israelite but his mother was a harlot, so his brothers threw him out. Jephthah went into exile and became chief of a group of bandits.

He became such a renowned warrior that when the Ammonites invaded Israel (claiming Israel had taken their land), the Israelites turned to Jephthah for help.

Jephthah then gave the Ammonites a summary of how Israel had come to possess the land. Unfortunately, his speech didn't convince them. "Then the Spirit of the LORD came on Jephthah. He. . .advanced against the Ammonites" (Judges 11:29 NIV). All good so far.

Jephthah foolishly vowed to sacrifice his daugher if God granted him victory.

Then Jephthah made a rash vow: if God helped him win, he'd sacrifice whatever came out his door when he got home. God gave Jephthah victory, but when he returned home, his daughter came out to greet him. It was a sin not to fulfill vows (Deuteronomy 23:21).

By keeping his vow, however, Jephthah committed a much *greater* sin. When the Israelites later sacrificed their children, God said, "I never commanded— nor did it enter my mind—that they should do such a detestable thing" (Jeremiah 32:35 NIV).

Be very careful not to speak hastily or make rash vows.

82. A STRONGMAN ARISES \\ JUDGES 13:1–14:20

» Philistines had lived in Canaan since Abraham's day (Genesis 21:34), but around 1177 BC a great wave of them settled the coast. Soon they overran the land and ruled Israel for forty years.

At this time Samson was born, and when he grew up, he fell in love with a Philistine woman. When he was going to visit her, a lion attacked him, but "the Spirit of the LORD came powerfully upon him so that he tore the lion apart with his bare hands" (Judges 14:6 NIV).

Samson later noticed a bees' nest inside the carcass, and ate some honey. At his wedding feast, therefore, he presented a riddle: "Out of the eater, something to eat; out of the strong, something sweet" (Judges 14:14 NIV).

Samson promised his guests that if they answered the riddle, he'd give them sixty garments. Otherwise, they had to give him sixty garments. The Philistines, however, forced Samson's wife to tell the answer.

Samson was furious. The Spirit of God empowered him and he went out, killed thirty Philistines, took their garments, and gave them to his guests. And the uprising began.

God sometimes uses imperfect people and odd circumstances to accomplish His purposes.

83. SAMSON BATTLES THE PHILISTINES \\ JUDGES 14:20; 15:1–20

» After Samson stormed out of his wedding feast, his father-in-law gave the bride to another man. *That* made Samson so mad that he caught three hundred foxes, tied torches to their tails, and set them loose in the grain fields. Soon half of Philistia was burning.

In retaliation, the Philistines burned down the house of Samson's wife, killing her and her father. This infuriated Samson. He roared, "Since you've acted like this, I swear that I won't stop until I get my revenge on you" (Judges 15:7 NIV). He slaughtered many Philistines. Then, with the entire country stirred up, he retreated to Judah.

A Philistine army marched into Judah, so to avoid trouble, the men of Judah talked Samson into surrendering to them. They bound his wrists and handed him over to the delighted Philistines.

Then the Spirit of the Lord came mightily on Samson and he snapped the ropes as if they were burned threads. "Finding a fresh jawbone of a donkey, he grabbed it and struck down a thousand men" (Judges 15:15 NIV).

Sometimes we don't think that we can overcome the many obstacles in our life, but with God's help we can accomplish amazing things.

» After several years, things seemed to settle down, so Samson went to the Valley of Sorek near Gath. There he fell in love with a woman named Delilah. We don't know if she was Hebrew or Philistine, but she had her price.

The Philistines offered her great rewards if she discovered the secret to Samson's strength and informed them. Samson refused to tell her at first, but Delilah "tormented him with her nagging day after day until he was sick to death of it" (Judges 16:16 NLT).

Samson finally revealed that his strength was due to his long hair. So while he slept, Delilah cut it off. Samson's strength immediately departed, and the Philistines captured and blinded him. They threw him in prison, forcing him to grind grain.

Samson fell in love with Delilah—and ultimately told her that his strength came from his uncut hair.

One day, however, they had a great feast and brought Samson out to mock him. But his hair had grown back, and in one final, mighty act, he pushed apart the two main pillars supporting the temple roof. The entire temple collapsed—killing thousands of leading Philistines.

Despite his incredible strength, Samson had a weakness for women, and it brought about his downfall. Know your weaknesses and avoid temptation.

85. A FOREIGN WIDOW IS REWARDED \\ RUTH 1:1–4:17

» Once there was a famine in Israel, so Naomi, her husband, and their two sons went to Moab. While there, their sons married Moabite women, Ruth and Orpah. Then after ten years, Naomi's husband and both sons died. Devastated, she headed back to Israel.

Ruth, now a young widow also, accompanied her—although Naomi had nothing but poverty to offer. In a stirring appeal, Ruth said, "Wherever you go, I will go; wherever you live, I will live. Your people will be my people, and your God will be my God" (Ruth 1:16 NLT).

The women arrived in Bethlehem during barley harvest, so Ruth went gleaning after the reapers, to get food. She happened to choose the field of Boaz, Naomi's wealthy relative, who was probably an older man (Ruth 3:10). Boaz was deeply moved by Ruth's selfless devotion and told her, "May the LORD. . .reward you fully" (Ruth 2:12 NLT).

To make a long, beautiful story short, Naomi urged Ruth to go to Boaz one night and propose marriage—and Boaz was delighted. They soon married, and their child was the grandfather of King David himself.

God *still* rewards people for selfless deeds. "Give, and it shall be given unto you" (Luke 6:38 KJV).

86. GOD GIVES HANNAH A SON \\ 1 SAMUEL 1:1–28

» Hannah was an ordinary woman with a painful dilemma. Her husband loved her dearly, but although she had persistently tried to get pregnant, she hadn't been able to.

To make matters worse, her husband's first wife was blessed with several children and constantly taunted Hannah, making her life miserable. Hannah wept and refused to eat.

When they went to the Lord's house to worship, Hannah prayed desperately. She promised God that if He gave her a child, she would dedicate that child to Him. Now, Eli the high priest noticed that although Hannah's lips were moving, she wasn't speaking a word. Indignant, he demanded, "How long are you going to stay drunk?"

Hannah replied, "I have not been drinking. . . . I have been praying here out of my great anguish and grief." So Eli responded, "Go in peace, and may the God of Israel grant you what you have asked of him" (1 Samuel 1:14–17 NIV).

Hannah believed that God would answer her prayer. She stopped grieving, began to eat, and was no longer sad. Not long after, she had a child—and no ordinary child: Samuel would be Israel's greatest prophet since Moses.

What a difference desperate prayer and simple faith make!

87. GOD SPEAKS IN THE NIGHT HOURS \\ 1 SAMUEL 2:12–17, 22–36; 3:1–21

» Eli was high priest, but he was old and quite overweight, so his two sons handled the day-to-day duties. The problem was that they were godless, and their abuses greatly offended many Israelites. Eli heard about their deeds, but he didn't stop them.

Samuel was still a child and was living at the house of God, helping Eli. One night when he was lying down to sleep, he heard a voice call, "Samuel!" He ran to Eli to see what he wanted, but the old man assured him that he hadn't called.

God spoke to Samuel in the middle of the night.

This happened two more times, and the last time, Eli realized that it was the Lord calling the child, so he told him what to answer. When God called again, Samuel responded, "Speak, for Your servant hears" (1 Samuel 3:10 NKJV).

God then gave Samuel a prophecy saying that He was going to judge Eli and his house for their sins. Fortunately, Eli accepted the message. "And all Israel. . .knew that Samuel had been established as a prophet of the LORD" (1 Samuel 3:20 NKJV).

May we too listen to God's "still small voice" (1 Kings 19:12 KJV) and obey Him.

88. THE ARK OF GOD IS CAPTURED \\ 1 SAMUEL 4:1–22

» For hundreds of years, ever since the ark of the covenant had been made, it had symbolized the presence of the Lord. God sometimes descended and appeared between the two golden cherubim on its cover.

Now, the Philistines were oppressing Israel, so the Israelites went out to battle them. But the Philistines defeated them and killed four thousand men. Shaken, the Israelites decided to bring the ark of God out to the battlefield.

They weren't desperately praying for God to help them. In fact, they had a very limited relationship with God at that point. They were treating the ark as an almost magical object.

At first the Philistines were terrified at its arrival, but their commanders realized that if they gave in to fear they were done for, so they ordered their troops to stand up like men and to fight as never before.

They did, and as a result, there was a very great slaughter of Israelites, so much so that the ark itself was captured.

God doesn't want us to trust in rituals, traditions, or outward forms. He desires us to have a daily relationship with Himself, the living God.

89. THE ARK WREAKS HAVOC IN PHILISTIA \\ 1 SAMUEL 5:1–12; 6:1–16

» The Philistines were ecstatic to capture the ark. It seemed like a victory over Israel's God. They took it to Ashdod and set it before their god, Dagon, in his temple.

But when the Philistines rose the next morning, they saw Dagon's idol fallen before the ark of God. Hoping it was an accident, they set their idol up again. The following morning Dagon had again fallen. This time he was broken in pieces.

Then a terrible disease—probably the bubonic plague, caused by rats—broke out in Ashdod. Many people there died.

Frantic, the Philistines carried the ark to Gath, but soon "the hand of the Lord was against the city with a very great destruction" (1 Samuel 5:9 NKJV).

The men of Gath took the ark to Ekron, but as Ekron began to be devastated, its people wailed in terror, "They have brought the ark of the God of Israel to us, to kill us and our people!" (1 Samuel 5:10 NKJV).

In total fear of the Lord, the Philistines returned the ark to Israel.

It's very foolish to disrespect God. We shouldn't do it, even in so-called jest.

90. ISRAEL INSISTS ON A KING \\ 1 SAMUEL 8:1–22; 12:13–25

» God had prophesied that the Israelites would one day have a king (Deuteronomy 17:14–20), but for centuries they'd been satisfied to be ruled by God through judges.

One day the Israelites demanded a king. When Samuel prayed about it, God told him, "Do everything they say to you, for it is me they are rejecting, not you. They don't want me to be their king any longer" (1 Samuel 8:7 NLT). Nevertheless, God told Samuel to warn them of the downsides of having a king.

"But the people refused to listen. . . . 'No!' they said. 'We want a king over us. Then we will be like all the other nations, with a king to lead us'" (1 Samuel 8:19–20 NIV).

The day that Samuel anointed Saul as king, it was wheat harvest. So

Samuel called out to God, and God sent thunder and heavy rain that made reaping impossible, "and all the people greatly feared the Lord and Samuel" (1 Samuel 12:18 NASB).

They got the message: they could have a king, but both they and their king had to be *very* careful to obey God. We today must do the same.

Samuel anointed Saul as ruler when the Israelites demanded a king to lead them.

» When the Israelites gathered, Samuel revealed that God had chosen Saul as king. Saul was good looking, muscular, and tall, but he was also painfully shy and a lowly farmer's son. Some men complained, "How can this fellow save us?" (1 Samuel 10:27 NIV). Sure enough, after the meeting, Saul returned home and. . .continued farming.

Then Nahash, king of the Ammonites, besieged the city of Jabesh Gilead. The Israelites there offered to surrender to him, but Nahash said he'd agree on one condition: if they let him gouge out all of their right eyes.

When Saul heard this news, he was furious, and the Spirit of God came upon him in great power. He commanded all Israel to come at once then marched an army to Jabesh Gilead. Just before sunrise, he attacked the Ammonite camp, slaughtering and scattering them.

After this tremendous victory, all Israel rejoiced to proclaim Saul king, and they built him a fortress in his hometown of Gibeah. The kingdom was established.

The secret to Saul's success in his early days was that he didn't depend upon his looks and physical prowess for his victories but was inspired by God's Spirit.

92. SAUL PANICS AND DISOBEYS \\ 1 SAMUEL 13:1–22

» At this time the Philistines dominated Israel, so when Saul's son Jonathan attacked their garrison in Geba, the Philistines marshaled to crush the revolt.

Saul had a mere three thousand men, but the Philistines arrived with an innumerable army. In addition, only Saul and Jonathan had iron swords, but all the Philistines were armed to the teeth with state-of-the-art weapons.

The Israelites were in terrible danger, and thousands fled or hid. Even Saul's small army "followed him trembling" (1 Samuel 13:7 NASB).

Samuel had said he'd come to sacrifice and pray for God's help, but when the prophet didn't show up on time, Saul became frantic and offered the sacrifice himself. No sooner had he finished, however, than Samuel arrived.

Yes, the situation was dire, but God would have done a tremendous miracle. That's why Saul's faith and obedience were more important than the size of the Philistine army. But Saul gave in to fear and foolishly took the prophet's job into his own hands.

Samuel then informed him that his kingdom wouldn't continue, but that God had chosen "a man after His own heart" as king (1 Samuel 13:14 NKJV)—a man who would do things God's way.

93. JONATHAN ATTACKS THE PHILISTINES \\ 1 SAMUEL 14:1-23

» Jonathan was different from his father. After Saul's fearful sacrifice, there never was a battle. Instead, Saul withdrew his trembling army to Gibeah and *avoided* any confrontation with the Philistines.

Not so Jonathan. Without telling Saul, he and his armor bearer headed to a Philistine garrison atop a cliff. Jonathan said, "Perhaps the LORD will help us, for nothing can hinder the LORD. He can win a battle whether he has many warriors or only a few!" (1 Samuel 14:6 NLT).

They showed themselves to the Philistines, who dared them to climb up. This was the sign Jonathan had been waiting for, so they climbed up. Then Jonathan attacked, and the two men killed twenty Philistines.

At that very moment God sent an earthquake, all the countryside shook greatly, and the terrified Philistines fled. "Then Saul and all his men rushed out to the battle and found the Philistines killing each other. There was terrible confusion everywhere" (1 Samuel 14:20 NLT). All the Israelites joined the attack and gained a tremendous victory that day.

That's the kind of miracle God could have done for Saul earlier—but Saul lacked faith. May God help *us* to trust Him.

» God still used Saul to defend Israel, and Saul "fought valiantly. . . delivering Israel from the hands of those who had plundered them" (1 Samuel 14:48 NIV). But, unfortunately, he also continued to disobey God's explicit instructions.

One day Samuel ordered Saul to wipe out Israel's ancient enemies, the Amalekites. These desert raiders had been the first to attack Israel and, in the ensuing centuries, had never ceased raiding and pillaging them. Their day of judgment had finally come. Even their livestock was not to be spared.

"But Saul and the army spared Agag and the best of the sheep and cattle. . .everything that was good. These they were unwilling to destroy" (1 Samuel 15:9 NIV). Agag was the chief of the Amalekites. He of all men should have been destroyed.

When Samuel confronted Saul about it, at first he argued that he *had* obeyed God. When Samuel pressed his point, Saul finally confessed, "I have sinned, for I have transgressed the commandment of the LORD and your words, because I feared the people and obeyed their voice" (1 Samuel 15:24 NKJV).

It can be very difficult at times, but we *cannot* be people pleasers. We must please God.

» After the Amalekite incident, Samuel mourned greatly that Saul wasn't the king he could have been. One day God told the aged prophet to stop mourning, but to go to Bethlehem. God had chosen one of Jesse's sons as king.

Samuel asked, "How can I go? If Saul hears it, he will kill me" (1 Samuel 16:2 NKJV). Another indication that Saul was no longer fit to be king.

God told Samuel to take a heifer as if he were merely going to sacrifice. So he did. When Jesse and his sons came to the sacrifice, Samuel took one look at Eliab, Jesse's oldest son, a tall, handsome man, and thought that he was God's choice.

God chose Jesse's youngest and least important son to be Israel's second king.

But God told Samuel, "Do not consider his appearance or his height, for I have rejected him. The LORD does not look at the things people look at. People look at the outward appearance, but the LORD looks at the heart" (1 Samuel 16:7 NIV).

David was Jesse's youngest, least esteemed son, and when he was finally summoned, God instructed Samuel to anoint *him* as king.

God still looks at our hearts, not our outward appearance.

96. DAVID SLAYS A PHILISTINE GIANT \\ 1 SAMUEL 17:1–54

» One day when the Philistines were arrayed in battle against the Israelites, Goliath strode forward and bellowed out a challenge. Goliath was from Gath and was one of the last of a race of giants called Anakim (Joshua 11:21–22 KJV).

Goliath dared any Israelite soldier to face him in single combat. Whichever champion lost, his people would become slaves of the other side. For forty days, Goliath repeated his challenge, but no Israelite dared step forward.

One day, David came to the battle lines. When he heard the challenge, he asked for permission to fight, and Saul granted it. As David advanced, he proclaimed, "You come against me with sword and spear and javelin, but I come against you in the name of the LORD Almighty" (1 Samuel 17:45 NIV).

Goliath was not only monstrous but was covered in protective armor. David rushed toward him without armor. As he ran, he swung his sling and sent a stone slamming into the giant's forehead. Goliath dropped like a rock. The Philistine army fled, and God gave the Israelites a great victory.

As we go forth against giants, truly trusting in God's name, He will go with us.

97. DAVID RUNS FROM SAUL \\ 1 SAMUEL 18:5–16; 19:1–18; 22:1–2

»After killing Goliath, David served in King Saul's army. He made a great name for himself, so that "all Israel and Judah loved David because he was so successful at leading his troops into battle" (1 Samuel 18:16 NLT).

David also spent time as Saul's court musician, playing tunes to soothe the king's troubled spirit. In addition, David married Saul's youngest daughter, Michal. This gave him a claim to the throne—though that wasn't David's motive for marrying her.

When Saul became obsessed with killing him, David fled the palace and hid in the wilderness.

Saul was insanely jealous of David and began to see him as a threat to his rule, so he tried to kill him with a javelin. After the second attempt, David fled the palace and stayed in the wilderness. There a group of valiant warriors gathered around him.

Saul then repeatedly led his army out to hunt David down. He became obsessed with trying to kill him (1 Samuel 23:7–8, 14).

There may be times in your life when, although you have done nothing wrong, jealous people will seek to harm you. Take heart from David's example: God protected him and eventually made him king, just as He had promised.

» Saul was determined to destroy David, but Jonathan remained his loyal friend and constantly spoke up to defend him. When Saul insisted that David must die, Jonathan asked, "Why should he be put to death? What has he done?" (1 Samuel 20:32 NIV).

Saul tried to appeal to Jonathan's desire to rule, saying, "For as long as the son of Jesse lives on the earth, neither you nor your kingdom will be established" (1 Samuel 20:31 NASB).

Jonathan refused to betray his friend. Instead, he warned David about his father's intentions and made an eternal covenant of friendship with David.

When Saul was pursuing David in the wilderness, Jonathan slipped away from the army, met David secretly, and encouraged him. "'Don't be afraid,' he said. 'My father Saul will not lay a hand on you. You will be king over Israel, and I will be second to you. Even my father Saul knows this'" (1 Samuel 23:17 NIV).

Indeed Saul did! He just had an entirely different reaction to it.

Jonathan had an outstanding degree of selflessness and integrity. We *all* wish for friends like that! But we should seek to *be* friends like that as well.

» David would go from being a fugitive to king of an empire stretching from Egypt to the Euphrates. God was *with* him! Also, while David was in the wilderness, God raised up warriors of almost superhuman strength and ability to help him.

While David was staying at a stronghold in the wilderness, warriors from Gad defected from Saul and joined him. "These Gadites were army commanders; the least was a match for a hundred, and the greatest for a thousand" (1 Chronicles 12:14 NIV).

One man, chief among David's captains, "was called Adino the Eznite, because he had killed eight hundred men at one time" (2 Samuel 23:8 NKJV).

Then there was Shammah. The Philistines had gathered together into a troop—a regiment of fifty soldiers—in a lentil field. Shammah's men were frightened and fled, but he took a stand alone in the middle of that field and killed all the Philistines who attacked.

God gave these men extraordinary strength and skill to establish David as king and to help him build his kingdom.

Our abilities aren't always to elevate ourselves. Often they're to help other people achieve God's will.

100. BATTLE AT BETHLEHEM'S WELL \\ 1 SAMUEL 22:1–2; 2 SAMUEL 23:13–17

» In places, the wilderness of Judah is a bewildering maze of wadis, rock formations, and natural caves. And David took refuge in a giant natural cavern called the cave of Adullam.

Then, at harvesttime, three mighty warriors went to David's hiding place and joined him. Now, an army of Philistines was camped in the valley just north of David's hometown, and they had established a garrison in Bethlehem itself.

One day David sighed and said, "Oh, that someone would give me a drink of the water from the well of Bethlehem, which is by the gate!" (2 Samuel 23:15 NKJV).

So the three mighty men broke through the Philistines' line of defense, drew water from the well of Bethlehem, while fighting off the entire garrison, and brought it to David.

But he refused to drink it, saying, "Far be it from me, O LORD, that I should do this! Is this not the blood of the men who went in jeopardy of their lives?" (2 Samuel 23:17 NKJV). So David poured out the water as an offering to the Lord.

Love and devotion cause us to willingly make tremendous sacrifices.

» Tests and opportunities reveal what's in our hearts, and on two occasions the Israelites got a look into David's heart—and saw both compassion and a fear of God.

For years, Saul had been hunting David. At one point, God told David, "I will give your enemy into your hands for you to deal with as you wish" (1 Samuel 24:4 NIV).

One day when David and some men were hiding in a cave, Saul went into the cave alone, to rest. David's men urged him to kill Saul. But

David, because he trusted God, refused two chances to kill Saul.

though David had been called to replace Saul as king, Saul was—for the present—still king. So David refused to take his life.

Some months later, David and some men entered Saul's camp at night. They tiptoed up to where Saul was sleeping, and Abishai begged David to let him kill Saul. Again, David refused. David trusted that God would take Saul in His time, so he refused to take matters into his own hands.

God may have great things planned for us, but He may also test us to see if we'll try to force things in our own strength and wisdom.

102. FARMER'S WIFE STOPS A SLAUGHTER \\ 1 SAMUEL 25:2–42

» There was an ill-tempered man in the south of Judah named Nabal ("fool"). He had great riches, however, so Abigail's parents had given their beautiful daughter to him in marriage.

David's men had camped in the wilderness near Nabal's pastures and had protected his sheep from wild beasts and robbers. Thus, when it came time for the feast at shearing time, David sent young men to ask Nabal to share of his bounty.

Nabal not only refused but insulted David, so David was furious. He ordered his men to arm themselves and prepare to wipe out every male in Nabal's household.

One of Nabal's shepherds told Abigail what had happened—and she immediately loaded donkeys with food and drink and went out to meet David. She persuaded him, since he was going to be king one day, to not to act in anger now, or he'd always look back on this day in regret. So saying, she wisely talked David out of taking revenge.

Not long after, when Nabal heard of the near disaster, he had a heart attack and died. David then took Abigail as his wife.

May God give us wisdom like Abigail!

103. DAVID LIVES AMONG THE PHILISTINES \\ 1 SAMUEL 27:1–28:2; 29:1–11

» Even godly people get discouraged. After years of barely staying one step ahead of Saul's armies, David began to doubt that God would protect him, let alone make him king.

"David kept thinking to himself, 'Someday Saul is going to get me. The best thing I can do is escape to the Philistines. Then. . .I will finally be safe'" (1 Samuel 27:1 NLT).

There's no indication that David prayed about this decision, but the next thing we hear, he and his six hundred men and their families had gone to Gath. To be accepted, David had to swear to be King Achish's servant (1 Samuel 27:5; 28:2).

For a while, there were no consequences, and David's men settled in Ziklag. One day, however, the Philistines gathered their armies to fight Israel—and Achish summoned David and his men. To prove their loyalty, they had to obey, even if it meant killing their own people.

Fortunately, the other Philistine lords didn't trust David, so Achish reluctantly sent him back to Ziklag. David's decision made while despairing would yet cause great grief.

When God has given you definite promises, the "best thing you can do" is to continue trusting Him.

104. SAUL CONSULTS A MEDIUM \\ 1 SAMUEL 28:3–25; 31:1–10

» Saul, meanwhile, also gave in to despair. When the Philistines invaded, he gathered the fighting men of Israel. Then he saw what he was up against.

"When Saul saw the Philistine army, he was afraid; terror filled his heart. He inquired of the LORD, but the LORD did not answer him" (1 Samuel 28:5–6 NIV). Saul had not listened to God for many years, so God had stopped speaking to him.

Desperate to know what to do, Saul went to a medium and told her to summon the departed prophet Samuel. The woman prepared

Saul was punished with death and defeat after consulting a medium.

to fake it. But to her amazement, Samuel's spirit actually appeared. Samuel told Saul that Israel would be defeated and he'd die.

Sure enough, in the terrific battle that followed, Saul and many Israelites were slain. The disaster was so great that countless Israelites abandoned their cities and fled.

"Saul died because he was unfaithful to the LORD; he did not keep the word of the LORD and even consulted a medium for guidance" (1 Chronicles 10:13 NIV).

Like Saul, many people start out with great promise but eventually reap the results of a lifetime of disobedience and evil thoughts.

105. DAVID BATTLES THE AMALEKITES \\ 1 SAMUEL 30:1–31

» David's men had only been gone from Ziklag for a few days, but when they returned, they found the town burned and all their wives and children gone. David and his men "wept until there was no strength in them to weep" (1 Samuel 30:4 NASB).

Then his men blamed David for bringing them to the land of the Philistines in the first place. They were so furious that they spoke of stoning him. David was in deeper despair than he'd ever been before— but instead of giving up, "David encouraged himself in the LORD his God" (1 Samuel 30:6 KJV).

David then asked God if they should pursue the Amalekites, if they could possibly find or overtake them at this late date. God answered that they would not only overtake the raiders but recover everyone. So David and his men set out.

They found the Amalekite camp, attacked it, and fought furiously. True to God's promise, they recovered everyone. They also recovered great spoil that the raiders had taken, which David then shared with many Israelite towns.

When you're thoroughly discouraged and at your wit's end, look to God. He can help you.

106. CIVIL WAR IN ISRAEL \\ 2 SAMUEL 2:1–3:1

» After their disastrous defeat and the Philistine invasion of their land, Israel was broken. Their king had been killed. However, Saul's son Ish-Bosheth had survived, so Abner, commander of Saul's army, brought him to a city across the Jordan River and made him king. However, Ish-Bosheth was a weak ruler. Abner was the real power.

Meanwhile, David went to Hebron in Judah. The men of Judah, knowing the prophecies about David, anointed him king over their tribe. The stage was now set for a protracted struggle for the throne of all Israel.

"The war between the house of Saul and the house of David lasted a long time. David grew stronger and stronger, while the house of Saul grew weaker and weaker" (2 Samuel 3:1 NIV). This simmering civil war lasted seven years.

David could have mounted a major assault, but this would have resulted in many Israelite deaths. So he settled for a slow, steady campaign. He had the faith to wait for God to act.

Often when the goal is finally in sight, we lose patience and try to quickly wrap things up. But even in the final lap we need patience and faith.

107. JOAB MALICIOUSLY MURDERS ABNER \\ 2 SAMUEL 2:17–23; 3:6–39

» During a battle at Gibeon, David's men outfought Ish-Bosheth's men. Soon Abner and the Israelites were in full retreat. Joab's brother Asahel pursued Abner and, despite Abner's warnings, refused to turn back—so Abner struck him with his spear, killing him.

Joab, son of Zeruiah, never forgave this. Now, sometime later, Abner had a falling out with Ish-Bosheth and decided to give his allegiance to David instead. While Joab was away on a raid, Abner visited David in Hebron and agreed to rally all Israel to his side.

When Joab found out that Abner had just been there, he was furious. He sent messengers after him and called him back to Hebron. He then took Abner aside as if to speak to him and fatally stabbed him.

Joab did this to avenge his brother, not caring what negative ramifications such a devious, self-serving murder would have on the kingdom.

David had treated Abner with respect and honor, and he now openly mourned Abner, saying that "these men, the sons of Zeruiah, are too harsh for me" (2 Samuel 3:39 NKJV).

Revenge and deceit were not David's way. May they not be ours either.

》 With the death of Abner, Ish-Bosheth was greatly weakened, and not long after he was assassinated by his own servants. Soon all Israel accepted David as king.

David now needed a more central capital, so he chose the Canaanite stronghold of Jebus, formerly called Jerusalem. However, Jebus had high walls, and its inhabitants mocked David, saying that he wouldn't be able to take their city.

But David had grown up nearby and knew a detail that the Canaanites didn't consider important. The city's water supply was just outside the walls, and a small opening led under the city— and from there a water shaft went straight up.

King David established Israel and became an ancestor of Jesus Christ.

David sent his men through the opening and they scaled the vertical water shaft. Once inside, they fought their way to a gate and opened it for the army. Joab, who had fallen out of favor and had lost his job, made sure to lead the attack, winning back his position again. David then took the city—and renamed it Jerusalem, which became known as "the city of David."

When a full-frontal assault simply won't work, look for a back-door solution.

109. DAVID DEFEATS THE PHILISTINES
\\ 2 SAMUEL 5:17–25; 1 CHRONICLES 14:8–17

》 For seven years, the Philistines had gladly watched the Israelites' civil war. After all, a divided enemy was a weak enemy.

But when David became king of all Israel, they were alarmed. They decided to crush Israel once again, so they massed their army in the Valley of Rephaim, just south of Jerusalem.

When David prayed, God promised victory, so he attacked and defeated them. David said, "God has broken through my enemies by my hand like a breakthrough of water" (1 Chronicles 14:11 NKJV). They called the place *Baal Perazim*, meaning "master of breakthroughs."

The Philistines advanced again, and when David prayed, God told him to circle behind them and to attack only when he heard a sound in the treetops.

"So David did as God commanded him, and they drove back the army of the Philistines. . . ." David then "attacked the Philistines and subdued them" (1 Chronicles 14:16; 2 Samuel 8:1 NKJV).

This was the breakthrough David needed to end the power of the Philistines over Israel—and he got it by listening to and obeying God. When we need a breakthrough, we too must listen to God and obey.

110. THE ARK COMES TO JERUSALEM
\\ 2 SAMUEL 6:1–19; 1 CHRONICLES 13:1–14; 15:1–28

» One day David decided to bring the ark of God to Jerusalem. It was a wonderful idea, but he failed to read the scriptures that specified *how* to transport the ark (Exodus 25:10–14; Numbers 4:5–6, 15). So some men

David brings the ark to Jerusalem.

simply placed it on an oxcart and headed down the road.

David had gathered priests and Levites from all over Israel, and they were singing and rejoicing with all their might when suddenly the oxen stumbled. A man steadied the ark, to keep it from falling, and was immediately struck dead.

David was afraid to bring the ark into his city, so that's as far as it got. All the Levites went home. Years passed and David had built his palace before he attempted to move the ark again. By then he knew that *Levites* had to carry it.

Once again David gathered Levites from all over Israel, and once again they sang and rejoiced as they moved the ark. But this time they did it the *right* way! And they brought it safely into Jerusalem.

Exuberance and joy are wonderful, but we must also deeply respect the things of God.

111. DAVID BUILDS A VAST EMPIRE \\ 2 SAMUEL 8:1–14

» After David's victory over the Philistines, "the LORD brought the fear of him on all the nations" (1 Chronicles 14:17 NASB). David then defeated Moab. "So the Moabites became subject to David and brought him tribute" (2 Samuel 8:2 NIV).

The Aramean kingdoms to the far north were battling each other, so David chose this strategic moment to launch an attack far beyond his borders—and utterly defeated much greater armies.

With such an assault, he fulfilled an ancient prophecy that God would give the Israelites not just Canaan, but all lands from the Red Sea to the Euphrates River (Exodus 23:31). Even Joshua hadn't fulfilled this.

David also seized a vast amount of plunder, articles of silver, gold, and bronze, from the peoples he conquered—Edomites, Moabites, Amalekites, Ammonites, Arameans, and Philistines. These he dedicated to the Lord. David then became wealthy from the ongoing tribute these subjugated lands paid him.

David and Solomon would rule over this far-reaching empire for nearly seventy years. Even the Persians, some five hundred years later, would hear of the fame of this empire (Ezra 4:20).

When God is with you, you can accomplish absolutely astonishing things!

112. GOD'S COVENANT WITH DAVID
\\ 2 SAMUEL 7:1–29; 1 CHRONICLES 22:1–19

» After David had finished his wars and was settled in his palace, he said to the prophet Nathan, "Here I am, living in a house of cedar, while the ark of God remains in a tent." Nathan replied, "Whatever you have in mind, go ahead and do it, for the LORD is with you" (2 Samuel 7:2–3 NIV).

God indeed *was* with David, but Nathan had spoken hastily. That night, God told the prophet that because David had fought many wars and shed much blood, the task of building Him a house was reserved for David's son.

However, God vowed that *He* would build *David's* house: "The LORD declares to you that the LORD himself will establish a house for you . . . 'Your house and your kingdom will endure forever before me; your throne will be established forever'" (2 Samuel 7:11, 16 NIV).

This promise would be ultimately fulfilled in Jesus Christ, the Son of David, who would live and reign forever (Luke 1:31–33).

Although David couldn't build a temple, he made extensive preparations for Solomon. If you can't be first fiddle, be content to play backup for the one who is.

113. BATTLING AN AMMON-ARAM COALITION \\ 2 SAMUEL 10:1–19

» David didn't battle Ammon because Nahash, their king, was his ally. But when Nahash died and David sent mourners to Hanun, his son, Hanun accused them of being spies and treated them disgracefully.

Hanun then realized his serious mistake. So he took all his gold and sent it to two Aramean kingdoms, to hire them to fight for him.

Joab arrived with a medium-sized army, only to find himself surrounded before and behind by over thirty-two thousand soldiers. He therefore divided his army and put half of it under the command of his brother Abishai. He then said: "If the Arameans are too strong for me, then come over and help me. . . . And if the Ammonites are too strong for you, I will come and help you. Be courageous! Let us fight bravely. . . . May the LORD's will be done" (2 Samuel 10:11–12 NLT).

The men of Israel fought so courageously and well that the enemy fled from them. The Arameans later returned in great numbers, and this time David led the armies of all Israel out—and decisively defeated them.

You can win against vastly superior forces if you plan wisely, fight well, and have your brother's back.

114. DAVID STEALS URIAH'S WIFE \\ 2 SAMUEL 11:1–12:15

» You'd think that with all these great victories, David would have been keenly aware of God's presence and power. But David had been so highly honored that he began to think he was entitled to whatever he desired.

One evening when he was on his palace roof, he glanced down into a neighboring courtyard and saw a beautiful woman named Bathsheba bathing. David immediately had her brought to him and committed adultery with her.

When Bathsheba became pregnant, David summoned her husband home from the war, hoping that he'd sleep with her then think that the child was his.

But when Uriah didn't do that, David plotted his death. He had Uriah placed in the heaviest fighting, then had the army withdraw from him, leaving him to die. David then took Bathsheba as his own wife.

David had always followed the Lord's commands—until he fell in love with Uriah's wife, Bathsheba.

This affair was a blot on his life. "David had done what was right in the eyes of the LORD and had not failed to keep any of the LORD's commands all the days of his life—except in the case of Uriah the Hittite" (1 Kings 15:5 NIV).

Avoid transgressions that can tarnish an otherwise flawless record.

>> David had a son named Amnon, and Amnon lusted so much for his half sister Tamar that one day he violated her. "When King David heard all this, he was furious" (2 Samuel 13:21 NIV). Amnon was David's first-born, destined to be king (2 Samuel 3:2). No longer.

For Absalom, Tamar's full brother, this wasn't enough. Two years later, he had Amnon murdered then fled to Geshur.

After three years, however, David's temper cooled and he invited Absalom back to Jerusalem. A little later, David fully reinstated him.

Absalom rewarded his father by plotting to murder him too. After all, wouldn't Absalom make a great king? Wasn't he better at meting out justice? And wasn't he strikingly handsome with five pounds of long, beautiful hair? (2 Samuel 14:25–26).

Absalom began to flatter all the Israelites who came seeking justice, telling them that there was no one to hear their complaints, but that *he* would help them if *only* he had the authority. "So Absalom stole the hearts of the men of Israel" (2 Samuel 15:6 NKJV).

Outwardly, Absalom appeared righteous and beautiful—but pride and murder lurked in his heart. Beware of sweet-talking deceivers with an agenda.

>> By the time David heard of Absalom's conspiracy, there was barely time to flee. So he quickly left, leaving his ten concubines to keep the palace. When Absalom arrived in Jerusalem, his first act was to set up a tent on the palace roof and publicly ravish all ten women.

David had fled across the Jordan River with a small army of elite fighters, so Absalom gathered a large army and pursued him. They met in the woods of Ephraim, and the battle raged there all day.

David's forces were fierce, professional fighters. Furthermore, they were "enraged in their minds, like a bear robbed of her cubs" (2 Samuel 17:8 NKJV). Soon Absalom's hastily assembled army was fleeing.

Absalom was riding through the forest when he met some of David's men. He raced away, but as his donkey passed under a tree, Absalom's long hair caught in the branches. And he hung there! His hair had been his pride, and turned out to be his downfall.

When Joab arrived, he killed Absalom then blew a trumpet. The war was over. God is able to deliver us from proud enemies, just as He delivered David.

Absalom was killed after he was caught in a tree by his long hair.

117. CENSUS CAUSES A NATIONWIDE PLAGUE
\\ 2 SAMUEL 24:1–25; 1 CHRONICLES 21:1–30

» One day Satan inspired David to number all Israel, to know how strong he was. Now, there was technically nothing wrong with a census. In the very last battle David had numbered the fighters who were with him (2 Samuel 18:1). And God had twice told Moses to count Israel's warriors (Numbers 1:1–3; 26:1–2).

But even Joab knew that David's motives were wrong and protested, "Why, my lord the king, do you want to do this? . . .Why must you cause Israel to sin?" (1 Chronicles 21:3 NLT).

Nevertheless, David insisted, so it was done. But "God was very displeased with the census, and he punished Israel for it" (1 Chronicles 21:7 NLT).

God sent a plague on Israel, and seventy thousand people died. Soon the angel causing the plague arrived at Jerusalem. When David saw him, he prayed for God to spare the people, because he—not they—had sinned. So God halted the judgment.

Sometimes, like David, we can do a reasonable thing with wrong motives. When God has done miracles for us, He wants us to continue to trust Him, not to depend on our own strength and resources.

118. SOLOMON BECOMES KING \\ 1 KINGS 1:1–52; 2:10–12

» When David was seventy years old, he was sick and about to die. Now, David had promised that Solomon would reign after him, and this promise was widely known.

But Adonijah decided to claim the throne. He persuaded Joab, Abiathar the high priest, and all his brothers that since he was David's oldest living son he had the right. But they had to act quickly "for the good of the kingdom" before Solomon was crowned. So the conspirators held a secret feast and proclaimed Adonijah king.

They made a point of not inviting Solomon, the prophet Nathan, or the captain of David's guard. They didn't tell David either. They counted on his being too sick to interfere.

David may have been old and sick, but when he learned what was happening, he took decisive action and immediately had Solomon declared king.

The city was soon in a joyous uproar—and when news of Solomon's coronation reached Adonijah's feast, his guests scattered. Soon Adonijah was bowing before Solomon, pledging his loyalty.

Don't try to wheel and deal yourself into a position of power—even if common sense tells you that you deserve it and must seize it.

119. SOLOMON PRAYS FOR WISDOM \\ 1 KINGS 3:1–15

» King Solomon started out his rule on a terrific note, for "Solomon loved the Lord" (1 Kings 3:3 NASB) and obeyed all His commandments. At this time, although the ark was in Jerusalem, the altar of sacrifice was in Gibeon, so Solomon went there and sacrificed to the Lord.

That night while he was sleeping, God appeared to Solomon in a dream and told him, "Ask for whatever you want me to give you" (1 Kings 3:5 NIV).

Solomon could have asked for great riches or victory over his enemies. Instead he unselfishly asked for the wisdom to rule and judge God's people. The Lord replied, "I will do what you have asked. I will give you a wise and discerning heart, so that there will never have been anyone like you, nor will there ever be" (1 Kings 3:12 NIV).

God also gave Solomon what he had *not* asked for—tremendous riches, honor, and peace in his kingdom.

Now, God won't necessarily give you great riches or unparalleled wisdom, but He *has* promised all of us, "If any of you lacks wisdom, let him ask of God. . .and it will be given to him" (James 1:5 NKJV).

120. SOLOMON BUILDS GOD'S TEMPLE \\ 1 KINGS 5:1–6:9, 37–38; 7:13–14

» David had made extensive preparations for the temple (1 Chronicles 22:2–5), and once Solomon became king, he requested King Hiram of Tyre to send the final cedar.

Then, in his fourth year, Solomon began building, and Hiram sent skilled architects and stonemasons to help him.

Solomon needed artisans to create pillars, statues of oxen, carts, a great basin, and other articles of bronze—as well as objects of gold and silver. A skilled bronze worker named Huram (an Israelite) was living in Tyre, so King Hiram sent him as well.

Seven years later, the temple was complete, paneled inside with cedar boards and covered with gold. And all the articles for the temple were finished.

The priests placed the ark of God in the holy place inside the temple. Then Solomon

Solomon completed impressive building projects.

dedicated God's house. When he finished praying, fire fell from heaven and consumed the sacrifices! And the cloud of the Lord's presence completely filled the temple (1 Kings 8:1–11; 2 Chronicles 7:1–3).

When God ordains a project, He puts His presence and His blessing upon it—even if they're not manifested as visibly or dramatically as they were for Solomon.

121. SOLOMON FALLS INTO IDOLATRY \\ 1 KINGS 9:1–9; 11:1–13

» Afterward, God appeared to Solomon again. He promised that if Solomon loved and obeyed Him, He would bless him; but if Solomon or his sons turned to worship other gods, God would abandon this temple he had built.

For most of his life Solomon *was* faithful, so God fulfilled His promise to make him wealthier, wiser, and more glorious than all other kings on earth.

"King Solomon, however, loved many foreign women. . . . He had seven hundred wives of royal birth. . .and his wives led him astray. As Solomon grew old, his wives turned his heart after other gods" (1 Kings 11:1, 3–4 niv).

Solomon compromised to please his pagan wives. As a result, the Spirit of God lifted from his life and his wisdom departed. God determined to remove most of his kingdom, leaving only Judah to David's line. Worst of all, Solomon led all Israel into great sin.

Solomon himself had written, "The fear of the Lord is the beginning of wisdom, and the knowledge of the Holy One is understanding" (Proverbs 9:10 nasb). When Solomon ceased to fear the Lord, he lost true wisdom. May we learn from his bad example!

122. REHOBOAM'S FOOLISH BOAST \\ 1 KINGS 11:26–12:24

» God had vowed to tear most of the kingdom away from David's descendants. So while Solomon was still king, God sent the prophet

Ahijah to anoint Jeroboam (one of Solomon's officers) king over the northern ten tribes.

After Solomon died, all Israel gathered to make his son Rehoboam king. But first they complained that his father had imposed heavy taxes and labor requirements on them; if Rehoboam would lighten their load, they would serve him faithfully.

When Rehoboam asked his older advisors what to do, they urged him to listen to the people. But when Rehoboam asked his young companions for advice, they convinced him to show he was boss by declaring that he'd make their load even *heavier*. When the northern tribes heard this answer, they revolted. Then Jeroboam stepped up and became their king.

Rehoboam was preparing for war, but the prophet Shemaiah gave him a message from God: "Do not go up to fight. . .for this is my doing" (1 Kings 12:24 NIV). Yes, God had used even Rehoboam's foolish boast to accomplish His will.

God can use setbacks and mistakes to accomplish His will today as well—especially His plans for our lives.

God used Rehoboam's boast to accomplish His own will.

123. JEROBOAM SETS UP IDOLS \\ 1 KINGS 11:35–38; 12:25–33; 14:1–20

>> When Ahijah had anointed Jeroboam king of northern Israel, He explained that God had ordained this occasion to judge the nation for its idol worship. What a clear warning!

God then promised Jeroboam: "If you do whatever I command you and walk in obedience to me. . .I will be with you. I will build you a dynasty as enduring as the one I built for David" (1 Kings 11:38 NIV). What powerful promises!

But when Jeroboam realized that his people would continue going to Jerusalem to worship God, he worried that they'd eventually give their allegiance to Rehoboam.

Had Jeroboam sought the Lord, He would've inspired him with a godly way to keep his subjects loyal. God *had* promised him an enduring dynasty, after all. But instead of seeking God, "on the advice of his counselors" (1 Kings 12:28 NLT) Jeroboam set up golden calves as gods, so his people wouldn't go to Judah to worship.

This led the Israelites into blatant idolatry, and God warned that He'd judge Jeroboam and his entire kingdom as a result.

God has wonderful plans for our lives, but these can be completely derailed by our disobedience and carnal reasoning.

124. GOD'S PROPHETS DISOBEY \\ 1 KINGS 13:1–32

» Soon after Jeroboam set up the calf idol and an altar in Bethel, a prophet of God arrived from Judah and prophesied against the altar.

King Jeroboam pointed at the prophet and ordered, "Arrest him!" Immediately the king's arm withered and the altar split apart. Talk about miracles! Jeroboam begged for mercy, so the prophet prayed and Jeroboam's arm was restored.

Jeroboam then invited him for a meal and a reward. He wanted to buy God off. However, God had commanded the prophet not to eat or drink anything there, but to return straight to Judah. So he left.

Then an old prophet rode after him and lied, saying that an angel had told him to bring him back to eat and drink. But when the young prophet followed him home, the old prophet rebuked him for disobeying God. On his way south, a lion killed the young prophet.

God dealt so strictly with him because He'd done outstanding miracles through him and had spoken clearly to him—yet the young prophet had disobeyed.

It's vital to obey what we know to be God's will and not allow even other believers to talk us into compromising.

» After Rehoboam became king of Judah "and he had become strong, he and all Israel with him abandoned the law of the LORD. Because they had been unfaithful to the LORD, Shishak king of Egypt attacked Jerusalem" (2 Chronicles 12:1–2 NIV). Shishak took all the gold out of the king's palace and from God's temple.

Judah had not simply neglected to worship God, but had begun worshiping idols on every high hill and in groves everywhere.

Then a prophet told the rulers of Judah that because they had forsaken the Lord, the Lord would forsake them and leave them in the hands of Shishak.

When the Israelites turned away from their idols, God protected them from Shishak.

To their credit, Rehoboam and the other leaders took this warning to heart, humbled themselves, and said, "The LORD is righteous" (2 Chronicles 12:6 NKJV). As a result, God turned away His anger and didn't allow Shishak to destroy them.

As long as they humbled themselves before the Lord, things went well in Judah.

God also gives us warnings when we slip into idolatry. We may think that we're in no danger of worshipping idols, but Paul warns that covetousness and materialism are outright idolatry (Colossians 3:5).

126. ASA REIGNS (MOSTLY) RIGHTEOUSLY
\\ 1 KINGS 15:9–24; 2 CHRONICLES 14:2–16:14

» Asa was Rehoboam's grandson, and "Asa did what was good and right in the eyes of the LORD his God" (2 Chronicles 14:2 NIV). He not only removed the altars of pagan gods and demolished their idols, but also deposed his own grandmother for making an idol of Asherah.

When the Ethiopians invaded Judah with a vast army, Asa cried out, "LORD, it is nothing for You to help, whether with many or with those who have no power; help us, O LORD our God, for we rest on You" (2 Chronicles 14:11 NKJV). And God mightily helped Asa defeat them.

Then God gave Asa peace for many years from all his enemies.

But later, to defend himself from northern Israel, Asa took the gold from the temple's treasury and sent it to the Arameans, to get them to help him. God sent a prophet to Asa reminding him that He had helped him against the Ethiopians and telling him how foolish he was now.

From then on, Asa had wars.

"Having begun by the Spirit, are you now being perfected by the flesh?" (Galatians 3:3 NASB). No. We must *continue* trusting God.

127. KINGS OF ISRAEL RULE RUTHLESSLY \\ 1 KINGS 15:25–34; 16:1–28

» The kings of Israel ruthlessly seized power—even if it meant shedding much blood. "Nadab the son of Jeroboam began to rule over Israel" and "immediately slaughtered all the descendants of King Jeroboam, so that not one of the royal family was left" (1 Kings 15:25, 29 NLT).

Baasha, the next king, died peacefully. But when his son Elah was king, while he was drunk his servant Zimri assassinated him. "Zimri [then] immediately killed the entire royal family of Baasha. . . . He even destroyed distant relatives and friends" (1 Kings 16:11 NLT).

But after Zimri had reigned one week, Omri besieged his palace, and Zimri burned the palace down around himself, dying in the inferno rather than letting Omri have it.

Omri then became king, and because the royal palace was burned, he made Samaria the new capital of Israel and built another palace there.

Israel had gone from being a spiritual kingdom of God's holy people to being a carnal, bloody nation—just like the rest of the sinful world.

As Christians, our lives have been transformed by Christ (2 Corinthians 5:17), so let's be sure that we don't do business the world's unscrupulous way.

» After Omri died, Ahab became king, and he "did more evil in the eyes of the LORD than any of those before him" (1 Kings 16:30 NIV). He not only worshipped the golden calves, but he married Jezebel, a Canaanite princess from Sidon, and worshipped her gods.

Ahab built a temple for Baal in Samaria, and soon 450 prophets of Baal and 400 prophets of Asherah ate daily at Jezebel's table and promoted idol worship in Israel. Jezebel then launched a campaign to massacre every prophet of God (1 Kings 18:13, 19). Fortunately, a royal servant hid a hundred prophets in a cave.

One day, Ahab desired the vineyard of an Israelite named Naboth, and when Naboth declined to sell it, Jezebel had false witnesses testify that he had "blasphemed God" (1 Kings 21:10 NKJV). Innocent Naboth was then stoned for blasphemy, and Ahab—the *real* blasphemer—took his vineyard.

"There was never anyone like Ahab, who sold himself to do evil in the eyes of the LORD, urged on by Jezebel his wife" (1 Kings 21:25 NIV).

Ahab and Jezebel worshipped golden calves and other gods, such as Baal.

When people continue making major disobedient decisions, they begin to travel down the broad way to destruction.

» At one point only seven thousand Israelites remained faithful to God and refused to worship Baal (1 Kings 19:18). But God still loved His people and sent them a powerful prophet—Elijah.

One day Elijah stormed in and declared to Ahab: "As the LORD, the God of Israel, lives, whom I serve, there will be neither dew nor rain in the next few years except at my word" (1 Kings 17:1 NIV). This drought was more than just a punishment for sin. For forty-two months, it was a daily reminder of the power of God.

It also showed the effectiveness of prayer. "The effective, fervent prayer of a righteous man avails much. Elijah. . .prayed earnestly that it would not rain; and it did not rain on the land for three years and six months. And he prayed again, and the heaven gave rain" (James 5:16–18 NKJV).

The entire nation suffered during this drought, because almost the entire nation was guilty and needed to return to God.

Even today, God sends troubles to bring His people back to Him. "As many as I love, I rebuke and chasten. Therefore be zealous and repent" (Revelation 3:19 NKJV).

130. AN AMAZING MIRACLE IN ZAREPHATH \\ 1 KINGS 17:8–24

» After warning of the coming drought, Elijah hid. Ahab sent men to every nation looking for him, but couldn't find him (1 Kings 18:10–11). He never *dreamed* Elijah was in Zarephath, just eight miles south of Jezebel's hometown of Sidon.

When he arrived in Zarephath, Elijah asked a Canaanite widow for bread. She answered, "As the LORD your God lives, I do not have bread, only a handful of flour in a bin, and a little oil in a jar" (1 Kings 17:12 NKJV).

Elijah told her not to fear, and promised that if she shared the last of her food with him, God would do a miracle and make her meager supply of flour and oil last for *years*. And He did!

The widow believed the word of the Lord and "she and he and her household ate for many days. The bin of flour was not used up, nor did the jar of oil run dry" (1 Kings 17:15–16 NKJV). Jesus Himself spoke of God's tender care for this Canaanite woman (Luke 4:25–26).

It can take great faith to obey God's counterintuitive instructions— but there are also great rewards for doing so.

❯❯ At God's command Elijah sent a message to Ahab, telling him to gather the Israelites—and all the prophets of Baal and Asherah—on Mount Carmel.

Both Elijah and the false prophets built an altar, piled wood on top, and put a sacrifice on that. Elijah then stated: "You call on the name of your god, and I will call on the name of the LORD, and the God who answers by fire, He is God" (1 Kings 18:24 NASB). All the people agreed.

Now, Baal was a storm god. Lightning was supposedly his forte. But though Baal's prophets prayed from morning till evening, there was no answer. Finally they gave up.

The Israelites acknowledged the one true God after a fire from heaven burned down on Elijah's sacrifice on Mount Carmel.

Then Elijah soaked the wood of his altar with water three times and prayed to God. Immediately fire blazed down from heaven and burned up the sacrifice, the wood, the stones, and the dust. It even vaporized the water on the ground.

Then all the people cried out, "The LORD—he is God! Yes, the LORD is God!" (1 Kings 18:39 NLT).

The Lord is *indeed* the one true God, whether or not He does an awe-inspiring miracle to prove it to us.

132. ELIJAH FLEES TO MOUNT SINAI \\ 1 KINGS 18:40–46; 19:1–14, 18

❯❯ At Elijah's command, the people killed all the false prophets. Then Elijah prayed for rain, and God sent a heavy rainstorm. The drought was over! Many Israelites were convinced that the Lord was actually God. Even Ahab was moved by this miracle.

Jezebel, however, was furious. She immediately sent word to Elijah that she was going to have him killed within one day.

If Elijah had hoped that the miracle would cause a nationwide revival, he was disappointed. Instead of a multitude of Israelites rallying around him, he found himself alone.

Elijah became depressed. He fled south, and in the desert he prayed, "It is enough! Now, LORD, take my life" (1 Kings 19:4 NKJV). Instead, God sent an angel to strengthen him. Eventually Elijah arrived at Mount Sinai.

God sent a great wind, then an earthquake; then fire swept across the mountain. But the Lord was not in these things. Then God spoke to Elijah in "a still small voice" (1 Kings 19:12 KJV) and mightily encouraged him to continue.

After serious spiritual tests, we too need time alone to hear God's Spirit speaking gently to our spirits, encouraging us.

133. ELIJAH CHOOSES A SUCCESSOR \\ 1 KINGS 19:15–21

» When Elijah spoke with God on Mount Sinai, God told him, "Anoint Hazael to be king of Aram. Then anoint Jehu grandson of Nimshi to be king of Israel, and anoint Elisha. . .to replace you as my prophet" (1 Kings 19:15–16 NLT).

Elijah departed, found Elisha out plowing a field, and called him to follow. So Elisha "set out to follow Elijah and became his servant" (1 Kings 19:21 NIV). He was a genuine servant. One of his jobs was to pour water on Elijah's hands when he washed (2 Kings 3:11).

In later years, after Elijah departed from this life, Elisha finished his mission for him: he announced Hazael as the new king of Aram, and he sent a young prophet to anoint Jehu as king of Israel (2 Kings 8:7–15; 9:1–13).

Elisha was a great prophet. And because he received a double portion of Elijah's anointing (2 Kings 2:9, 12), he did twice as many miracles as Elijah had.

But he had to be a servant before he could become an outstanding man of God. The same is true of us today. "Anyone who wants to be first must be. . .servant of all" (Mark 9:35 NIV).

» Ahab allowed his wife Jezebel to lead him deep into idolatry, and he'd stood by when she killed prophets of God. Yet after fire fell on Mount Carmel, proving that the Lord was God, Ahab listened carefully when God's prophets spoke.

One day the king of Aram made such oppressive demands that Ahab couldn't comply. This meant war, and Ahab was anxious.

Then God sent a prophet to Ahab, saying, "Thus says the LORD: 'Have you seen all this great multitude? Behold, I will deliver it into your hand today, and you shall know that I am the LORD" (1 Kings 20:13 NKJV). Ahab believed God, went to battle, and defeated the Arameans.

The next year a huge Aramean army returned. Again a prophet of God told Ahab, "I will deliver all this great multitude into your hand, and you shall know that I am the LORD" (1 Kings 20:28 NKJV). Again Ahab believed God, went to war, and defeated the Arameans.

You may wonder why God mercifully delivered someone like Ahab, who was so

Cain committed the world's first murder by killing his brother.

far from Him. But God is patient. He still has mercy on us today, despite *our* failings.

» It was *after* these battles that Jezebel murdered Naboth and Ahab took over his vineyard. So Elijah told Ahab, "Now the LORD says, 'I will bring disaster on you'" (1 Kings 21:21 NLT). The time for mercy was over.

Three years later, Jehoshaphat king of Judah visited Ahab, and Ahab asked if he'd help him take back one of his cities from the Arameans. Jehoshaphat first wanted to hear from the prophets. All four hundred of them encouraged Ahab to go to battle, saying he'd be victorious.

But when pressed on this point, a final prophet named Micaiah bluntly told Ahab that it was God's will that he die in battle, so God "put a deceiving spirit in the mouths of all these prophets of yours. The LORD has decreed disaster for you" (1 Kings 22:23 NIV).

Ahab was alarmed. He still went to war but disguised himself as a common charioteer. Nevertheless, God saw to it that "a certain man drew a bow at random" and this "random" arrow fatally wounded Ahab (1 Kings 22:34 NKJV).

God often has mercy for years, but if people *persist* in not repenting, He finally sends judgment.

136. ELIJAH IS SWEPT UP TO HEAVEN \\ 2 KINGS 2:1–18

Elijah was taken to heaven in a chariot of fire and a whirlwind.

» One day the Lord prepared to take Elijah up to heaven. Elisha knew this was going to happen, and refused to leave Elijah's side.

When they came to the Jordan River, Elijah rolled up his cloak, struck the waters, and they parted so that the two prophets could cross over.

When Elijah asked Elisha what he wanted, Elisha asked for a double anointing of his spirit. Moments later, "a chariot of fire and horses of fire appeared and separated the two of them, and Elijah went up to heaven in a whirlwind" (2 Kings 2:11 NIV).

Elisha picked up Elijah's cloak that had fallen, walked back to the river, and struck the waters with it. They immediately parted. The prophets who witnessed this said, "The spirit of Elijah is resting on Elisha" (2 Kings 2:15 NIV).

Only one other time in the Old Testament did God transport a living man to heaven. "And Enoch walked with God: and he was not; for God took him" (Genesis 5:24 KJV). In the New Testament, Jesus ascended to heaven after His resurrection (Luke 24:50–51; Acts 1:9).

One day, when Jesus returns, we too shall be caught up to heaven.

137. MOAB REBELS AGAINST ISRAEL \\ 2 KINGS 3:1–24

» After Ahab died, his son Ahaziah reigned for only two years (1 Kings 22:51). When he died, his younger brother Jehoram became king (2 Kings 3:1). Moab was subject to Israel, and the Moabites took advantage of Israel's internal turmoil to revolt.

Jehoram wasn't strong enough to reconquer Moab, so he asked Judah for help. Jehoshaphat agreed, suggesting that they attack Moab from the south. After seven days of having no water, however, their armies were ready to perish.

Elisha was in their midst, and prophesied that they should dig ditches throughout the valley and God would fill them with water.

He added, "And this is a simple matter in the sight of the LORD; He will also deliver the Moabites into your hand" (2 Kings 3:18 NKJV).

So the thirsty soldiers dug ditches all over. The next morning, water rushed south and filled the ditches. The Moabites saw the red sunrise on the water and thought it was blood. Thinking the attackers had killed one another, they rushed into the valley—and were ambushed.

God's instructions will sometimes make no sense, but remember: He knows facts that we can't know. Our job is simply to obey.

138. A GOOD KING MAKES BAD FRIENDS
\\ 2 KINGS 3:9–14 ; 2 CHRONICLES 19:1–3; 20:35–37

» Jehoshaphat of Judah was a good king, but he had his weaknesses: although he knew that God was determined to destroy Ahab, he still helped Ahab fight the Arameans (1 Kings 22:20–23, 29). And Ahab died.

After the battle, a prophet told Jehoshaphat, "Should you help the wicked and love those who hate the LORD? Therefore the wrath of the LORD is upon you" (2 Chronicles 19:2 NKJV).

Jehoshaphat didn't take this to heart. "After this Jehoshaphat. . .allied himself with Ahaziah king of Israel. He acted wickedly in so doing." They made a fleet of trading ships. Another prophet declared, "Because you have allied yourself with Ahaziah, the LORD has destroyed your works." And all his ships were wrecked (2 Chronicles 20:35, 37 NASB).

And after *this*, Jehoshaphat joined Ahab's wicked son Jehoram in his battle against Moab. Although God did a miracle and gave them an initial victory, in the end they failed to reconquer Moab.

Like Jehoshaphat, we may sincerely love the Lord but displease Him by forming alliances with the ungodly. God warns us, "Do not be unequally yoked together with unbelievers" (2 Corinthians 6:14 NKJV).

139. PRAISE WINS A BATTLE \\ 2 CHRONICLES 17:1–19; 20:1–30

» Despite Jehoshaphat's compromises, "the LORD was with Jehoshaphat . . ." The reason for this was because "his heart took delight in the ways of the LORD" (2 Chronicles 17:3, 6 NKJV).

One day, not long after Moab's revolt against Israel, the armies of Moab, Ammon, and Edom banded together and invaded Judah—probably in retaliation for Jehoshaphat helping invade Moab. God was also punishing Jehoshaphat (2 Chronicles 19:2).

But Jehoshaphat poured out his heart in desperate prayer: "Our God, will you not judge them? For we have no power to face this vast army that is attacking us. We do not know what to do, but our eyes are on you" (2 Chronicles 20:12 NIV).

The Lord heard him and said, "the battle is not yours, but God's. . . . You will not need to fight in this battle" (2 Chronicles 20:15, 17 NKJV). Jehoshaphat believed God, so when he went out he had singers go *ahead* of his army, praising the Lord. The result: God caused the invading forces to fight among themselves and destroy each other.

God can still do mighty miracles today when we take delight in the Lord, pray desperately, believe His Word, and praise Him.

140. THE MIRACLE OF THE WIDOW'S OIL \\ 2 KINGS 4:1–7

» A group of prophets were in the habit of following Elijah— and now Elisha—to learn from him. There were fifty of them living in Jericho alone (2 Kings 2:7).

Then one of these prophets died, and his sudden passing left his wife and two children deeply in debt. The wife came to Elisha and told him, "My husband is dead, and you know that he revered the LORD. But now his creditor is coming to take my two boys as his slaves" (2 Kings 4:1 NIV).

Elisha asked what she had in her house. The poor lady was down to just one jar of oil. Elisha said, "Go around and ask all your neighbors for empty jars. Don't ask for just a few" (2 Kings 4:3 NIV). Elisha told her to then pour oil into the jars. She obeyed.

God supplied a widow with oil to sell so that her sons would not be taken as slaves.

The oil miraculously kept flowing until *all* the empty jars were filled. Elisha then told her to sell the oil, pay her debt, and live on the money that remained.

God commands us to provide for our families. This we must do. However, when adverse circumstances cause a financial crisis, God can supply miraculously.

141. ELISHA REVIVES A DEAD BOY \\ 2 KINGS 4:8–37

» There was a wealthy woman of Shunem who was very hospitable to Elisha, so in return God miraculously gave her a son, even though her husband was old.

Then one day the boy was out in the sun watching his father's men harvesting, when he was overcome, possibly by sunstroke. His father had him taken to the house, where he died in his grief-stricken mother's arms.

The woman mounted a donkey and quickly rode to Mount Carmel, twenty-five miles away. There she told Elisha the news. Elisha sent his servant Gehazi ahead with his staff and told him to lay it on the boy to raise him up. But this was unsuccessful.

Late in the day Elisha and the woman arrived at the house. The boy's corpse was now cold. Elijah prayed fervently then stretched himself out on the body until it became warm. Then Elisha paced back and forth. He stretched himself out again. Suddenly the boy sneezed and opened his eyes. He was alive again!

Elijah had performed a similar miracle years earlier in Zarephath (1 Kings 17:17–24). When Jesus was on earth, He raised *three* people from the dead!

142. NAAMAN'S LEPROSY IS HEALED \\ 2 KINGS 5:1–19

» The Arameans had fought several pitched battles with Israel. At the moment, however, there was a cessation of hostilities.

Now, Naaman, commander of the Aramean army, was mighty and honorable. But he was a leper. One day a Hebrew slave said, "I wish my master would go to see the prophet in Samaria. He would heal him of his leprosy" (2 Kings 5:3 NLT). Soon Naaman was outside Elisha's house.

Elisha sent a man out with this message: "Go and wash yourself seven times in the Jordan River. Then. . .you will be healed of your leprosy."

Naaman was enraged. "'I thought he would certainly come out to meet me!' he said. 'I expected him to wave his hand over the leprosy and call on the name of the LORD his God and heal me!'" (2 Kings 5:10–11 NLT).

Naaman was about to leave, but his servants pointed out that, after all, he'd been told to do something easy. It was worth trying. So Naaman washed. . .and was healed!

Often we have preconceived ideas about how God should answer prayer. But we must be open to His answering in ways that surprise and humble us.

143. ANGEL ARMY ARRAYS AROUND DOTHAN \\ 2 KINGS 6:8–23

» For some time after Naaman's healing, there was peace with Israel. But then Ben-Hadad, king of Aram, renewed hostilities and sent raiding parties to ambush the king of Israel. But God showed his plans to Elisha, who repeatedly warned the king.

Ben-Hadad wondered who was betraying his secret plans, but his servants explained that Elisha the prophet was actually the one warning the king of Ben-Hadad's secret plans.

Ben-Hadad decided that Elisha had to be eliminated. Since Elisha was in the city of Dothan, he sent a great army and many chariots there.

God sent a heavenly army to protect Elisha from Ben-Hadad.

When Elisha's servant saw that they were surrounded, he was alarmed. But Elisha told him, "Don't be afraid. Those who are with us are more than those who are with them." Then Elisha prayed, "Open his eyes, LORD, so that he may see." Suddenly the servant saw flaming horses and chariots all around them (2 Kings 6:16–17 NIV).

Elisha then prayed for God to strike the Aramean army blind, and they all immediately lost their sight.

The Bible promises us even today: "The angel of the LORD encamps around those who fear him, and he delivers them" (Psalm 34:7 NIV).

144. BREAKING THE SIEGE OF SAMARIA \\ 2 KINGS 6:24–7:20

» After this, Ben-Hadad gathered his army and besieged Samaria, the capital of Israel. And there was a severe famine in Samaria.

Finally, the king of Israel had enough. Elisha had evidently promised that God would deliver them, but the king said, "Surely this calamity is from the LORD; why should I wait for the LORD any longer?" (2 Kings 6:33 NKJV). He wanted to kill Elisha.

However, Elisha told him that by this time tomorrow the siege would be over and there would be more than enough food for everyone.

One of the king's officers mocked, "Look, if the LORD would make windows in heaven, could this thing be?" (2 Kings 7:2 NKJV). Elisha assured him that it would indeed happen, but he wouldn't eat any of it.

That night, God caused the Aramean besiegers to hear the noise of many chariots and horses. Thinking that it was the Egyptian army arriving, the Arameans fled, leaving all their tents and food behind.

The next day while the officer was standing in the gate, the people rushed out to get food, and he was trampled to death. It simply doesn't pay to doubt and mock God.

145. HAZAEL ASSASSINATES BEN-HADAD \\ 2 KINGS 8:7–15

» Although Ben-Hadad was a cruel, pagan king, God waited years before judging him. Now Ben-Hadad was sick. The time had finally come to anoint Hazael as king in his place (1 Kings 19:15).

Elisha then made a surprise visit to Damascus, the Aramean capital. When Ben-Hadad heard that Elisha was in the city, he sent his official

Hazael to see him. Hazael brought forty camels loaded down with gifts for Elisha.

Hazael asked him the king's question: "Will I recover from this sickness?"

Elisha replied, "Go, say to him, 'You will surely recover,' but the LORD has shown me that he will certainly die." Elisha stared at Hazael for so long that Hazael became embarrassed. Then Elisha began crying.

When Hazael asked why he was weeping, Elisha answered, "Because I know the evil that you will do to the sons of Israel . . . . You will be king over Aram" (2 Kings 8:8–13 NASB).

Hazael couldn't wait to rule. He returned to the palace, smothered Ben-Hadad, and became king in his place. God planned to use Hazael to judge His sinful people, Israel.

God is concerned with the affairs even of pagan nations, especially if they affect believers.

This ivory image may depict Hazael after he became king.

146. JEHU BECOMES KING \\ 2 KINGS 9:1–10:17

» Elijah had warned Ahab of Jezebel's doom and that all his descendants would be killed (1 Kings 21:21–24). Now the time had come for these chilling prophecies to be fulfilled. And they both were tied directly into Jehu's becoming king (1 Kings 19:16).

Elisha sent a prophet to Jehu to anoint him king of Israel and inform him that he was to execute vengeance on Ahab's wicked house. Jehu was commander of the army and used to shedding blood, so he had no qualms.

Jehu's underofficers gladly proclaimed him king. He then raced to Jezreel in his chariot and slew King Joram (Ahab's son) and Ahaziah king of Judah (Ahab's relative) when they rode out to meet him.

When Jehu arrived in the city, Jezebel looked out a tower window and began cursing him, but Jehu commanded the servants beside her to hurl her down—and they did. Jehu then threatened to besiege the city where Ahab's seventy sons were and persuaded the fearful elders to behead them.

Jehu was a very violent man, but he was an instrument of vengeance on the house of Ahab for all the evil they had done for so many years.

147. JEHU DESTROYS BAAL WORSHIP \\ 2 KINGS 10:18–31

» Jehu was ruthless by nature and didn't hesitate to use deception. Subterfuge was a very common military tactic and he, as army commander, was adept at it. So when he determined to wipe out the lascivious worship of Baal, he said: "Now summon all the prophets of Baal, all his servants and all his priests. See that no one is missing, because I am going to hold a great sacrifice for Baal" (2 Kings 10:19 NIV). Delighted, all the servants of Baal came.

After Jehu destroyed the temple of Baal, he turned it into a public latrine. This image above is a similar latrine built later in Ephesus.

Jehu ordered the person in charge of the wardrobe to give a robe to each of the Baal worshippers. This was to clearly identify them. Soon the temple was crowded. Jehu then commanded eighty soldiers to go inside and slay everyone.

They then burned the temple and tore it apart. Thus Jehu destroyed Baal worship in Israel.

"Yet Jehu was not careful to keep the law of the LORD. . .with all his heart" (2 Kings 10:31 NIV). He refused to get rid of the golden calves—and this doomed the nation.

Like Jehu, we may be zealously fighting some evil, but God knows whether we are truly motivated by His zeal or our own.

148. JEHOIADA AND MATTAN VIE FOR POWER
\\ 2 CHRONICLES 22:11; 23:17; 24:7

» When Jehoiada was high priest there were very difficult times. Jehoiada was a very old man. He was about ninety years old at this point, and had seen kings come and go. And things took a turn for the worst when Jehoshaphat died and his wicked son Jehoram ruled.

Jehoram had married Athaliah, daughter of Jezebel, and Athaliah led Jehoram to worship Baal. In fact, they built a temple to Baal right in Jerusalem, and Mattan was its priest.

But Jehoram's daughter Jehosheba loved God, and one day she and Jehoiada had gotten married. That marriage was the best thing that could've happened, as we shall soon see.

After Jehoram died, his son Ahaziah became king. Ahaziah was as bad as his father, and his mother, Athaliah, had him break into God's temple and steal its treasures so Mattan could use them to worship Baal. And things were about to get even *worse*!

Sometimes when evil and evil people are winning and good seems weak and ineffective, we give up hope. But don't despair. "God chose the weak things of the world to shame the strong" (1 Corinthians 1:27 NIV).

149. WICKED QUEEN USURPS THE THRONE
\\ 2 KINGS 11:1–3; 2 CHRONICLES 22:10–12

» After two years, Ahaziah died. His son should have become king, but Ahaziah's mother, Athaliah, enraged over the death of Jezebel and the destruction of Baal worship in Israel, decided *she* would rule. So she sent soldiers to murder all her grandsons.

Princess Jehosheba was in the palace when the order was given. She only had time to save *one* child, so she grabbed her nephew, baby Joash, and hid him and his nurse in another bedroom.

Jehosheba was the wife of the high priest, Jehoiada, and he agreed to bring the baby to the temple. So, risking her life, Jehosheba smuggled Joash out of the palace, and he was hidden in the temple for the next six years. No one—not even the temple guards—knew about Joash.

For six years Athaliah ruled Judah and enforced Baal worship on the nation, and for six years Jehoiada and Jehosheba secretly taught young Joash to worship the true God. A confrontation was coming, and it would be dramatic.

Jehoiada would live to be 130 years old, and as long as he was alive, Joash worshipped and served God (2 Chronicles 24:2, 15). Thank God for selfless protectors and mentors!

150. JEHOIADA PULLS OFF A COUP \\ 2 KINGS 11:4–21; 2 CHRONICLES 23:1–21

» Jehoiada finally made his move. He called the commanders of the temple guards, showed them Prince Joash, and had them swear loyalty. Then he sent them throughout Judah to gather the priests and rulers. They all agreed that Joash should be king.

Each commander had a hundred guards. Normally when one shift ended, new guards replaced them. But now when fresh guards arrived, Jehoiada retained the old ones. He even armed the priests inside the temple.

Jehoiada had a third of the guards protect the temple, a third watch the palace, and a third watch the city gate. Then Jehoiada crowned Joash and shouted, "Long live the king!" (2 Chronicles 23:11 NKJV).

When Athaliah heard the noise, she rushed to the temple and cried, "Treason! Treason!" The guards executed her.

Then a crowd of people stormed across the city and tore down the temple of Baal. Meanwhile, Joash sat on the throne. He was only seven, but he had Jehoiada to advise him.

Jehoiada was so honored that when he died at age 130, he was buried in the tombs of the kings. Remember this: you're never too old for God to use you mightily.

151. ELISHA PROPHESIES ON HIS DEATHBED
\\ 2 KINGS 13:10–25; 14:23–27

» In the beginning of King Jehoash's reign, northern Israel was suffering bitter oppression from the Arameans, so God had mercy on them. For over forty years, Elisha hadn't prophesied or done miracles. But when he was old and sick, he summoned the king to his bedchamber.

Elisha had Jehoash take up a bow; then, placing his hands over the king's hands, he shot an arrow out the window, calling it "the arrow of victory over Aram" (2 Kings 13:17 NIV).

Elisha then told Jehoash to grab a bundle of arrows and strike the floor. Jehoash struck three times and stopped. Elisha was angry, saying that he should have continued striking five or six times. Then he would have utterly defeated the Arameans.

Sure enough, Jehoram defeated Aram only three times.

After Jehoash died, Jeroboam II became king. Then God sent the prophet Jonah to declare that Jeroboam would restore the size of the kingdom—and he *did* (2 Kings 14:23–26). Jeroboam did what Jehoash had failed to do.

When God has given you a job, do it with your whole heart! There may *not* be someone to finish the job if you fail.

152. JEHOASH DEFEATS PROUD AMAZIAH
\\ 2 KINGS 14:1–16; 2 CHRONICLES 25:1–28

» When he became king of Judah, Amaziah worshiped the Lord. Therefore, God gave him a great victory over the Edomites. He even conquered their capital. Then, astonishingly, he brought back the idols of Edom, bowed down to them, and worshiped them as his own gods.

A prophet of God rebuked the king for foolishly worshipping idols that hadn't even been able to save the Edomites from *him*. Amaziah ordered the prophet to shut up. He then sent a message to Jehoash, king of Israel: "Come, let us face each other in battle" (2 Kings 14:8 NIV).

Jehoash warned that Amaziah would be trampled like a thistle in battle.

Jehoash answered, "You have indeed defeated Edom and now you are arrogant. Glory in your victory, but stay at home! Why ask for trouble and cause your own downfall and that of Judah also?" (2 Kings 14:10 NIV).

But Amaziah again refused to listen, and in the battle that followed, God made *sure* that Judah was defeated. And Amaziah was imprisoned in Samaria for several years. After Jehoash's death, Amaziah was released and returned to Judah.

The lessons in this story are clear. God doesn't always judge pride and sin this quickly, but He *does* judge them.

153. PROPHET JONAH RUNS AWAY \\ JONAH 1:1–4:11

» Jonah had prophesied that Jeroboam II would defeat Aram, and he did. Israel was now larger, stronger, and more prosperous than it had ever been.

But a mighty warring empire to the north was an imminent threat. The Assyrians were the cruelest, most violent empire the world had ever seen, and Jonah knew this. So at first he was delighted when God told him to go to Nineveh and preach, "Forty days from now Nineveh will be destroyed!" (Jonah 3:4 NLT).

Then Jonah got the inescapable feeling that the Assyrians would repent if they heard this warning. Then God would have mercy and *not* destroy them (Jonah 4:2). Jonah therefore took a ship to Tarshish, to make *sure* Nineveh was destroyed.

We know the rest of the story: God sent a storm, the sailors threw Jonah overboard, he was swallowed by a great sea creature, was finally vomited on the shore. . .and once again was ordered to go warn Nineveh. This time he obeyed.

And precisely as Jonah had feared, Nineveh repented and God delayed His judgment.

When God has given you a message, speak what He tells you to speak, and leave the results in His hands.

154. THE RISE AND FALL OF UZZIAH \\ 2 KINGS 15:1–7; 2 CHRONICLES 26:1–23

» Uzziah (also known as Azariah), became king of Judah when his father was imprisoned in Samaria. After his father was released, they shared the throne. After his death, Uzziah again was sole ruler.

Now, Uzziah "sought God in the days of Zechariah. . .and as long as he sought the Lord, God made him prosper" (2 Chronicles 26:5 NKJV).

Uzziah was "exceedingly strong" and conquered all his enemies. "So his fame spread far and wide, for he was marvelously helped till he became strong. But when he was strong his heart was lifted up, to his destruction" (2 Chronicles 26:8, 15–16 NKJV).

One day Uzziah thought that he was *so* special that he went into the temple and offered incense on the altar of incense. The astonished priests told him that this job was *only* for the priests.

Uzziah became furious, and in that instant, leprosy broke out on his forehead. The priests chased him out of the temple. From then on he couldn't live in his palace. He had to live in an isolated house by himself.

Often we too are "marvelously helped" by God. Let's not ruin a good thing by giving in to pride.

155. THE FATE OF THE JUDEAN CAPTIVES \\ 2 CHRONICLES 28:1–15

» Ahaz, Uzziah's grandson, was a wicked king. He not only worshipped the Baals, but sacrificed his children in the fire to pagan gods. He led Judah greatly astray. Then Pekah, king of Israel, together with Aram, invaded Judah "because Judah had forsaken the LORD" (2 Chronicles 28:6 NIV).

The Israelites took a great amount of plunder. They also captured two hundred thousand women and children from their fellow Israelites and took them back to Samaria to make them slaves.

But a prophet met the army and said that because the Lord was angry with Judah, He had helped Israel conquer them. But, as he pointedly stated, "Are you not also guilty before the LORD your God? Now hear me, therefore, and return the captives. . .for the fierce wrath of the LORD is upon you" (2 Chronicles 28:10–11 NKJV).

The Israelites were deeply moved. They then clothed all the captives who needed clothes, gave them sandals, gave them food and drink, and took them back to Judah, letting the weak ride on donkeys.

Even the people of Samaria who weren't walking with God were moved to acts of great compassion. How much more should *we* be Good Samaritans?

156. ISAIAH PROPHESIES THE VIRGIN BIRTH \\ ISAIAH 7:1–14

» Now, Ahaz was an especially idolatrous king, so you'd think that God wouldn't have cared for him. But the fact that Ahaz believed in

Isaiah, as envisioned by an early twentieth-century artist.

signs and the supernatural meant that he was also open to appreciating the power of the true God— if he saw it.

One day Ahaz heard that Aram and Israel would invade Judah again, "so the hearts of Ahaz and his people were shaken, as the trees of the forest are shaken by the wind" (Isaiah 7:2 NIV). But the prophet Isaiah assured him, "This invasion will never happen" (Isaiah 7:7 NLT).

Isaiah challenged Ahaz to ask God for a sign of confirmation. The sign could be as difficult as he wished. But Ahaz refused to ask.

God *wanted* to give a sign. He wanted to demonstrate His power. But when Ahaz wasn't interested, God gave a sign that was fulfilled in the distant future: "Behold, the virgin shall conceive and bear a Son, and shall call His name Immanuel [God with us]" (Isaiah 7:14 NKJV).

Ahaz didn't see this sign, but it has encouraged millions of people since then to believe that Jesus is God's Son and is God with us (Matthew 1:21–23).

157. THE NORTHERN KINGDOM FALLS \\ 2 KINGS 15:27–30; 17:1–23

» A prophet had told Israel that "the fierce wrath of the LORD is upon you" (2 Chronicles 28:11 NKJV), and it was. It had finally come time to pay for *centuries* of sins and idol worship.

Therefore, during Pekah's reign, Tiglath-Pileser of Assyria attacked Israel and sacked many cities. He also conquered the regions of Gilead, Galilee, and the north, and took many captives. Then there was a brief reprieve.

After Hoshea became king of Israel, however, the Assyrians returned—this time to stay—and Hoshea was forced to pay heavy tribute for several years.

Then Hoshea tried to get Egypt's help to break free. The Assyrians discovered his plot and invaded the entire country. After a three-year siege, Samaria itself fell. Then the Assyrians took all Israel captive. . .and that was the *end* of the northern kingdom.

"This disaster came upon the people of Israel because they. . .had done many evil things, arousing the LORD's anger. Yes, they worshiped idols, despite the LORD's specific and repeated warnings" (2 Kings 17:7, 11–12 NLT).

God loves you and is at work in your life, specifically and repeatedly convicting you of disobedience as well.

» Now, Sargon II, king of Assyria, deported people from other lands and settled them in the towns of Israel. When they first arrived, these newcomers didn't worship the Lord, so He sent lions that slew many of them.

When this report reached the king of Assyria, he ordered: "Have one of the priests you took captive from Samaria go back to live there and teach the people what the god of the land requires" (2 Kings 17:27 NIV).

Therefore, one of the priests who had been exiled from Samaria came to live in Bethel and taught the pagan settlers how to worship God. And the lion attacks stopped. However, they "worshiped the LORD, but they also served their own gods" (2 Kings 17:33 NIV).

By Jesus' day, the Samaritans had stopped worshipping other gods and worshipped only the true God. They still didn't know Him very well. Jesus pointed out, "You Samaritans worship what you do not know" (John 4:22 NIV).

But when the early church evangelized Samaria, thousands of Samaritans became Christians (Acts 8:4–8, 12).

The work of that one Israelite priest, centuries earlier, had far-reaching ramifications. Our work for God can too.

» Hezekiah became king of Judah and revolted against Assyria and refused

When Sennacherib conquered the cities of Judah, Hezekiah gave him all of his gold and silver.

to pay tribute when Hoshea did. But while Israel was crushed and deported, things went differently for Judah.

The reason? Hezekiah trusted God and was "faithful to the LORD in everything. . . . So the LORD was with him, and Hezekiah was successful in everything he did" (2 Kings 18:6–7 NLT). He became so strong that he even conquered the Philistines.

Seven years after Samaria fell, however, Sennacherib invaded Judah and conquered all its cities. Only Jerusalem withstood. Hezekiah then sent this message: "I have done wrong. I will pay whatever tribute money you demand if you will only withdraw" (2 Kings 18:14 NLT).

Sennacherib demanded eleven tons of silver and a ton of gold—so Hezekiah handed over all the silver in his palace and the temple. He even stripped the gold from the doors of God's temple and gave that.

It looked like a humiliating defeat for a godly king. . .and things were about to get even *worse*! But the darkest hour was just before dawn.

When God is with you and gives you success, He may allow you to be severely tested, but continue trusting Him.

160. ASSYRIANS FOOLISHLY MOCK GOD
\\ 2 KINGS 18:17–19:37; 2 CHRONICLES 32:1–23

» Hezekiah had paid an exorbitant tribute for Sennacherib to withdraw from Judah. But after Sennacherib received it, he treacherously reneged. He sent an army commander to Jerusalem demanding its surrender—saying that he'd deport everyone to a distant land.

Hezekiah encouraged his people, "With him is only the arm of flesh, but with us is the LORD our God to help us and to fight our battles" (2 Chronicles 32:8 NIV).

The Assyrian commander mocked, "Don't let him fool you into trusting in the LORD. . . . What god of any nation has ever been able to save its people from my power? So what makes you think that the LORD can rescue Jerusalem from me?" (2 Kings 18:30, 35 NLT).

He even put this boast in writing. Hezekiah went into the temple, spread the letter out before the Lord, and prayed desperately. As a result, Isaiah prophesied that God would miraculously deliver the city.

A few nights later, God sent an angel into the Assyrian camp and wiped out 185,000 soldiers. The Assyrians who survived fled.

God is *still* with us today to help us and to fight our battles, so we can trust Him.

161. HEZEKIAH GETS A LEASE ON LIFE
\\ 2 KINGS 20:1–19; 2 CHRONICLES 32:23–31

» After God saved Hezekiah from the Assyrians, "he was exalted in the sight of all nations" and many foreigners brought offerings for God (2 Chronicles 32:23 NASB). God not only honored Hezekiah but restored riches to him.

Then Hezekiah became deathly sick from a boil. God sent Isaiah to tell him to put his house in order, for he would surely die. After Isaiah left his bedchamber, Hezekiah wept bitterly and prayed.

God stopped Isaiah before he reached the middle court and sent him back with this message: "I have heard your prayer, I have seen your tears; surely I will heal you. . . . And I will add to your days fifteen years" (2 Kings 20:5–6 NKJV). And He did!

Despite his miraculous healing, "Hezekiah did not repay according to the favor shown him, for his heart was lifted up; therefore wrath was looming over him." But just when he seemed doomed once again, "Hezekiah humbled himself," and once again God held back His judgment (2 Chronicles 32:25–26 NKJV).

Time and again when we deserve to be judged, repentance and sincere prayer cause God to have mercy.

162. WICKED MANASSEH RULES JUDAH
\\ 2 KINGS 21:1–18; 2 CHRONICLES 33:1–9

» After Hezekiah died, his son Manasseh became king. When the Assyrians again threatened Judah, Manasseh surrendered and became a vassal. He was then obliged to send troops to help the Assyrian king, Ashurbanipal, crush uprisings in Egypt—in 667 BC and again in 664 BC.

Manasseh was forced to serve the Assyrians because he didn't trust God to save him. The fact was, he worshipped Baal and other pagan gods and even built them altars in God's temple. He practiced witchcraft, consulted mediums, and killed many innocent people.

Manasseh was more wicked than the Canaanites Israel had displaced, so God vowed to irrevocably destroy Judah, no matter how much they repented later (2 Kings 23:26–27).

Then, in 653 BC, Pharaoh Psamtik I revolted and drove the Assyrians from Egypt. Emboldened by this success, the Babylonians also rebelled from 652 to 648 BC. Manasseh may have been suspected of treason in this, because after the Assyrians crushed the Bab-

Manasseh consulted mediums, practiced witchcraft, and burned his son as an offering to pagan gods.

ylonians, they put him in prison. His life was one long disaster—all because he despised the Lord.

Often when people make self-serving "rational decisions" when in trouble, their real reason is that they don't love or trust God.

163. MANASSEH IS BROUGHT DOWN \\ 2 CHRONICLES 33:10–20

» The Assyrians suspected that Manasseh had been plotting against them, so they imprisoned him in far-off Babylon. There he languished under arrest, remembering the many prophets of God who had warned him.

Then in a total change of heart, Manasseh turned to the God he had so grievously rebelled against. Remember, Manasseh had been into the worst evil imaginable.

"In his distress he sought the favor of the Lord his God and humbled himself greatly before the God of his ancestors." God heard him, cleared him of the charge of treason, and had the Assyrians restore him to his throne. "Then Manasseh knew that the Lord is God" (2 Chronicles 33:12–13 niv).

Manasseh removed an idolatrous object from God's temple. He tore down all the altars he had built on the temple hill and in Jerusalem. Then he restored the altar of the Lord and made offerings on it. And he commanded all Judah to serve the Lord.

God is still in the business of redeeming and transforming people lost in deep darkness—in fact, now more than ever! "Therefore, if anyone is in Christ, he is a new creation" (2 Corinthians 5:17 NKJV).

164. FINDING THE LOST LAW \\ 2 KINGS 22:1–20; 2 CHRONICLES 34:1–28

❯❯ God's temple had been neglected for many decades and had fallen into disrepair. When Josiah, Manasseh's grandson, had been king for eighteen years, he had workmen repair it.

It was at this time that the high priest found the long-lost law of Moses. A scribe took it to Josiah, saying, "Hilkiah the priest has given me a book" (2 Kings 22:10 NIV). The scribe then read it out loud.

The law had been lost for many decades, and Josiah had never heard it. So when the scribe began reading God's warnings in Deuteronomy 28:15–68, Josiah became afraid. Israel had disobeyed God greatly, and judgment was imminent.

Josiah asked the prophetess Huldah what God would do, and she prophesied, "I am going to bring disaster on this place and its people— all the curses written in the book" (2 Chronicles 34:24 NIV). But God promised that because of Josiah's tender heart, the disaster wouldn't happen in his day.

When we haven't read our Bible for a long time, we forget what it says—and since we don't know what it says, we don't obey it. God help us to read His Word daily.

165. JOSIAH PURGES THE LAND OF IDOLS
\\ 2 KINGS 23:1–25; 2 CHRONICLES 34:29–33

❯❯ Until he heard the details described in the law of Moses, Josiah had let things slide—but no longer! When he knew how abhorrent idol worship was to God, Josiah was shocked into action. He gathered his people together and reaffirmed their commitment to the Lord.

That's when he realized that there were idols and pagan altars right in the temple of God. The worshippers of Asherah had their own weaving room in God's house. Josiah immediately cleared them out.

He dragged the Asherah carving from the temple and burned it. He also got rid of the idolatrous priests who burned incense to Baal throughout Judea.

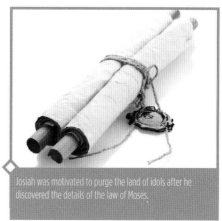

Josiah was motivated to purge the land of idols after he discovered the details of the law of Moses.

Once he had a clear understanding of what God required, Josiah did a thorough house-cleaning. "Neither before nor after Josiah was there a king like him who turned to the LORD as he did—with all his heart and with all his soul and with all his strength" (2 Kings 23:25 NIV).

And so "Josiah removed all detestable idols from the entire land of Israel" (2 Chronicles 34:33 NLT). May we also be spurred to recommit ourselves, obey God's commands, and clean up our lives.

166. JUDAH'S PRETEND REVIVAL \\ JEREMIAH 3:6–15

>> Josiah was a godly king and led a nationwide revival for more than ten years, and many Israelites returned to God. But people were deeply entrenched in idol worship, and many were loathe to change their ways. Although they couldn't stop Josiah from destroying all the idols, they "set up their idols in their hearts" (Ezekiel 14:3 NKJV).

As Jeremiah prophesied, "The LORD said also to me in the days of Josiah the king. . .'Judah has not turned to Me with her whole heart, but in pretense'" (Jeremiah 3:6, 10 NKJV). They went through the motions of worshipping God, but for many, it was just an act.

What about northern Israel, which was mercifully able to share in Judah's revival, even after their kingdom had fallen? God stated, "And I said, after she had done all these things, 'Return to Me.' But she did not return" (Jeremiah 3:7 NKJV).

This was why, despite Josiah's best efforts to rid the nation of idolatry, its doom was sealed and its fate determined.

Jesus said similar things about the scribes and Pharisees of His day—that they were only pretending to worship God (see Mark 7:6–7). May the same not be true of us!

167. PROPHET OF DOOM ARISES \\ JEREMIAH 1:1–19

» In the thirteenth year of King Josiah, when Jeremiah was a youth, God told him, "Before I formed you in the womb I knew you, before you were born I set you apart; I appointed you as a prophet to the nations" (Jeremiah 1:5 NIV).

When Jeremiah protested that he was too young, the Lord told him, "Do not say, 'I am too young.' You must go to everyone I send you to and say whatever I command you" (Jeremiah 1:7 NIV).

God then showed Jeremiah an ominous vision of a boiling pot in the north, tilted toward Judea. The Lord told him that He was summoning powerful kingdoms against His people, and from the north judgment would be poured out on the inhabitants of the land.

God told Jeremiah, "Get yourself ready!" (Jeremiah 1:17 NIV) and warned that he'd face tremendous opposition. But Jeremiah was not to be terrified by his adversaries, because God was with him and would make him like a "fortified city" to withstand their attacks.

Sometimes we feel as if we're under siege, attacked by those around us. But God, who created us and called us to serve Him, is also there to protect us.

168. JOSIAH'S MIGHTY RISE AND FALL
\\ 2 KINGS 23:28–30; 2 CHRONICLES 35:20–25

» Josiah committed his life to the Lord, and God richly rewarded him. In 627 BC, the Assyrian strongman Ashurbanipal died, and his once-mighty empire went into decline and came under attack by enemies like the Babylonians.

The Assyrians were forced to abandon northern Israel. With them gone, Josiah expanded his kingdom. It was the first time since Solomon's day that all Israel was ruled by the house of David. The first thing Josiah did was abolish idols throughout the north. All Israel seemed to be experiencing a revival.

Josiah was killed in battle at Tel Megiddo.

Then in 609 BC, Pharaoh Neco led an army out of Egypt to help the Assyrians fight the Babylonians. Pharaoh preferred a weak Assyria to a powerful Babylon.

Josiah tried to intervene, but Pharaoh warned him, "I am on my way to fight another nation. . . . Do not interfere with God, who is with me, or he will destroy you" (2 Chronicles 35:21 NLT). God had indeed spoken to Pharaoh, and Josiah *suspected* this—which is why he went into battle disguised. But he died in that battle.

Loving God is definitely the *most* important thing. But it's also important to obey God in the details.

169. TWO EMPIRES CONQUER JUDAH
\\ 2 KINGS 23:28–37; 2 CHRONICLES 36:1–4

» The Egyptians continued north, crossed the Euphrates, and beseiged the city of Haran. But the Babylonian army outmaneuvered them, so Neco was forced to retreat.

After Josiah's death, Jehoahaz became king—but only reigned three months before the Egyptians deposed him and set up Jehoiakim as puppet king. Pharaoh demanded that they pay tribute, so Jehoiakim taxed everyone to raise the money.

Jehoiakim didn't love God as Josiah had, and during his reign, worship of Baal and Asherah flourished once more.

Meanwhile, in 606 BC, Pharaoh Neco again attacked the Babylonians. At first he was winning, but at the Battle of Carchemish in 605 BC, his army was badly mauled (Jeremiah 46:2). That same year, Nebuchadnezzar became king of Babylon.

Following this battle, Pharaoh Neco lost control of Syria, Phoenicia, and Israel (2 Kings 24:7; Daniel 1:1-2). After that, Neco didn't venture outside Egypt. Not only was Judah ruled by an idolatrous king, Jehoiakim, but it fell under Babylonian control. Things did *not* look good.

In this time of confusion, darkness, and distress, a prophet named Jeremiah spoke out. We too are called upon to courageously proclaim God's message, even during troubled times.

170. JEREMIAH STANDS TRUE \\ JEREMIAH 26:1–24

» Early in the reign of Jehoiakim, Jeremiah went to the temple and warned that God's house would be destroyed and Jerusalem would be abandoned. No sooner had he finished speaking, however, than the priests and prophets crowded around him and shouted, "You must die!" (Jeremiah 26:8 NIV).

They pointed out that King Jehoiakim had just finished killing a

The people believed Jeremiah when he said that Jerusalem would be abandoned.

prophet named Uriah who had prophesied the same kinds of things. Although Uriah had fled to Egypt, Jehoiakim had sent men after him to arrest him; they had brought him back, and the king had him killed.

Jeremiah warned them, "Be assured, however, that if you put me to death, you will bring the guilt of innocent blood on yourselves and on this city" (Jeremiah 26:15 NIV).

The officials and people believed Jeremiah. They reminded the priests and prophets that during the days of King Hezekiah, a man named Micah had prophesied doom against Jerusalem (Micah 3:9–12). Instead of killing him, Hezekiah had repented, and God relented from sending destruction.

A nobleman named Ahikam supported Jeremiah, so he wasn't put to death.

When it comes time to stand up for what is right, make sure that your voice is heard.

171. COLDHEARTED KING BURNS SCRIPTURE \\ JEREMIAH 36:1–32

» Josiah had been a godly king and had greatly repented when he'd heard God's warnings (2 Kings 22:11–13). His son Jehoiakim had an entirely different reaction.

One day, God told Jeremiah to record all the prophecies he'd received. So Jeremiah dictated them to the scribe Baruch, who wrote them in a scroll. Jeremiah then sent Baruch to the temple to read his warnings. Jeremiah could no longer go there.

Jehudi and other noblemen heard Baruch and were afraid. They knew what they had to do. Jehudi took the scroll into Jehoiakim's palace and began reading it to him.

It was wintertime, so the king had a fire burning, and every time Jehudi had read three or four columns, Jehoiakim would cut that section off and toss it in the fire. He did this until the entire scroll was burned.

If Jehoiakim had repented at the warnings, God would've had mercy, just as He'd had mercy on Josiah. But because he rejected God's Word, his judgment was certain. Jeremiah then gave Baruch another scroll and had him write the words again.

God still either blesses or chastises us depending upon how we react to His Word.

172. DANIEL TAKES A STAND IN BABYLON \\ DANIEL 1:1–20

» When Nebuchadnezzar conquered Judah in 605 BC, he took several members of the royal house and noble families back to Babylon. Among them were four youths—Daniel and his friends, whose Babylonian names were Shadrach, Meshach, and Abednego.

In a three-year crash course, Daniel and friends were taught the language and literature of the Babylonians. Fortunately, they were quick learners.

However, there was a serious challenge: they were given food from the king's table, yet this included food forbidden to the Jews (Leviticus 11) and meat from which the blood hadn't been drained. So "Daniel resolved not to defile himself with the royal food and wine" (Daniel 1:8 NIV).

His supervisor was afraid to change the king's orders and have the Israelites look sickly, but Daniel suggested that he and his friends have only vegetables and water for ten days, and after that the supervisor could judge the results. Sure enough, after ten days, the four Israelite youths were in excellent health!

It took great courage to stand up to the king's orders, but Daniel and his friends were serious about loving and obeying God. May we also be willing to take unpopular stands for our faith.

173. NEBUCHADNEZZAR'S FANTASTIC DREAM \\ DANIEL 2:1–49

» One night King Nebuchadnezzar had a mysterious dream—and to make matters worse, when he woke up, he couldn't remember it. So he called his wise men and demanded that they tell him *what* he had dreamed *and* its interpretation.

They protested that he was asking an impossible thing, but this made the king so mad that he ordered the execution of all the wise men. Daniel, however, asked Nebuchadnezzar for time and promised that he'd do what he asked.

Then Daniel prayed desperately—because this truly *was* an impossible task. And that night God did a miracle and revealed the king's dream to him.

The next day, Nebuchadnezzar asked him, "Are you able to tell me what I saw in my dream and interpret it?" Daniel answered that this mystery was beyond *his* ability to solve, then said, "But there is a God in heaven who reveals mysteries" (Daniel 2:26, 28 NIV).

When Daniel revealed what God had showed him, Nebuchadnezzar was astonished. He exclaimed, "Truly, your God is the greatest of gods" (Daniel 2:47 NLT).

Are you at your wit's end? God is still God. He can *still* solve problems that are beyond human power and understanding.

174. ISRAELITES HURLED INTO A FURNACE \\ DANIEL 3:1–30

» One day, King Nebuchadnezzar had a ninety-foot-high golden idol made. He then commanded that everyone bow down and worship it. But Shadrach, Meshach, and Abednego refused.

Nebuchadnezzar summoned them and gave them one last chance to obey him. If they didn't, they'd be hurled into a burning furnace. He assured them that no god would be able to deliver them then.

They answered, "If we are thrown into the blazing furnace, the God whom we serve is able to save us. . . . But even if he doesn't, we want to make it clear to you, Your Majesty, that we will never. . . worship the gold statue you have set up" (Daniel 3:17–18 NLT).

Nebuchadnezzar's face contorted with rage, and he ordered the furnace heated even hotter.

Nebuchadnezzar threw Shadrach, Meshach, and Abednego into a fiery furnace when they refused to worship his golden idol.

Then Shadrach, Meshach, and Abednego were hurled into the flames. To the king's astonishment, moments later, the three men were walking around inside the furnace. And a fourth man appeared with them!

They came out of the furnace completely unharmed.

Now, God may not always deliver *you* from every accident and danger, but the point is: "even if he doesn't," you need to be faithful to Him.

175. EZEKIEL SEES GOD'S MAJESTY \\ 2 KINGS 24:1–17; EZEKIEL 1:1–28

» In Judah, King Jehoiakim rebelled against the Babylonians, so Nebuchadnezzar captured Jerusalem and took him to Babylon. His son Jehoiachin then reigned. But only three months later, Jehoiachin was also taken to Babylon.

Several other Jews went to Babylon with him; among them was a Levite named Ezekiel. Soon Ezekiel was living with other Jews along the Kebar Canal. There, five years later, he had an astonishing vision.

The heavens opened and Ezekiel saw "a whirlwind was coming out of the north, a great cloud with raging fire engulfing itself; and brightness was all around it and radiating out of its midst like the color of amber" (Ezekiel 1:4 NKJV).

Ezekiel then saw four heavenly creatures called cherubim. Each one had four faces, and "their appearance was like burning coals of fire. . .and out of the fire went lightning" (Ezekiel 1:13 NKJV).

Above the four creatures was a throne, and the Lord sat on the throne, gleaming brilliantly like fire with a rainbow around Him.

God then called Ezekiel to be a prophet to the Israelites (Ezekiel 2:2–3).

God calls us to serve Him as well—to obey Him and to speak His truth to others.

176. PROPHET PERFORMS PERPLEXING SKITS \\ EZEKIEL 12:1–16

» After Jehoiachin went to Babylon, Zedekiah became king. The people wanted to believe that they weren't sinning, that things would be okay.

So false prophets arose, assuring them that very soon the exiles would return from Babylon.

They claimed, "The LORD has raised up prophets for us in Babylon" (Jeremiah 29:15 NIV). God *had* raised up a true prophet in Babylon, Ezekiel, but the Jews were listening to the false prophets. When they did listen to Ezekiel, they didn't obey (Ezekiel 33:31–32). So God instructed Ezekiel to do a series of silent skits. No words, just actions.

In one pantomime, Ezekiel dug through the clay wall of his house in broad daylight. Then he crawled through the hole with all his belongings, set the pack on his shoulder, and carried it to another place.

The Jews asked, "What are you doing?" Ezekiel answered, "I am a sign to you. As I have done, so will it be done to them. They will go into exile as captives" (Ezekiel 12:9, 11 NIV). Sure enough, Zedekiah later rebelled, Jerusalem was besieged, and the *rest* of the Jews went into exile in Babylon.

Sometimes actions really *do* speak louder than words.

177. JEREMIAH THROWN IN PRISON \\ 2 KINGS 25:1–2; JEREMIAH 37:1–21

» In the ninth year of his reign, Zedekiah rebelled, so Nebuchadnezzar sent an army to besiege Jerusalem. Then Pharaoh led an army out of Egypt, and when the Babylonians heard about it, they broke off their siege.

The Jews were delighted, thinking that they'd been rescued. They once again opened the gates and people came and went.

But Jeremiah warned Zedekiah that God was still determined to judge them for their sins: "Do not fool yourselves into thinking that the Babylonians are gone for good. They aren't! Even if

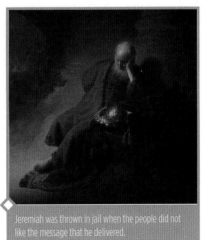

Jeremiah was thrown in jail when the people did not like the message that he delivered.

you were to destroy the entire Babylonian army, leaving only a handful of wounded survivors, they would still stagger from their tents and burn this city to the ground!" (Jeremiah 37:9–10 NLT).

Then Jeremiah decided to head to his home village, but as he was going out the gate, a guard said, "You are defecting to the Babylonians!" (Jeremiah 37:13 NLT). Jeremiah denied the charge, but he was arrested anyway. The officials had him flogged and imprisoned in a dungeon cell, where he remained for many days.

Jeremiah had an unpopular job, constantly warning people not to have false hopes. We may be called to do the same.

178. A PRISONER BUYS SOME LAND \\ JEREMIAH 32:1-44

» Pharaoh's army returned to Egypt without helping the Jews, so the Babylonians continued besieging Jerusalem. Soon food was scarce and expensive. Things looked grim. Zedekiah, beginning to get desperate, had compassion and moved Jeremiah to a better prison in the courtyard in the palace.

One day Jeremiah's cousin Hanamel came to Jeremiah. He said, "Please buy my field at Anathoth" (Jeremiah 32:8 NLT). Apparently he needed money for food. God had *told* Jeremiah that Hanamel would do this, so he bought the field for seventeen pieces of silver.

It seemed foolish to buy land outside the city. Jerusalem was under siege and its inhabitants starving. It appeared like a waste of money to buy that field.

But God told Jeremiah that although Jerusalem was doomed and the Jews were about to go in exile to Babylon, one day He would bless them again and return them to their land. God wanted Jeremiah to buy the field as a sign of hope in Judah's darkest hour.

As God asked: "I am the LORD, the God of all mankind. Is anything too hard for me?" (Jeremiah 32:27 NIV). May this promise also give *us* hope during our dark days.

» As the siege continued and famine ruled the city, even Zedekiah was forced to concede that they couldn't withstand the Babylonian army. The city was doomed.

Jeremiah, meanwhile, continued prophesying: "Whoever stays in this city will die by the sword, famine or plague, but whoever goes over to the Babylonians will live" (Jeremiah 38:2 NIV).

Finally, the officials had heard enough. They insisted that Jeremiah be put to death. Zedekiah felt unable to stop them, so he handed Jeremiah over.

The officials decided to make Jeremiah suffer greatly until he died. They dropped him into a deep cistern (reservoir). All the water was gone and there was only deep mud there. Jeremiah sank in the mud and couldn't get free. This looked like the end.

But an Ethiopian named Ebed-melech heard what they'd done, went to the king, and got permission to rescue Jeremiah. With the help of several men, Ebed-melech lowered a rope. He attached a harness made of old clothes to it, and told Jeremiah to put this under his arms. Then they pulled him up.

You may be at your lowest point, stuck in troubles. It may look like the end is certain. But never give up hope!

» Finally the Babylonians broke through the wall and rushed into the city. Zedekiah then put his backup plan into operation. He and his army burst out from a secret gate, fought their way through the enemy lines, and fled toward Jericho.

It might have seemed like a clever plan, but God made sure that the Babylonians caught Zedekiah. His army was scattered, his sons were killed, and he himself was blinded and taken to Babylon.

Meanwhile, the Babylonians looted God's temple. One month later General Nebuzaradan burned the temple, the palace, and all the houses of Jerusalem. His army then broke down all the city's walls so it could never rebel again.

He then took most of the surviving Jews as prisoners to Babylon.

God had delayed His judgment of Jerusalem, but the city did fall when the Babylonians invaded.

The judgments that had been threatened in Deuteronomy 28:15–68 had finally arrived. God's punishment had been mercifully delayed time and again, but it finally came.

God has mercy and patience today as well—but will eventually judge the world. "The Lord is not slow about His promise. . .but is patient toward you, not wishing for any to perish but for all to come to repentance" (2 Peter 3:9 NASB).

181. GOVERNOR GEDALIAH IS ASSASSINATED
\\ 2 KINGS 25:22–26; JEREMIAH 40:1–16; 41:1–3

» The Babylonians released Jeremiah from prison. Nebuzaradan knew Jeremiah had warned the Jews to surrender to the Babylonians, so he let him live wherever he wished to.

Now, a Jew named Gedaliah had been appointed governor of Judea, and he resided in Mizpah, so Jeremiah went there. The royal princesses and other Jews were there also (Jeremiah 43:6).

It was harvesttime, and the land was overflowing with ripe figs, grapes, and dates, so the surviving Jews had their pick of the best of the land. Gedaliah therefore urged everyone to settle down peacefully and serve the Babylonians.

Despite everything that had happened, they could *still* enjoy a very good life in the land that God had given to their ancestors.

But a surviving royal prince, Ishmael, wanted to rule. He came to Mizpah with a group of followers, pretending to be peaceful. Then he assassinated Gedaliah. He took the princesses and other Jews and headed for Ammon—thus destroying the last hope of the Jews in Judea.

After we've suffered great losses, we need to learn to be satisfied and not wreck a good thing, even if it's not quite what we were used to.

182. JEREMIAH IS TAKEN TO EGYPT \\ JEREMIAH 41:11–18; 42:1–22; 43:1–7

» When an army officer named Johanan heard about what Ishmael had done, he and his men pursued him and rescued the royal princesses and the others.

Ishmael fled to Ammon, but he was no longer their concern. After the massacre at Mizpah, Johanan and his men were afraid that the Babylonians would retaliate against them. They were worried that it was no longer safe for them in Judah, so they took all the people and headed for Egypt.

They stopped near Bethlehem and asked Jeremiah if God had clear direction for them. They vowed, "Whether it is pleasing or displeasing, we will obey the voice of the LORD our God to whom we send you" (Jeremiah 42:6 NKJV).

Jeremiah waited on the Lord for ten days. Finally God spoke, telling the people not to be afraid of the Babylonians. He told him to stay in Judah, and He would be merciful to them and bless them—yes, even now.

This was *not* the answer Johanan and his fellow officers had expected, and they angrily continued to Egypt. How often we too claim to be seeking God's will, yet insist on our own way.

183. GOD DRIVES A PROUD KING INSANE \\ DANIEL 4:1–37

» Meanwhile, in Babylon, Nebuchadnezzar had a dream about a mighty tree spreading out its branches far and wide. Then an angel descended and shouted to cut the tree down—and went on to give an ominous, mysterious message.

Nebuchadnezzar asked Daniel what this dream meant, and Daniel warned that the proud king would lose his mind, be driven from his palace, and eat grass like a cow "until you learn that the Most High rules over the kingdoms of the world" (Daniel 4:25 NLT).

When Nebuchadnezzar boasted about his power, God drove him to insanity.

Nebuchadnezzar soon forgot Daniel's warning. One day as he looked out over the city, he boasted, "Look at this great city of Babylon! By my own mighty power, I have built this beautiful city as my royal residence to display my majestic splendor" (Daniel 4:30 NLT).

No sooner had Nebuchadnezzar spoken than God judged him. . . and he lost his mind. He lived out with wild animals, exposed to the elements. Only when the allotted time was up did God restore his sanity—and his throne.

We too must recognize that God is the one who gives us all that we have and enjoy—or He might take it away so we can learn.

184. BABYLON FALLS SUDDENLY \\ DANIEL 5:1–31

» Years passed, and Nabonidus became king. Shortly afterward, he abandoned Babylon and left his heir Belshazzar in charge.

Belshazzar reigned poorly and lost most of his empire to the Medes and Persians. Soon their armies were camped around Babylon itself. But Belshazzar was confident that the capital was impregnable and could never fall, so one evening he threw a drunken party. He even used the golden goblets taken from God's temple to drink wine in.

Suddenly a disembodied hand wrote ominous words on the palace wall. Belshazzar shook with fear. He quickly summoned Daniel and asked him to interpret the handwriting.

Daniel first reminded him about Nebuchadnezzar: "When his heart became arrogant and hardened with pride, he was deposed from his royal throne. . . . But you, Belshazzar, have not humbled yourself, though you knew all this" (Daniel 5:20, 22 NIV).

Daniel then informed him that the handwriting declared that God had brought his reign to an end and given his kingdom to the Medes and Persians. That very night their armies broke through the city's defenses and Belshazzar was killed.

If we don't learn the lessons of history, we're doomed to repeat them.

185. CYRUS CREATES A MIGHTY EMPIRE
\\ ISAIAH 45:1–4; DANIEL 7:5; 8:1–4, 20

» The Persian king, Cyrus II—also called Cyrus the Great—conquered much of the Middle and Near East. The Persians were an ancient people of Iran. They were first subject to the Medes, but Cyrus rebelled in 554 BC and captured the Median capital Ecbatana four years later.

Fifteen years before Babylon fell (while Cyrus was still subject to the Medes, in fact), Daniel had a dream of his kingdom as a ferocious, hungry bear (Daniel 7:5). Two years later, Daniel dreamed of it as a great horned ram (Daniel 8:1–4, 20).

Cyrus then conquered Babylon—and went on to carve out the Persian Empire, an empire that stretched from the border of India in the east to Greece in the west, and Egypt in the south.

Amazingly, around 680 BC, some 130 years earlier, Isaiah had prophesied that Cyrus would rule: "Thus says the LORD to His anointed, to Cyrus, whose right hand I have held—to subdue nations before him. . . I have even called you by your name" (Isaiah 45:1, 4 NKJV).

God accurately declares the future far in advance—then moves mightily among the nations to bring about His will!

» Cyrus placed Darius the Mede (perhaps also known as Gubaru) in charge of the conquered Babylonian territories. Darius favored Daniel and appointed him as one of the three top rulers of the kingdom.

This made many governors and satraps jealous, and they plotted against Daniel. They "sought to find some charge against Daniel. . .but they could find no charge or fault, because he was faithful" (Daniel 6:4 NKJV).

Then they had an idea: they told Darius that he should enact a law

Daniel was faithful to God, and he was protected when he was thrown into the lions' den.

that no one should pray to any god for thirty days—only to Darius. All offenders should be thrown to the lions. Darius foolishly agreed.

Daniel, of course, continued praying faithfully to God. When the governors and satraps told Darius about it, he tried to rescue Daniel—but the law couldn't be broken. So, with a heavy heart, he ordered Daniel thrown into the lions' den.

Early the next morning, after a sleepless night, Darius called to Daniel, asking if he was still alive. Daniel answered that, yes, God had sent an angel to shut the lions' mouths. Darius then threw Daniel's accusers to the lions.

Let's be found faithful, both to other people and to God.

187. CYRUS LETS THE EXILES RETURN
\\ ISAIAH 44:24–28; 45:1–13; EZRA 1:1–11

» Also around 680 BC, about 130 years before the Medes and Persians conquered Babylon, Isaiah prophesied "to His anointed, to Cyrus"

(Isaiah 45:1 NKJV), saying, "I have raised him up. . .he shall build my city, and he shall let go my captives" (Isaiah 45:13 KJV).

God also declared, "I am the LORD. . .who says of Cyrus, 'He. . .shall perform all My pleasure, saying to Jerusalem, "You shall be built," and to the temple, "Your foundation shall be laid"'" (Isaiah 44:24, 28 NKJV).

The amazing thing is, at the time of these prophecies, Jerusalem was still intact, the temple was still standing, and the Jews hadn't gone into captivity. That changed in 586 BC when the Babylonians burned the temple, destroyed Jerusalem, and took the Jews to Babylon. For decades the Jews were captives in a foreign land.

In 538 BC Cyrus gave a decree, allowing the Jews to return home. This decree also fulfilled a prophecy by Jeremiah (2 Chronicles 36:22–23). Cyrus accepted his divine mandate and declared: "The LORD. . .has appointed me to build a temple for him at Jerusalem" (Ezra 1:2 NIV).

Fulfilled, detailed prophecy proves the omniscience—and loving care—of God.

188. ENEMIES OPPOSE REBUILDING GOD'S TEMPLE
\\ EZRA 3:8–13; 4:1–24

» Shortly after the Jews returned to Judea, Zerubbabel, the civil ruler, and Jeshua, the high priest, led the priests and Levites in laying the foundation of the new temple.

When the Samaritans heard, they said, "Let us build with you, for we seek your God as you do" (Ezra 4:2 NKJV). Now, the Samaritans did seek God, but not *quite* "as you do," because they worshipped their other gods alongside the Lord.

The Jews refused to let them help, because they knew that such a partnership would open wide the door to idolatry in their worship—and after being exiled for idol worship, they were determined never to repeat such a mistake.

This angered the Samaritans. Then they "set out to discourage the people of Judah and make them afraid to go on building" (Ezra 4:4 NIV).

They finally sent a letter to the new Persian king, Artaxerxes, complaining that this building threatened the peace of his kingdom.

Unfortunately, Artaxerxes believed them and commanded the Jews to stop building.

We too will face opposition as we obey the Lord. "Yes, and everyone who wants to live a godly life in Christ Jesus will suffer persecution" (2 Timothy 3:12 NLT).

189. TEMPLE BUILDING RECOMMENCES \\ EZRA 5:1–2; HAGGAI 1:1–15

» Cyrus had written an edict telling the Jews to rebuild their temple, so they had a *right* to build. But the present ruler was against them. So the people postponed things for a more favorable season, saying, "The time has not yet come to rebuild the LORD's house" (Haggai 1:2 NIV).

Zerubbabel and Jeshua were bold enough to start rebuilding God's temple.

But God spoke through the prophet Haggai: "Why are you living in luxurious houses while my house lies in ruins?" God then judged them to get their attention: "You have planted much but harvest little. . .our wages disappear as though you were putting them in pockets filled with holes!" (Haggai 1:4, 6 NLT).

God was withholding His blessings because His people were putting their needs first and taking the easy way out. They were afraid to stand up for the Lord. But God ordered them to boldly start building once again.

The prophet Zechariah echoed this message. Then Zerubbabel and Jeshua took courage and started to rebuild, "and the prophets of God were with them, helping them" (Ezra 5:2 NKJV).

We have a God-given right and obligation to serve the Lord. Let's not take it lying down if someone tries to deny us that right.

190. SEARCHING FOR A MISSING EDICT \\ EZRA 5:3–17; 6:1–12

» The Jews not only obeyed their prophets, but they carefully thought through their legal defense, because they knew that trouble would surely come.

They didn't have a copy of Cyrus's official edict, but they *knew* that one existed, so when Tattenai the governor asked them, "Who authorized you to rebuild this temple and to finish it?" (Ezra 5:3 NIV), they replied that King Cyrus had.

Tattenai therefore wrote to Darius, the new Persian king: "Now if it pleases the king, let a search be made in the royal archives of Babylon to see if King Cyrus did in fact issue a decree to rebuild this house of God in Jerusalem" (Ezra 5:17 NIV).

A search in the royal archives of Babylon turned up nothing. The original edict had been either lost or misplaced. But the officials kept searching—and eventually a scroll bearing the edict was found in the distant city of Ecbatana.

Darius then told the Jews to continue rebuilding and warned of serious punishments to anyone who opposed them—and the temple was finished four years later!

Have courage and obey God, but also do your homework and know your legal rights.

191. JEWESS BECOMES QUEEN OF PERSIA \\ ESTHER 1:1–22; 2:1–18

» Just before King Xerxes (also known as Ahasuerus) launched an invasion of Greece (482–479 BC), he hosted an extravagant banquet for 180 days. This assembly was also to plan his war.

One evening he commanded Queen Vashti to appear before his guests to display her beauty, but Vashti refused to come. As a result, she was deposed as queen. Xerxes then busied himself with preparations for war.

The campaign was a disaster, so when Xerxes returned, history tells us that he consoled himself by indulging in pleasures. One of the things he did was to search for beautiful young virgins. The woman who pleased him would be his queen instead of Vashti.

Xerxes made Esther queen after Vashti displeased him.

Now, in the capital lived a Jew named Mordecai. Mordecai had a beautiful young cousin named Hadassah (Esther), and when her parents died, Mordecai had taken her in as his own daughter. Esther was brought to the king's palace with the other women.

"Now the king was attracted to Esther more than to any of the other women," so he "made her queen" (Esther 2:17 NIV).

God can even use the world's setbacks and disasters to bring His people to the stage to fulfill His will.

192. A PLOT TO WIPE OUT THE JEWS \\ ESTHER 3:1–15

» Ever since Persian officials had plotted against Daniel, there appears to have been an undercurrent of hatred against the Jews. This is why "Esther had not revealed her nationality and family background, because Mordecai had forbidden her to do so" (Esther 2:10 NIV).

Mordecai was a government official of some standing, with access to the palace courts, and one day he heard two of the king's officers conspire to assassinate Xerxes. He quickly reported the incident, and the men were arrested and found guilty.

Mordecai's fears about anti-Semitism were well-founded. Not long after this incident, Xerxes appointed Haman, an Amalekite, as his right-hand man.

All the king's officials were supposed to bow down and honor Haman, but Mordecai refused, because the Amalekites were bitter enemies. Haman became furious at Mordecai and, when he found out that he was Jewish, decided to kill not only him but every Jew throughout the Persian Empire.

Xerxes trusted Haman and loaned him his signet ring to seal a royal decree ordering the Jews to be exterminated.

The devil has frequently inspired evil men to murder God's people—but God has always had a plan to eventually rescue them.

193. ESTHER RISKS DEATH \\ ESTHER 4:1–17; 5:1–8

» When Mordecai heard the terrible news, he sent a message to Esther telling her to plead with the king to spare their people.

Esther replied that anyone who went into the inner court uninvited was put to death. The person's life was spared only if the king held out his golden scepter. But she hadn't been called to see Xerxes in one month.

Mordecai answered, "If you remain completely silent at this time, relief and deliverance will arise for the Jews from another place. . . . Yet who knows whether you have come to the kingdom for such a time as this?" (Esther 4:14 NKJV).

Then Esther sent a reply to Mordecai, telling him to assemble all the Jews to fast for her. "And so I will go to the king, which is against the law; and if I perish, I perish!" (Esther 4:16 NKJV).

On the third day, Esther stood in the inner court. King Xerxes, sitting on his throne, held out the golden scepter. Her life was spared, and she was able to present a petition.

Sometimes we too will be called to abandon our personal comfort and safety to stand up for the defenseless.

» Esther invited Xerxes and Haman to a banquet, and there she pled for her life and the lives of her people. When the king demanded to know what man had dared plot such a massacre, Esther revealed that it was evil Haman.

Purim is celebrated in remembrance of when Esther saved the Jews from being massacred.

Haman had set up a great pole to impale Mordecai on, so the king commanded Haman to be executed on it instead. He then gave Haman's position and ring of authority to Mordecai.

When Esther asked Xerxes to countermand Haman's edict, he explained that no law of the Medes and Persians could be annulled. But there was something he *could* do: he immediately sent out a new message giving the Jews the right to defend themselves.

There was great rejoicing among the Jews when they read this edict. Meanwhile, their enemies—who had by now revealed themselves publicly—were terrified.

Mordecai became the king's new right-hand man, and Esther continued to enjoy great influence in the kingdom. And this day of the Jews' deliverance was established as a new feast day called Purim.

God can turn terrible near-disasters into great victories. But we must be courageous and faithful to do our part.

195. EZRA TRAVELS TO JUDAH \\ EZRA 7:1–28; 8:21–23, 31–32

»Despite Cyrus's edict allowing the Jews to return to Judea, many of them stayed in Babylon, and it became a major center of Jewish learning. Ezra was the foremost Jewish scholar during the reign of King Artaxerxes.

"Ezra was a scribe who was well versed in the Law of Moses," and he "had determined to study and obey the Law of the LORD and to teach those decrees and regulations to the people of Israel" (Ezra 7:6, 10 NLT).

When Ezra traveled to Israel to teach God's Word, "the king gave him everything he asked for, because the gracious hand of the LORD his God was on him" (Ezra 7:6 NLT). Artaxerxes sent a letter to his treasurers in the western provinces telling them to give Ezra whatever he needed.

The king wanted to ensure that he had the favor of Israel's God. He needed it. Egypt, right next to Judah, had just revolted and driven out the Persians. In the year of Ezra's trip, 458 BC, Artaxerxes was setting out to resubdue Egypt.

The gracious hand of the Lord is upon us today as well, if we too determine to study and obey the Bible.

196. SEPARATING FROM THE HEATHEN \\ EZRA 9:1–15; 10:1–17

❱❱ Ezra didn't decide to go to Judah on a whim. Judah was the Jewish homeland and boasted the temple of God, but many Jews living there were becoming involved in serious compromise.

In disobedience to the Law of Moses, they had begun marrying pagans who lived there (Exodus 34:15–16). It wouldn't be long before they began worshipping their gods and falling into idolatry all over again.

They had just survived judgment and exile in Babylon, and God had graciously allowed a remnant to survive and return to their land. And now *this*!

Ezra prayed, "What has happened to us is a result of our evil deeds. . . . Shall we then break your commands again and intermarry with the peoples who commit such detestable practices? Would you not be angry enough with us to destroy us, leaving us no remnant or survivor?" (Ezra 9:13–14 NIV).

This principle still applies to us today. God has had mercy upon us and rescued us from our sins and destructive ways—but let's not take His grace for granted. "For He will speak peace to His people and to His saints; but let them not turn back to folly" (Psalm 85:8 NKJV).

» During the twentieth year of King Artaxerxes, a Jew named Nehemiah was the king's cupbearer. It was his job to taste the king's wine before the king drank it, to make sure no one had poisoned it. So he was a highly trusted servant.

Then one of Nehemiah's relatives came from Judah, telling him news about the Jews living there: "The survivors. . .are there in great distress and reproach. The wall of Jerusalem is also broken down, and its gates are burned with fire" (Nehemiah 1:3 NKJV).

Although the temple had been rebuilt in Jerusalem, most of the city, destroyed by the Babylonians 140 years earlier, was still in utter ruins (Nehemiah 2:17; 7:4). And because it had no walls around it, the Jews were defenseless against their many enemies.

Nehemiah requested that the king allow him to go to Jerusalem to rebuild the city—and especially the walls. Artaxerxes therefore appointed Nehemiah governor of Judah, giving him real authority, and sent him there (Nehemiah 5:14).

Even today, certain of God's people may be living in "the promised land" but suffering distress and oppression. We need to be concerned about this and do what we can to help.

198. NEHEMIAH REBUILDS A FALLEN WALL
\\ NEHEMIAH 2:11–20; 4:1–23; 6:15–16

» After arriving in Jerusalem, Nehemiah inspected the walls then gathered all the Jews and told them his vision. So they began to build.

This was no easy task. They had nothing to build with other than the burned stones buried under tons of rubble. So they dug them out and began setting them in place. It didn't look like much, but it was a wall.

When the laborers nearly gave up because there was too much rubble, Nehemiah urged them on. And they kept working. "So we rebuilt the wall. . .for the people worked with all their heart" (Nehemiah 4:6 NIV).

Their enemies, meanwhile, became determined to stop them. They threatened to attack. They sent other Jews, ten times, to tell them that an attack was imminent. They threatened to report them to the king. But Nehemiah refused to give in to fear and kept building.

Nehemiah led the team that rebuilt the walls of Jerusalem.

Day after day, they "continued the work. . .from the first light of dawn till the stars came out" (Nehemiah 4:21 NIV). Finally, the wall was completed, giving the Jews tremendous joy.

There will be times when we also will need to persevere in serving God, despite intense opposition.

199. ALEXANDER CONQUERS A VAST EMPIRE \\ DANIEL 8:5–8, 15–21

» Around 552 BC Daniel had an astonishing dream: a he-goat "with a prominent horn between its eyes came from the west. . . . And [he] saw it attack the ram furiously, striking the ram and shattering its two horns" (Daniel 8:5, 7 NIV).

The angel Gabriel then told Daniel, "The ram which you saw with the two horns represents the kings of Media and Persia. The shaggy goat represents the kingdom of Greece, and the large horn that is between his eyes is the first king" (Daniel 8:20–21 NASB).

In 333 BC, Alexander the Great came from the west (Greece) and in 332 BC fought the Persian army at Issus, utterly defeating them. Then he headed down the Mediterranean coast conquering cities, and came to Jerusalem.

Instead of fighting the Greeks, the Jews opened the gates for them. The high priest led a procession out to meet Alexander and showed him Daniel's prophecy that declared that God had ordained him to conquer the world.

Alexander, meanwhile, had had a dream about a priest, dressed in white, coming to give him a message from God.

God plans history and moves powerfully to bring His will to pass among the nations—for the benefit of His people.

200. THE MACCABEES REVOLT \\ DANIEL 8:8, 22; 11:31–35

» Just as Daniel had dreamed, after the death of Alexander his empire was divided into four kingdoms. The Seleucid Empire ruled over Judah. Things were peaceful for many years. However, in 175 BC, Antiochus Epiphanes became ruler.

Antiochus determined that the Jews must follow Greek customs and worship Greek gods. Daniel prophesied that a wicked king would

The Greeks were driven out of Israel during the Maccabean Revolt.

"defile the sanctuary. . .take away the daily sacrifices, and place there the abomination of desolation" (Daniel 11:31 NKJV). In 167 BC Antiochus set up an idol of Zeus in God's temple and sacrificed a pig on the altar.

Then there was great persecution against faithful Jews. Daniel had prophesied that they "will die by fire and sword, or they will be jailed and robbed" (Daniel 11:33 NLT).

But there was also a powerful promise: "But the people who know their God will be strong and will resist him" (Daniel 11:32 NLT). In 167 BC, a Jewish priest named Mattathias and his sons rose up and led a revolt, driving the Greeks out of Israel. This was the Maccabean Revolt.

God's prophets predicted the future accurately and in stunning detail. That's one way we know the Bible is the Word of God.

201. ROME RISES TO POWER \\ DANIEL 7:7; ROMANS 13:1–7

» The Maccabees wanted strong allies against the Greeks, so they turned to Rome. The Romans were rapidly conquering nations around the Mediterranean Sea and would soon conquer Greece and much of its eastern empire, including Egypt.

Later, Herod the Great was appointed ruler of Galilee, although he was not a Jew, but an Edomite. But when a ruling Jew named Antigonus drove him out, Herod fled to Rome where he persuaded the Roman Senate to declare him "King of the Jews."

Herod returned to Judah in 40 BC, and after three years of wars, with the help of the Roman army, he conquered all Israel. Herod was now king, but was a vassal of the Romans.

Daniel had dreamed about the Roman Empire, describing it as a "fourth beast—terrifying and frightening and very powerful. It had large iron teeth; it crushed and devoured its victims" (Daniel 7:7 NIV). This Roman beast soon completely swallowed up Israel.

Paul made it clear that although the Roman Empire was sometimes oppressive, God had ordained its rule, and His people were to obey it (Romans 13:1–7). This same principle applies to the government that rules our land today.

202. A MIGHTY ANGEL VISITS NAZARETH
\\ MATTHEW 1:18–25; LUKE 1:26–38

» In the days of King Herod a man named Joseph, living in the village of Nazareth, in Galilee, became engaged to a young woman named Mary.

One day the angel Gabriel appeared and greeted Mary, saying, "You will conceive and give birth to a son, and you are to call him Jesus. He will be. . .the Son of the Most High" (Luke 1:31–32 NIV). Mary was a virgin, so she asked how this was possible. The angel told her that the Spirit of God would come upon her and cause her to conceive.

When Mary became pregnant, Joseph was deeply troubled. Thinking that she had slept with another man, he decided to call off the marriage.

But an angel appeared to him in a dream, saying, "Joseph. . .do not be afraid to take to you Mary your wife, for that which is conceived in her is of the Holy Spirit. And she will bring forth a Son, and you shall call His name JESUS, for He will save His people from their sins" (Matthew 1:20–21 NKJV).

Isaiah's 730-year-old prophecy about a virgin bearing a son was about to be fulfilled (Isaiah 7:14; Matthew 1:22–23).

203. THE WORD BECOMES FLESH \\ JOHN 1:1–18; PHILIPPIANS 2:5–11

» Matthew 1:23 (NKJV) states, "'Behold, the virgin shall. . .bear a Son, and they shall call His name Immanuel,' which is translated, 'God with us.'" Yes, Jesus was *literally* "God with us."

"In the beginning was the Word, and the Word was with God, and the Word was God." We know that this Word is Jesus because "the Word became flesh and dwelt among us" (John 1:1, 14 NKJV).

John also declares, "All things were made through Him, and without

Jesus was the Word of God dwelling among us.

Him nothing was made that was made" (John 1:3 NKJV). God the Father created the universe by means of His Son (Genesis 1:1; Hebrews 1:2).

But how could the omnipotent, omnipresent God become a mortal man? How could infinite deity be contained in a finite human body? Jesus had to first empty Himself of His divine power and attributes.

"Christ Jesus, who, although He existed in the form of God, did not regard equality with God a thing to be grasped [held on to], but emptied Himself, taking the form of a bond-servant, and being made in the likeness of men" (Philippians 2:5–7 NASB).

God became a limited, mortal man because He loved us so much!

204. JOHN THE BAPTIST IS BORN \\ LUKE 1:5–25, 36–45, 57–66

» The angel Gabriel told Mary that her cousin Elizabeth, well past child-bearing years, was also pregnant. Here's what had happened.

One day while the elderly priest Zacharias was burning incense in the temple, the angel Gabriel appeared to him and said, "Your wife, Elizabeth, will give you a son, and you are to name him John. . . . He will prepare the people for the coming of the Lord" (Luke 1:13, 17 NLT).

Zacharias doubted that his wife, old as she was, could get pregnant, so the angel struck him mute.

In Elizabeth's sixth month, Mary arrived to visit her and stayed until the baby was born. Now, everyone wondered what the child would be named. Zacharias was mute, so they handed him a writing tablet, and he wrote, "His name is John" (Luke 1:63 NLT). Immediately Zacharias could speak again and prophesied: "And you, my little son, will be called the prophet of the Most High, because you will prepare the way for the Lord. You will tell his people how to find salvation through forgiveness of their sins" (Luke 1:76–77 NLT).

God's great plan for the salvation of mankind was now beginning to unfold!

205. JESUS IS BORN IN BETHLEHEM \\ LUKE 2:1–20

» After John's birth, Mary returned to Nazareth. Several months later, just as it came time to give birth, all Nazareth was astir with the news: Caesar Augustus had decreed that the entire Roman world would be taxed. Everyone had to return to the town of their birth to be registered.

Both Joseph and Mary were descended from King David and were from Bethlehem, so they had to return there. So Joseph and his very pregnant wife made the journey south.

When they arrived, Bethlehem was overflowing with people who had also come to register, so there was no room for them in the inn or with their relatives. Mary and Joseph were forced to take shelter in a cave that served as an animal stable. There Jesus was born.

Shepherds were watching their flocks in the nearby hills when an angel appeared exclaiming: "I bring you good news that will cause great joy for all the people. Today in the town of David a Savior has been born to you; he is the Messiah, the Lord" (Luke 2:10–11 NIV).

Suddenly a great multitude of angels appeared, praising God. The astonished shepherds immediately left their flocks, went to Bethlehem, and worshipped Jesus.

206. WISE MEN COME CALLING \\ MATTHEW 2:1–12

» Back in Moses' day, Balaam prophesied, "I perceive him, but far in the distant future. A star will rise from Jacob; a scepter will emerge from Israel" (Numbers 24:17 NLT).

Some fourteen hundred years later, wise men known as Magi, living in Persia, saw a bright star in the skies over Israel. There were many Jews living in Persia in those days, and Jewish scholars likely told the wise men that the star meant a great king had been born in Israel.

When the Magi arrived in Jerusalem, they went to King Herod's palace and asked, "Where is the newborn king of the Jews? We saw his

The Magi found and worshipped Jesus, but God warned them against telling Herod about the newborn king.

star as it rose, and we have come to worship him" (Matthew 2:2 NLT).

Herod was greatly disturbed. He summoned the priests and scribes and asked where the Messiah was supposed to be born. They answered, "In Bethlehem in Judea" (Micah 5:2, 4).

Herod then told the wise men to go to Bethlehem and search for the child, then tell him when they found Him. The Magi *did* find Jesus and worshipped Him. But they returned to their own country by another route, for God had warned them against returning to Herod.

207. NIGHTTIME FLIGHT FROM A MASSACRE \\ MATTHEW 2:13–23

» After the wise men left, an angel appeared in a dream to Joseph and told him, "Get up. . .take the child and his mother and escape to Egypt. Stay there until I tell you, for Herod is going to search for the child to kill him" (Matthew 2:13 NIV).

Joseph immediately got up and woke Mary. They hastily packed their belongings, bundled up baby Jesus, and abandoned their house in the middle of the night. They were already far to the south in the Sinai desert when Herod's soldiers rode into Bethlehem.

There were nearly one million Jews living in Egypt in those days, so one more small Jewish family melted into the crowd without anyone noticing.

About two years later, Herod died. The angel again appeared to Joseph and told him that it was now safe to return to Israel. But when Joseph arrived and heard that Herod's son Archelaus was king in Judea, he didn't know what to do.

Then, being warned in a dream, he returned north to Galilee and settled there. And so Jesus was raised in Nazareth.

It's vital to take precautions if you sense God is warning you of danger (Proverbs 22:3).

208. JESUS ASTONISHES THE TEACHERS \\ LUKE 2:41–50

» In Nazareth, as in all the towns and villages of Galilee and Judea, boys were taught the scriptures from an early age.

At age five, they attended a *bet ha-sefer* ("house of the book") where they studied God's Word from dawn until noon. At age ten, boys entered the *bet talmud* ("house of learning") where they studied the scriptures and the "oral law" in depth. This second level required some reasoning, but still mostly meant memorizing rote answers.

This was the state of Jesus' education when He went to Jerusalem with His parents at age twelve, to attend the Passover.

When Joseph and Mary departed with a crowd of fellow villagers, Jesus stayed at the temple. When His parents realized that Jesus wasn't with them, they hurried back to Jerusalem and searched for Him for three days.

They finally found Him in the temple, talking with the teachers.

Jesus was only twelve years old when He amazed the teachers at the temple with His knowledge of God.

"And all who heard Him were astonished at His understanding and answers" (Luke 2:47 NKJV). Jesus had outstanding wisdom, even at a young age.

Like the first disciples, we may not be highly educated, but we gain great wisdom if we spend time with Jesus (Acts 4:13) in Bible reading and prayer.

209. A WILD MAN PREACHES \\ MATTHEW 3:1–12; LUKE 3:1–18

» John the Baptist grew into a powerful prophet and began shouting in the deserts of Judea, "Repent, for the kingdom of heaven is at hand!" (Matthew 3:2 NKJV). The Messiah was coming to bring God's kingdom into their lives (Luke 17:20–21).

John preached a "baptism of repentance" (Luke 3:3 KJV). And people repented by the thousands. They confessed their sins and John baptized them in the Jordan River.

Some religious leaders tried to go through the motions to be associated with this popular movement. But John condemned their hypocrisy, saying, "Produce fruit in keeping with repentance." He warned that "every tree that does not produce good fruit will be cut down and thrown into the fire" (Matthew 3:8, 10 NIV).

John wasn't trying to gain followers—even though several disciples did gather around him. His whole purpose was to prepare Israel for the coming Messiah. He stated that although he baptized with water, one was coming who was far mightier than him, who would baptize them with the Holy Spirit and with fire (Matthew 3:11).

Jesus did baptize His disciples with the Holy Spirit after He was raised from the dead (Acts 1:5; 2:3–4).

210. JOHN BAPTIZES JESUS \\ MATTHEW 3:13–17; JOHN 1:29–34

» One day when He was about thirty, Jesus came from Galilee to where John was baptizing in the Jordan and asked John to baptize Him.

But Jesus had no sins to confess! As He stated of His Father, "I always do those things that please Him" (John 8:29 NKJV). Astonished, John realized that this man was the "Lamb of God, who takes away the sin of the world" (John 1:29 NIV).

John protested that he couldn't baptize Jesus, that he needed Jesus to baptize *him*. But Jesus insisted, so John proceeded.

John baptized Jesus in the Jordan River.

As soon as Jesus emerged from the water, heaven opened and the Spirit of God descended like a dove, alighting on Him. And God declared, "This is my Son, whom I love; with him I am well pleased" (Matthew 3:17 NIV).

John witnessed this as well. God had told him, "Upon whom you see the Spirit descending, and remaining on Him, this is He who baptizes with the Holy Spirit." So John said, "I have seen and testified that this is the Son of God" (John 1:33–34 NKJV).

When people's hearts open to the truth, they recognize that Jesus is the Son of God.

211. THE DEVIL TEMPTS JESUS \\ MATTHEW 4:1–11; LUKE 4:1–13

» When He took on a human body, Jesus emptied Himself of His divine power. Now, at His baptism, the Father anointed Him with the Holy Spirit to do miracles (Acts 10:38).

Then the Spirit led Jesus into the desert, where He fasted for forty days. Afterward the devil tempted Him, saying, "If You are the Son of God, command that these stones become bread," and "If You are the Son of God, throw Yourself down" (Matthew 4:3, 6 NKJV).

Satan wasn't hoping to make Jesus doubt that He was God's Son. Jesus *knew* who He was. He was "the one and only Son, who is himself God and is in closest relationship with the Father" (John 1:18 NIV).

Satan was trying to tempt Jesus to use His power for His *own* self-serving ends. But that's *not* why Jesus had come. He declared later that He had come down from heaven, not to do His own will, but to do the will of the Father who sent Him (John 6:38).

Jesus resisted all Satan's deceitful temptations. We can be comforted to know that He "has been tempted in every way, just as we are—yet he did not sin" (Hebrews 4:15 NIV).

212. JOHN'S DISCIPLES FOLLOW JESUS \\ JOHN 1:35–57

» After His temptation in the desert, "Jesus returned in the power of the Spirit" (Luke 4:14 NKJV) to the Jordan. John was standing with two of his disciples when he saw Him and said, "Behold the Lamb of God!" (John 1:36 NKJV).

The two disciples immediately followed Jesus and spent the day talking to Him. One of the men, Andrew, then found his brother Simon (Peter) and excitedly said, "We have found the Messiah" (John 1:41 NKJV). And he took Peter to Jesus.

The next day, Jesus prepared to return north to Galilee, so He told Philip to follow Him. Philip had been talking with Andrew and Peter, so he now quickly found Nathaniel, telling him that they had found the Messiah—Jesus of Nazareth.

Nathaniel quipped, "Can anything good come out of Nazareth?" (John 1:46 NKJV).

But when Nathanael met Jesus and Jesus described what he had been doing before he came, Nathaniel became convinced. He exclaimed, "Rabbi, You are the Son of God! You are the King of Israel!" (John 1:49 NKJV).

Jesus was no ordinary man, and His disciples were aware of this from the beginning. We also should never forget who He is.

213. AMAZING MIRACLE AT A WEDDING \\ JOHN 2:1–12

» Jesus hurried to Cana of Galilee with His first four followers and arrived there "on the third day" (John 2:1 NKJV). Apparently, sometime before His forty-day fast, He'd been invited to a wedding, and He hadn't forgotten about it.

While attending a wedding, Jesus turned water into wine.

The groom, however, wasn't as organized as Jesus. He had greatly miscalculated the amount of wine needed, and not far into the wedding, it was all gone.

Jesus' mother and brothers were present, and Mary was aware that her son was the Son of God (Luke 1:35). So she told Him, "They have no more wine."

Jesus replied, "Woman, why do you involve me?" Undeterred, Mary turned to the servants and ordered, "Do whatever he tells you." Mary truly believed in Him. Jesus then told the servants, "Fill the jars with water" (John 2:3–5, 7 NIV).

They filled six stone jars with about 150 gallons of water, and Jesus promptly turned it all into high-quality wine. Only a few days previously, when starving, He'd refused to turn stones into ordinary bread. Jesus refused to do a miracle unless it glorified God.

After He did this astonishing wonder, His new disciples believed in Him.

214. JESUS DRIVES OUT GREEDY MERCHANTS \\ JOHN 2:13–22

» Several months later, just before Passover, Jesus and His disciples went to Jerusalem. There He saw merchants selling cattle, sheep, and doves in the temple courts. Money changers had also set up their tables there.

Furious, Jesus braided a whip from some cords and beat them all out of the courts. He drove out the sheep and cattle, violently overturned the money changers' tables, and scattered their coins across the paving stones.

He turned to those who sold doves and shouted, "Take these things away! Do not make My Father's house a house of merchandise!" (John 2:16 NKJV).

The high priests were getting kickback from allowing merchants to be on the temple grounds, so they protested. Since Jesus was acting as if He had the right to drive them out, they wanted to see a miraculous sign as *proof* of that authority.

Jesus' authority rested in the fact that He was the Son of God with the power to rise from the dead, so He replied, "Destroy this temple, and in three days I will raise it up" (John 2:19 NLT).

Jesus made some bitter enemies that day. The priests remembered His statement and quoted it three years later, just before He was crucified (Matthew 26:60–61).

» While Jesus was in Jerusalem, a wealthy man named Nicodemus came to Him secretly one night. Jesus was controversial, and Nicodemus was a respected member of the Sanhedrin, the ruling Jewish council.

When Nicodemus declared that he knew Jesus was of God, Jesus abruptly told him, "Very truly I tell you, no one can see the kingdom of God unless they are born again" (John 3:3 NIV).

Nicodemus thought He was referring to a second *physical* birth, but Jesus clarified that He meant being "born of the Spirit" (John 3:8 NIV).

Jesus then described the heart of His message, explaining how a person could be born again: "For God so loved the world that He gave His only begotten Son, that whoever believes in Him should not perish but have everlasting life" (John 3:16 NKJV).

Nicodemus thought deeply about this simple truth—and evidently accepted it, because he later repeatedly stood up for Jesus and, together with Joseph of Arimathea, became a secret disciple (John 7:47–51; 19:38–42).

Have you been born again? Believe in Jesus and God will send the Spirit of His Son into your heart to bring eternal life to *your* spirit (Galatians 4:6).

» As Jesus and His handful of disciples returned north to Galilee, they stopped at Sychar in Samaria. Jesus rested at Jacob's well while His disciples went into the city to buy food.

As He rested, a woman came to draw water, so Jesus asked her to give Him a drink. The woman was surprised, since Jews and Samaritans despised one another. She bluntly asked why He, a Jew,

Jesus told the Samaritan woman that He wanted to give her "living water."

asked her, a Samaritan woman, for a drink.

Jesus answered, "If you knew the gift of God, and who it is who says to you, 'Give Me a drink,' you would have asked Him, and He would have given you living water" (John 4:10 NKJV). What *is* the "gift of God"? Paul wrote that "the gift of God is eternal life in Christ Jesus" (Romans 6:23 NKJV).

The woman thought He was talking about a perpetual supply of cool fresh water, but Jesus explained that He was referring to "a fresh, bubbling spring within them, giving them eternal life" (John 4:14 NLT).

Jesus ended up staying with the Samaritans for two days, and many of them believed in Him. He still longs to give us "living water" today.

217. JESUS HEALS FROM A DISTANCE \\ JOHN 4:46–54

» Jesus had only done one miracle in Galilee, but when He was in Jerusalem at the Passover, "many believed in His name when they saw the signs which He did" (John 2:23 NKJV). Now He returned to Cana in Galilee.

Thousands of returning pilgrims spread the news of Jesus' Jerusalem miracles throughout Galilee, and a nobleman of Capernaum heard. His son was dying of a high fever, so he hurried to Cana, eighteen miles away. He arrived there at 1:00 p.m.

He asked Jesus to come heal his son, but when He declined, the nobleman begged, "Sir, come down before my child dies!" Jesus therefore said, "Go your way; your son lives."

The nobleman believed Jesus and headed to Capernaum. That night he went to sleep, trusting. The next morning he met his servants on the road, and they told him that his son was cured (John 4:49–50).

When the nobleman asked when he'd recovered, they replied, "Yesterday afternoon at one o'clock his fever suddenly disappeared!" (John 4:52 NLT). So the nobleman and his entire household became believers.

God rewards those who trust in Him.

218. JESUS IS REJECTED AT NAZARETH \\ LUKE 4:16–31

» After the healing in Capernaum, Jesus went by Himself to Nazareth, His hometown. On the Sabbath, He entered the synagogue and was handed the scroll of Isaiah. Unrolling it, He read Isaiah 61:1–2 and 58:6. Then He said that this very day the scripture had been fulfilled.

The people were amazed. How could an ordinary local boy fulfill prophecy? They grumbled, "Isn't this Joseph's son?" (Luke 4:22 NIV). And they were *thinking*, "Do miracles here like those you did in Capernaum. *Then* we'll believe!"

Jesus responded that no prophet is ever accepted in his own hometown. He pointed out that although there were many starving widows in Israel during a famine, Elijah was only sent to provide for a Canaanite widow. And though there were many lepers in Israel in Elisha's day, only a foreign enemy, Naaman, was healed.

When they grasped that God was rejecting them, the people were furious. They seized Jesus, dragged Him to the cliff that their town was built on, and tried to hurl Him down. But Jesus escaped and went to Capernaum.

Sometimes those who have known us for years are the most skeptical about our new life in Christ (Matthew 10:34–37).

219. JESUS CALLS FOUR FISHERMEN \\ MATTHEW 4:18–22; MARK 1:16–20

» Jesus looked up Simon Peter and Andrew on the outskirts of Capernaum. They were fishermen, and although they'd followed Him for a while, they were now back at their jobs.

Peter and Andrew were partners with Zebedee and his sons, John and James—to whom they had talked nonstop about Jesus the Messiah.

Peter, Andrew, James, and John were fishermen eager to follow Jesus.

The four men determined to follow Jesus. They had apparently talked to Zebedee and his wife Salome about this, who agreed to help support Jesus' ministry (compare Mark 15:40-41; Matthew 27:55-56). Historians tell us that fishermen were wealthier than most Galileans, so they had the means.

And now the day had come.

As Jesus walked beside the Sea of Galilee, he saw Peter and Andrew casting a net into the water. Jesus said, "Come, follow me, and I will send you out to fish for people" (Mark 1:17 NIV). They immediately dropped their nets and followed.

James and John were in a boat nearby, preparing their nets. Jesus called them, and they left Zebedee in the boat with the hired men.

If you're going to follow Jesus, think your decision through carefully and plan *how* you're going to do it (Luke 14:28–30). Then do it.

220. JESUS DRIVES OUT DEMONS AND HEALS
\\ MARK 1:21–34; LUKE 4:31–41

» When the Sabbath came, Jesus entered the synagogue in Capernaum. He was teaching when suddenly a demon-possessed man screamed, "Let us alone! . . . Did You come to destroy us? I know who You are—the Holy One of God!"

Jesus commanded, "Be quiet, and come out of him!" (Mark 1:24–25 NKJV). The man convulsed violently on the synagogue floor and shouted out, and the demon left him. The people looking on were absolutely astonished.

From there, Jesus and His disciples went to Peter's house, where He healed Peter's mother-in-law of a high fever. Meanwhile, news of that morning's dramatic deliverance was sweeping throughout Capernaum.

No sooner had the sun gone down, ending the Sabbath, than the entire town gathered outside Peter's house. They brought everyone in the city who was sick or demon possessed.

Try to picture it: For hours, people shouted with joy as they were healed, and demoniacs shrieked in fear as Jesus drove evil spirits from them. The drama was likely lit by flickering torches and lamps. After this night, Jesus' reputation spread far and wide.

Often, when the devil attacks us, God then uses the opportunity to counterattack and get out a powerful Gospel message.

221. TWO FISHING BOATS NEARLY SINK \\ MARK 1:35–39; LUKE 5:1–11

» The crowds wanted Jesus to stay, but He replied that He had to preach in the surrounding towns and villages also. So He left.

Eventually they returned to Capernaum. While Jesus slept, Peter, Andrew, James, and John went out night fishing. They might as well have stayed home and slept too, because they didn't catch anything.

The next day while they wearily cleaned their nets, a crowd gathered around Jesus, so He sat in Peter's boat, had him push out a ways from shore, and taught.

Then Jesus said, "Put out into deep water, and let down the nets for a catch" (Luke 5:4 NIV). Peter replied that they'd worked all night but caught nothing. Nevertheless, he believed that Jesus was the Messiah, so they followed His instructions.

Immediately, their nets filled with so many fish that they began breaking. Peter hollered for help, and James and John rushed over. Soon both boats were so full of fish that they were sinking. Jesus then repeated, "From now on you will fish for people" (Luke 5:10 NIV).

Sometimes God makes our instructions clear, but we don't fully get it. So He reminds us.

222. JESUS CLEANSES A LEPER \\ MARK 1:40–45; LUKE 5:12–16

» One day a leper saw Jesus, rushed toward Him, and flung himself to the ground at His feet. He begged, "If You are willing, You can make me clean" (Mark 1:40 NKJV).

The man's flesh was deformed and literally "full of leprosy" (Luke 5:12 NKJV), so most people were repulsed. But Jesus compassionately stretched out His hand and *touched* him. He said, "I am willing; be cleansed" (Mark 1:41 NKJV).

The instant Jesus spoke, the man's many leprous sores vanished!

Jesus told a leper to keep silent about how he had been healed—but the man still told people about the miracle.

Jesus ordered, "See that you say nothing to anyone; but go your way, show yourself to the priest" (Mark 1:44 NKJV). Then Jesus sent him away before a crowd could gather.

However, the man went out publicly proclaiming the miracle. The result? Jesus could no longer openly enter cities without being mobbed. He was forced to stay in deserted places. Yet still people came to Him from every direction.

Jesus knew the effect that great miracles had on people—and He didn't want to *only* heal. He also wanted to teach people about God.

This episode demonstrates Jesus' deep compassion. It also shows that sometimes it's more effective to work quietly, without notoriety.

223. FORGIVING AND HEALING A PARALYTIC
\\ MARK 2:1–12; LUKE 5:17–26

» When Jesus returned to Capernaum, people heard that He was in a certain house. This was probably Peter's house. Jesus was so famous now that the crowds mobbed Him. They gathered in such large numbers that there was no room left, even outside the door.

Jesus was intent on teaching, but others were intent that He do healing miracles. Four men came, bringing a paralyzed friend. They couldn't get in the house, so they climbed up on the roof and dug through the ceiling. They then lowered their friend by ropes on his mat.

Jesus beheld the paralyzed man and said, "Son, your sins are forgiven" (Mark 2:5 NIV).

Some scribes were scandalized, thinking that Jesus was blaspheming. After all, who could forgive sins but God alone?

Jesus knew what they were thinking, so to prove that He *had* the authority to forgive sins, He said to the man, "Stand up, pick up your mat, and go home!" (Mark 2:11 NLT). Immediately the man jumped up, picked up his mat, and left.

Thank God that Jesus has the power to heal our bodies *and* to forgive our sins!

224. JESUS CALLS MATTHEW \\ MATTHEW 9:9–13; LUKE 5:27–32

» Jesus had been steadily gathering disciples (Matthew 8:19–22), and He now added one of His most infamous followers.

Jesus saw a Jew named Matthew (or Levi) working at the Roman tax office and said, "Follow Me." So he got up and followed (Matthew 9:9 NKJV). Matthew didn't make a sudden decision to follow a total stranger. Jesus had been turning Capernaum upside down with miracles and teachings for months, and Matthew had been quietly taking it all in.

Jesus had an enormous following in Capernaum. Now He risked losing it all by associating with a despised Roman collaborator. Worse, he ate a meal in Matthew's house, and many tax collectors and disreputable people came and sat down with Him.

The Pharisees demanded, "Why does your teacher eat with such scum?" But Jesus replied, "Healthy people don't need a doctor—sick people do. . . . For I have come to call not those who think they are righteous, but those who know they are sinners" (Matthew 9:11–13 NLT).

These so-called "scum" actually *repented*, whereas most "good citizens" of Capernaum—although they loved Jesus' miracles—*didn't* repent (Matthew 11:20–24; 21:31).

This same situation is often true in our world today.

» It was fall, and Jesus went to Jerusalem for a Jewish feast. Now, there was a pool there and a huge crowd of sick people waited near it, because an angel sometimes stirred up the water, and whoever stepped in first was healed.

Jesus saw a man there who had been sick for thirty-eight years, so He asked, "Do you want to be made well?" The man replied, "I have no

Religious leaders were angry that Jesus had healed a lame man on the Sabbath.

man to put me into the pool when the water is stirred up." So Jesus commanded, "Rise, take up your bed and walk" (John 5:6–8 NKJV).

Immediately the man was healed, picked up his mat, and walked off. Jesus then melted quietly into the crowd.

But the religious leaders indignantly informed the man that it wasn't lawful for him to carry a mat on the Sabbath. The man explained that the stranger who'd healed him had told him to. When he later learned who the stranger was, he told the leaders. They were furious that Jesus had healed on the Sabbath, persecuted Him, and sought to kill Him.

Jesus' compassion would repeatedly compel Him to ignore manmade traditions. We must be moved by love as well, even if it ruffles feathers.

226. JESUS OFFERS ETERNAL LIFE \\ JOHN 5:19–47

» Jesus was phenomenally popular as a miracle worker and was loved for His compassion on the poor and His denunciations of religious hypocrisy.

This disturbed the religious leaders, so they seized on the fact that He "broke the Sabbath" to argue that He wasn't of God.

Jesus not only argued that He *was* of God, but made the startling claim that God was His Father and that He was God's Son in whom they *must* believe: "Very truly I tell you, whoever hears my word and believes him who sent me has eternal life" (John 5:24 NIV).

Jesus informed them that He would one day judge them, and that everyone who heard His voice would have life. The religious leaders knew the Bible well, but as Jesus declared: "You study the scriptures diligently because you think that in them you have eternal life. These are the very scriptures that testify about me, yet you refuse to come to me to have life" (John 5:39–40 NIV).

It's still vital today to know that Jesus is more than a miracle worker or a great teacher. He's the Son of God, the only One who can give us eternal life.

227. JESUS HEALS A WITHERED HAND
\\ MATTHEW 12:9–14; MARK 3:1–6; LUKE 6:6–11

» In Jerusalem, Jesus had healed on the Sabbath, despite knowing that it would outrage His enemies. Not long after He returned to Galilee, He did the same.

One Sabbath Jesus was in a synagogue, and a man with a withered right hand was there. His enemies, seeking to trap Him, asked, "Is it lawful to heal on the Sabbath?" (Matthew 12:10 NKJV).

Jesus called the man to come stand in front of the entire congregation. Then He asked everyone, "If you had a sheep that fell into a well on the Sabbath, wouldn't you work to pull it out? Of course you would. And how much more valuable is a person than a sheep! Yes, the law permits a person to do good on the Sabbath" (Matthew 12:11–12 NLT).

He then commanded the man to stretch out his deformed hand. When the man obeyed, his hand was instantly restored.

Jesus' enemies became wild with rage and immediately began plotting to destroy Him.

We too must guard against falling into legalism. God wants us to be true to the scriptures, yes, but we must understand the scriptures correctly *and* love others.

228. JESUS CHOOSES TWELVE APOSTLES
\\ MARK 3:13–19; LUKE 6:12–16

» Jesus had been traveling around Israel, teaching and healing, for well over a year. He now had a large crowd of disciples following Him everywhere, learning from Him daily.

One winter's evening around the beginning of AD 28, as His disciples camped out in the open, Jesus climbed a high hill and spent the entire chilly night alone, praying to God.

When morning came, "he called his disciples to him and chose twelve of them, whom he also designated apostles" (Luke 6:13 NIV). Jesus had about eighty full-time disciples in total (Luke 10:1), but from this number He chose twelve as apostles.

The other seventy men were also disciples, but Jesus appointed twelve to be His closest followers, His primary ambassadors whom He would send out to preach the Gospel, perform healings, and drive out demons. In fact, *apostle* means "one sent out."

These men were: Simon Peter and Andrew, James and John, Philip, Bartholomew, Matthew, Thomas, James son of Alphaeus, Simon the Zealot, Judas son of James, and Judas Iscariot.

Even today, though all believers are disciples and ambassadors of Christ (2 Corinthians 5:20), God has appointed certain Christians as leaders.

229. FEMALE DISCIPLES FOLLOW JESUS \\ LUKE 8:1–3; MARK 15:40–41

» Apart from the eighty-plus male disciples constantly traveling around with Him, Jesus also had many faithful female followers.

Jesus set out on a tour of the towns and villages of Galilee, preaching the Good News. "He took his twelve disciples with him, along with some women who had been cured of evil spirits and diseases. Among them were Mary Magdalene. . .Joanna, the wife of Chuza, Herod's business manager; Susanna; and many others who were contributing from their own resources to support Jesus and his disciples" (Luke 8:1–3 NLT).

Mark names two other followers—Mary the mother of James and Joses (or Joseph) and Salome (Mark 15:40). Salome was Zebedee's wife, the mother of James and John (Matthew 20:20–21; 27:56).

These six women "and *many* others" were with Jesus as He went through every town and village. Their financial support, in fact, was crucial to keeping the entire show on the road.

Not only that, but these women undoubtedly handled most of the daily shopping and cooking for Jesus' huge group of disciples.

Never underestimate the power of women. Jesus' ministry and all His disciples wouldn't have lasted long without them—and neither will the church today.

230. SERMON ON THE MOUNT \\ MATTHEW 5:1–12; LUKE 6:17–26

» Jesus gave the Sermon on the Mount (Matthew 5–7) around this time. "Now when Jesus saw the crowds, he went up on a mountainside and sat down. His disciples came to him, and he began to teach them. He said: 'Blessed are the poor in spirit, for theirs is the kingdom of heaven'" (Matthew 5:1–3 NIV).

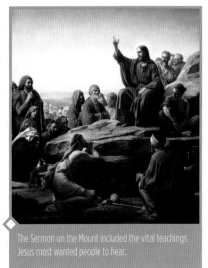
The Sermon on the Mount included the vital teachings Jesus most wanted people to hear.

Luke 6:17, 20 (NIV) describes a similar sermon: "He went down with them and stood on a level place" and said, "Blessed are you who are poor, for yours is the kingdom of God." Matthew says Jesus sat on a mountainside, while Luke says He stood on a plain. Also, Jesus' sayings in each, though similar, have striking differences. There's a reason for this.

The Sermon on the Mount contains the *heart* of Christ's teaching—on love, forgiveness, prayer, and obedience—so He repeated these important thoughts in different towns, villages, and open-air settings during the years of His public ministry. The slightly different sermon in Luke was given in a different setting on another date.

Jesus repeated these teachings because it was vital that *everyone* hear them—and they're still important for us to read today.

231. HEALING A CENTURION'S SERVANT \\ MATTHEW 8:5–13; LUKE 7:1–10

» When Jesus entered Capernaum, a Roman centurion's servant there was "paralyzed, dreadfully tormented. . .and ready to die" (Matthew 8:6; Luke 7:2 NKJV).

Being responsible for keeping the peace in Capernaum, the centurion had repeatedly watched Jesus perform astonishing healings in large crowds. So he had no doubt that Jesus could heal.

But he also knew that because he was a Gentile, Jesus couldn't enter his home (Acts 10:28). So he sent Jewish elders to plead his case. They told Jesus that *this* Gentile was deserving, because he loved the Jewish people and had built them a synagogue.

Jesus accompanied them. But just before He arrived, the centurion thought of a solution: he sent friends saying, "I am not worthy that You should enter under my roof. . . . But say the word, and my servant will be healed. For I also am a man placed under authority, having soldiers under me. And I say to. . .my servant, 'Do this,' and he does it" (Luke 7:6–8 NKJV).

Jesus marveled at the Roman's great faith—and his servant *was* healed! Like the centurion, we need to have faith not only in practical, everyday workings, but in the power of God.

232. JESUS RAISES THE DEAD AT NAIN \\ LUKE 7:11–17

» Soon after this miracle in Capernaum, Jesus traveled to a town called Nain, and His many disciples went with Him. A large crowd was also tagging along.

Just as they arrived there, a large funeral procession wound out the town gate, carrying a young man in an open bier to a waiting tomb.

His mother was a widow, and he, as her only son, had been supporting her. Now he too was dead. She was devastated and destitute.

Jesus' heart went out to her, and He said, "Don't cry" (Luke 7:13 NIV). He then took hold of the bier, signaling the bearers to stop. He commanded, "Young man, I say to you, get up!" (Luke 7:14 NIV). The youth immediately sat up and began talking.

The stunned crowds exclaimed, "A great prophet has appeared among us" (Luke 7:16 NIV). This was the first time Jesus raised a corpse to life, and the news spread like wildfire.

Jesus doesn't always restore our loved ones to life, but He says, "I know their sorrows" (Exodus 3:7 NKJV). He feels our grief and our pain. "In all their suffering he also suffered" (Isaiah 63:9 NLT).

233. JOHN THE BAPTIST IS THROWN INTO PRISON
\\ MATTHEW 14:3–5; MARK 6:17–20; LUKE 7:18–28

» Now Herodias had divorced Philip, Herod Antipas's brother, and Herod Antipas then married her. John the Baptist rebuked him for this, so Herod imprisoned him.

Herod considered killing John but was afraid the people would riot, because they believed he was a prophet. And as Herod listened to him, he began to believe that John *was* a prophet.

Now, John's disciples told him about Jesus raising the dead man at Nain. But Jesus wasn't rallying the people to overthrow the Romans and Herod as John expected He would.

John questioned whether Jesus was the Messiah.

John began to wonder therefore if Jesus were simply a great prophet. So he sent disciples to Him asking, "Are you the Messiah we've been expecting, or should we keep looking for someone else?" (Matthew 11:3 NLT).

While John's disciples watched, Jesus healed many sicknesses and gave sight to the blind, fulfilling Messianic prophecies (Isaiah 29:18–19; 35:5–6). Then He told John's disciples to go back and tell him what they'd seen.

Jesus didn't act as people *expected* the Messiah to act—and even today He doesn't always answer prayer the way we think He should. But He's definitely the Savior.

234. A SINFUL WOMAN ANOINTS JESUS \\ LUKE 7:36–50

» A Pharisee named Simon, eager to spend time with a prophet, invited Jesus to dinner, so Jesus reclined at his table.

When a prostitute heard that Jesus was there, she slipped into the house, knelt behind Him, wept over His feet, and wiped them with her hair. She kept kissing Jesus' feet and pouring expensive perfume on them.

Simon thought, "If this man were a prophet, he would know what kind of woman is touching him. She's a sinner!" (Luke 7:39 NLT).

Jesus, however, pointed out that when He'd entered his home, Simon hadn't washed the dust from His feet, yet this woman had washed them with tears. Simon had failed to greet Jesus with a customary kiss, but she hadn't stopped kissing His feet and anointing them with perfume.

Jesus concluded, "I tell you, her sins—and they are many—have been forgiven, so she has shown me much love. But a person who is forgiven little shows only little love." Then Jesus told her, "Your faith has saved you; go in peace" (Luke 7:47, 50 NLT).

Do you remember when your sins were forgiven? Make sure that you don't forget your "first love" (Revelation 2:4 NKJV).

235. PHARISEES BLASPHEME AND DEMAND A SIGN
\\ MATTHEW 12:22–40; MARK 3:20–30

» Most Jews acknowledged that Jesus' miracles were proof that He was of God (John 2:23; 3:2). Many declared, "A great prophet has appeared among us" (Luke 7:16 NIV).

The Pharisees were upset enough by *those* claims. But one day, Jesus cast a demon out of a blind, mute man, and the man instantly saw and talked. The astonished crowds started asking, "Could it be that Jesus is the Son of David, the Messiah?" (Matthew 12:23 NLT).

Alarmed about Jesus being proclaimed the Messiah, the Pharisees tried to squelch this speculation by arguing, "He is possessed by Beelzebul! By the prince of demons he is driving out demons" (Mark 3:22 NIV).

Jesus, however, assured them that He cast out demons by the Spirit of God. He pointed out that their own sons were exorcists and would therefore judge their blasphemous accusation.

Some Pharisees said, "Teacher, we want to see a sign from you" (Matthew 12:38 NIV). In other words, "Prove that you're of God!" What else did they *want*? He'd just raised the dead! He'd just healed a blind-mute!

"There are none so blind as they who refuse to see." May this saying never be true of us.

236. A SOWER GOES OUT TO SOW \\ MATTHEW 13:3–23; LUKE 8:5–15

» As people began to speculate that Jesus was the Messiah, the controversy intensified—yet He continued to calmly heal and teach.

Most listeners were farmers, so Jesus told this parable: "A sower went out to sow his seed. And as he sowed, some fell by the wayside; and it was trampled down, and the birds of the air devoured it. Some fell on rock; and as soon as it sprang up, it withered away because it lacked moisture. And some fell among thorns, and the thorns sprang up with it and choked it. But others fell on good ground, sprang up, and yielded a crop a hundredfold" (Luke 8:5–8 NKJV).

Jesus explained this parable to His disciples, but *not* to the crowds.

Jesus gave a full explanation of the parable of the seeds to His disciples.

He wanted them to think and pray about it until they finally understood it. Being simple, practical farmers, many of them eventually got it.

Jesus had prayed, "O Father. . . thank you for hiding these things from those who think themselves wise and clever, and for revealing them to the childlike" (Matthew 11:25 NLT).

Many wise people today fail to grasp the Gospel, but those who simply accept it enter God's kingdom (Matthew 18:3).

237. JESUS CALMS A TERRIFIC STORM
\\ MATTHEW 8:23–27; MARK 4:35–41; LUKE 8:22–25

» When evening came, Jesus said to His twelve apostles that they should cross over to the other side of the lake. So they climbed into a boat, and as they sailed, Jesus fell asleep on a cushion in the stern.

Suddenly a furious storm swept down on the lake, and powerful waves broke over the boat so that it began to fill with water.

Jesus was soaked but was so exhausted that He slept on. The disciples frantically woke Him, shouting, "Lord, save us! We're going to drown!" Jesus didn't seem concerned, so they cried out, "Teacher, don't you care if we drown?" (Matthew 8:25; Mark 4:38 NIV).

Finally getting up, Jesus commanded the winds and raging waters: "Peace, be still!" (Mark 4:39 NKJV). Instantly, the wind died down and it was calm. Looking at the disciples, Jesus asked, "Where is your faith?"

In amazement they asked one another, "Who is this man? When he gives a command, even the wind and waves obey him!" (Luke 8:25 NLT).

They *knew* who He was—the Messiah, the Son of God—but in their fear they had forgotten. We often do the same today.

238. JESUS EXORCIZES TWO DEMONIACS
\\ MATTHEW 8:28–34; MARK 5:1–20

» When Jesus and His disciples arrived at the other side of the lake, two fierce demon-possessed men came rushing out of the tombs. One of them screamed, "Why are you interfering with us, Son of God? Have you come here to torture us before God's appointed time?" (Matthew 8:29 NLT).

The leader of the two men was supernaturally strong, able to break iron chains, so Jesus asked him, "What is your name?" And he answered, "My name is Legion; for we are many" (Mark 5:9 NKJV).

Some distance away a herd of about two thousand swine was rooting and feeding. So the demons begged Jesus, if He drove them out, to send them into the herd of pigs.

Jesus said, "Go." Fleeing the two men, the demons swarmed into the swine. The entire herd went berserk and, trying to escape, stampeded down the steep bank into the lake, where they all drowned. The terrified swineherds fled.

Jesus is more powerful than the worst nightmare in the world today. We don't need to fear "because He who is in you is greater than he who is in the world" (1 John 4:4 NKJV).

239. WOMAN SECRETLY TAPS INTO HEALING
\\ MARK 5:25–34; LUKE 8:43–48

» When Jesus crossed back over the lake, a huge crowd met Him and thronged about Him. They were almost crushing Him at times.

There was a woman who'd had a flow of blood for twelve years but was too embarrassed to publicly confess her condition. She now made her way through the crowd.

She thought, "If I just touch his clothes, I will be healed." She quickly reached down and brushed her fingertips against Jesus' cloak. Immediately her bleeding stopped. Jesus abruptly turned and asked, "Who touched my clothes?" (Mark 5:28, 30 NIV).

The disciples were baffled. A multitude was crowding Him and pressing against Him.

A woman was healed simply by touching the clothes that Jesus wore.

But Jesus insisted, "Someone deliberately touched me, for I felt healing power go out from me" (Luke 8:46 NLT). Then the woman, trembling with fear and embarrassment, came forward and confessed what had happened.

She started a trend. Later on, people "begged Him that they might only touch the hem of His garment. And as many as touched it were made perfectly well" (Matthew 14:36 NKJV).

Often we too want to tap into Jesus' miraculous power without a personal encounter with Him, but Jesus wants a heart-to-heart meeting first.

240. JAIRUS'S DAUGHTER DIES AND REVIVES
\\ MARK 5:21–24; 35–43, LUKE 8:40–42, 49–56

» A synagogue leader named Jairus came to Jesus pleading, "My little daughter is dying. Please come and put your hands on her so that she will be healed and live" (Mark 5:23 NIV).

While Jesus went with him, however, messengers came running up, saying, "Your daughter is dead." Jesus immediately told Jairus, "Don't be afraid. Just have faith" (Mark 5:35–36 NLT).

The crowd was swayed by the news, so Jesus didn't let them follow Him to the house. He even ordered His disciples to stay outside. He took just Peter, John, James, and Jairus and his wife inside.

The house was filled with mourners wailing loudly, but Jesus said, "Stop the weeping! She isn't dead; she's only asleep." The mourners mocked Jesus because they knew she had died—so He ordered them all to leave the house.

Then Jesus took the girl by the hand and said, "My child, get up!" (Luke 8:52, 54 NLT). Immediately her life returned and she arose.

Jesus only allowed those with faith to be with Him. Then He did the miracle. We too must have faith if we expect Jesus to answer prayer.

241. THE TWELVE ARE SENT OUT \\ MATTHEW 10:1–42; LUKE 9:1–5

>> Jesus had been healing and teaching for two years. He now called His twelve apostles and "gave them power and authority to drive out all demons and to cure diseases" and "sent them out to proclaim the kingdom of God" (Luke 9:1–2 NIV).

Jesus instructed them not to take anything as they journeyed throughout the towns and villages—no walking stick, no food, no extra clothes, not even money. They were to trust that God would lead people to supply them meals and places to sleep.

The Twelve went out and began healing people just as Jesus had done. And after two years of listening to Him teach, they knew His message well and could preach it.

This was a great help to Jesus. But, unfortunately, He also had reason to be sad. Cities like Capernaum, in which He'd done most of His mighty miracles, still hadn't repented. The people heard His teachings but didn't *obey* them wholeheartedly (Matthew 11:20–24).

Worse yet, Jesus reminded His apostles that He'd recently been accused of being Beelzebul, so they shouldn't be surprised if they sometimes were disrespected (Matthew 10:25).

We too need to be willing to be rejected for Jesus' sake.

>> When his birthday came, Herod hosted a banquet for his officials and commanders and rulers. And Salome, the daughter of Herodias, danced for Herod and his dinner guests. Herod, his judgment perhaps befuddled by wine, was so taken by her seductive dance that he swore, "Whatever you ask I will give you, up to half my kingdom."

The girl could've asked for a great many things, but probably decided she'd better check with her mother first. So she hurried out of the chamber and asked, "What shall I ask for?" (Mark 6:23–24 NIV). Herodias, consumed with hatred for John, wanted only *one* thing—and told her.

Herod had John the Baptist beheaded to fulfill a promise he made to Herodias's daughter.

So Salome went back into the banquet hall and announced, "Give me here on a platter the head of John the Baptist" (Matthew 14:8 NIV).

Herod had sworn an oath, and now all his party guests were watching. So he sent an executioner who beheaded John and returned carrying his head on a platter. He presented it to Salome, and she gave it to her mother.

Beware of making rash promises. "Herod learned the truth of this proverb: "You have been trapped by what you said, ensnared by the words of your mouth" (Proverbs 6:2 NIV).

>> The twelve apostles had just returned and were telling Jesus their experiences when John the Baptist's disciples came, bringing news of his execution.

Jesus therefore left Galilee and entered the province of Gaulanitis, which was not under Herod's rule. He went to a deserted region, but people saw Him go and flocked to Him there.

Then, as it became late, His disciples urged Him to send the people away to buy food in the nearby villages, because they were in a desolate place.

Jesus replied, "They do not need to go away. You give them something to eat." The disciples answered, "We have here only five loaves of bread and two fish" (Matthew 14:16–17 NIV).

Jesus then gave thanks, broke the bread and fish, and had His disciples distribute them. Some five thousand men (not counting women and children) ate until they were full.

The devil had once tempted Jesus to create a couple of loaves (Matthew 4:3), but Jesus refused. Now He did it on a vast scale to feed a multitude and bring glory to God. Years later, the apostle Paul would write that we, too, should "do all to the glory of God" (1 Corinthians 10:31 NKJV).

244. CROWD ATTEMPTS TO CROWN JESUS KING \\ JOHN 6:1-15

» With the shock of John's execution still fresh, the speculation swirling around Jesus intensified: "Could it be that Jesus is the Son of David, the Messiah?" (Matthew 12:23 NLT).

When the crowds became aware of the tremendous miracle He had done, feeding over five thousand people bread in a desolate region, they needed no further sign.

Some fourteen hundred years earlier in Moses' day, God had fed the Israelites with manna—"bread from heaven"—in the desert (Exodus 16:4, 14–15).

Moses had prophesied, "The LORD your God will raise up for you a prophet like me from among you" (Deuteronomy 18:15 NIV). Now Jesus had miraculously provided bread—just as Moses had done! The crowds exclaimed, "This is truly the Prophet who is to come into the world" (John 6:14 NKJV).

This Prophet was the Messiah, so the crowds prepared to proclaim Jesus king. "Jesus, knowing that they intended to come and make him king by force, withdrew again to a mountain by himself" (John 6:15 NIV).

Jesus *is* the Prophet, greater than Moses, and the King of Israel, but He refuses to let *us* crown Him and try to make Him rule the way we want Him to.

245. JESUS WALKS ON WATER \\ MATTHEW 14:23–33; MARK 6:47–52; JOHN 6:16–21

» After sending the crowds away, Jesus sent His disciples across the sea. He Himself stayed to pray. After a while, a strong wind rose, and the disciples were soon fighting heavy waves far from land.

About three o'clock in the morning, Jesus came walking on the water in the darkness. When the disciples saw Him, they shouted out in terror, "It's a ghost!" (Matthew 14:26 NLT).

But Jesus assured them that it was He Himself, so not to fear.

Peter, impetuous as always, said that if it *was* really Jesus, to call him

When Jesus walked on water and caused the wind to stop, the disciples declared that He was the Son

to walk out on the water to Him. So Jesus said, "Come."

Peter stepped out of the boat and, to his utter amazement, walked on the waves. But when he had gone a ways on the surging water, he lost faith and started to sink. "Jesus immediately reached out and grabbed him" (Matthew 14:31 NLT).

"When they climbed into the boat, the wind stopped. Then the disciples worshipped him. 'You really are the Son of God!' they exclaimed" (Matthew 14:32–33 NLT).

The disciples gained a very clear idea of who Jesus was and worshipped Him. May we also have this clear understanding of who He is.

246. MANY DISCIPLES ARE SCANDALIZED \\ JOHN 6:22–69

» Not everyone had dispersed when Jesus sent them away. Some die-hard kingmakers had stayed. But the next morning, when they realized Jesus wasn't there, they sailed to Capernaum and found Him teaching in the synagogue.

Jesus bluntly told them that the only reason they were looking for Him was because they wanted more free bread—whereas God wanted them to seek the *true* bread.

He declared, "I am the living bread that came down from heaven. Whoever eats this bread will live forever." Then Jesus shocked them, saying, "Whoever eats my flesh and drinks my blood has eternal life" (John 6:51, 54 NIV).

After that, many disciples left Him. Yet just one day earlier they'd professed that He was the King of Israel.

"Then Jesus said to the twelve, 'Do you also want to go away?' But Simon Peter answered Him, 'Lord, to whom shall we go? You have the words of eternal life. Also we have come to believe and know that You are the Christ, the Son of the living God" (John 6:67–69 NKJV).

There are "hard sayings" in the Gospels, but if we trust that Jesus is God's Son, we won't be offended by them.

247. HEROD SEEKS FOR JESUS \\ MATTHEW 14:1–2; MARK 6:14; LUKE 9:7–9

» Just after John's death, all eyes were on Jesus. That's when Herod first heard about His mighty miracles—lepers cleansed, the blind seeing, and the dead raised to life.

"I beheaded John," Herod said, "so who is this man about whom I hear such stories?" (Luke 9:9 NLT). Rumors were flying. Many said that Jesus was Elijah finally come (Malachi 4:5). Others said that one of the old prophets had come back to life (Luke 9:7–8).

Herod's guilty conscience overreacted. When his servants told him the reports, Herod insisted, "John the Baptist is risen from the dead, and therefore these powers are at work in him" (Mark 6:14 NKJV).

"So he sought to see Him" (Luke 9:9 NKJV). But Herod wasn't about to personally travel around Galilee to find Jesus. "Seeing" Jesus meant soldiers apprehending Him and bringing Him bound to Herod. Herod later even sought to kill Jesus (Luke 13:31).

Ranking Romans such as the centurion in Capernaum (Matthew 8:5) undoubtedly alerted Jesus to Herod's intentions, and Jesus quickly took the necessary precautions.

Even today, "a prudent man foresees evil and hides himself" (Proverbs 22:3 NKJV).

248. CANAANITE WOMAN SHOWS GREAT FAITH
\\ MATTHEW 15:21–28; MARK 7:24–30

» It wasn't safe in Galilee, so Jesus departed from Herod Antipas's territory once again. He traveled far to the north, to Phoenicia.

Jesus blessed the Canaanite woman when He saw the strength of her faith.

Jesus secretly entered a house, but a Canaanite woman heard He was there, rushed in, and bowed down. Addressing Jesus as the Messiah, she told Him that her daughter was severely demon possessed and repeatedly asked Him to deliver her.

The woman was not simply a Gentile, but a Canaanite, so Jesus said, "I was not sent except to the lost sheep of the house of Israel." The woman repeated, "Lord, help me!" (Matthew 15:24–25 NKJV).

Jesus said, "Let the children be filled first, for it is not good to take the children's bread and throw it to the little dogs" (Mark 7:27 NKJV).

The woman responded, "Yes, Lord, yet even the little dogs eat the crumbs which fall from their masters' table." Jesus answered, "O woman, great is your faith! Let it be to you as you desire" (Matthew 15:27–28 NKJV). And it was!

Jesus had to show God's power to the Jews *first*, but the Canaanite woman's persistence and faith brought her the blessing ahead of the scheduled time.

249. JESUS FEEDS FOUR THOUSAND \\ MATTHEW 15:29–38; MARK 8:1–9

» After Phoenicia, Jesus still didn't return to Galilee; He traveled through the province of Decapolis, carefully avoiding setting foot in Herod's jurisdiction (Matthew 15:29; Mark 7:31).

He went to a remote place there, and people came from near and far, so Jesus taught them and performed healings. After they'd been there three days without food, Jesus refused to send them away hungry, lest they collapse along the way. Some of them had come a long distance.

But His disciples asked, "Where could we get enough bread in this remote place to feed such a crowd?" (Matthew 15:33 NIV).

When they told Jesus that they only had seven loaves and a few small fishes, He ordered the people to sit down, and *again* He miraculously multiplied the food. This time the number of people who ate was four thousand men, not including women and children—which probably meant a total of eight thousand.

Then Jesus left them, got into a boat with the apostles, and crossed to the other side of the lake—not into Galilee, but to Bethsaida in Gaulanitis (Mark 8:13, 22).

Jesus had stupendous, miraculous powers, true, but He still took commonsense precautions. So should we.

250. PETER DECLARES JESUS IS THE MESSIAH
\\ MATTHEW 16:13–20; LUKE 9:18–21

» Jesus now headed north again, to the region of Caesarea Philippi. He had previously moved freely throughout Galilee with over eighty disciples, but He was now traveling everywhere *but* Galilee with just the twelve apostles.

While there, Jesus asked them who the crowds said He was.

They answered, "Some say John the Baptist; others say Elijah; and still others, that one of the prophets of long ago has come back to life" (Luke 9:19 NIV).

Jesus asked, "But who do you say I am?"

"Simon Peter answered, 'You are the Messiah, the Son of the living God'" (Matthew 16:15–16 NLT).

Jesus replied, "Blessed are you, Simon Bar-Jonah, for flesh and blood has not revealed this to you, but My Father who is in heaven" (Matthew 16:17 NKJV). Now, the disciples *had* declared that Jesus was the Messiah, the Son of God, from the beginning (John 1:41, 49)—but many had since lost faith because Jesus wasn't acting as they expected the Messiah to.

It took a revelation, the light of God continually burning in their hearts, to still believe that Jesus was God's Son. We too must persevere in our faith.

251. JESUS PREDICTS HIS DEATH \\ MATTHEW 16:21–26; MARK 8:31–37

» After Peter confessed that Jesus was the Messiah, Jesus commanded His apostles to tell this to no one. These were dangerous times, and though it was God's will for Jesus to be crucified, this had to happen in Jerusalem and at a set time—during the Passover.

It was at this point that Jesus began to explain to His disciples what would happen in less than one year. He told them plainly that it was God's will that He go to Jerusalem where He'd suffer many things at the hands of the elders, the chief priests, and the scribes.

Jesus then shocked His disciples by announcing that He'd then be killed. . .but on the third day rise from the dead.

All Peter heard was the "killed" part. He abruptly took Jesus aside and reprimanded Him. "'Heaven forbid, Lord,' he said. 'This will never happen to you!'"

Jesus responded, "Get away from me, Satan! . . . You are seeing things merely from a human point of view, not from God's" (Matthew 16:22–23 NLT).

God still allows suffering and problems that we can't understand. We must trust Him, not merely look at our circumstances from a human point of view.

252. JESUS GLOWS LIKE THE SUN \\ MATTHEW 17:1–9; MARK 9:2–10; LUKE 9:28–36

» Several days later, Jesus climbed a high mountain with Peter, James, and John. This was likely Mount Hermon, towering over nearby Caesarea Philippi.

There, Jesus was transfigured. His face blazed like the sun, and his clothes became dazzling white, bright as lightning. Then two men appeared—Moses and Elijah—and began talking with Jesus about His soon-coming death.

It would be the Feast of Booths soon, so Peter—completely overwhelmed—offered to build three booths, one for each man.

Suddenly a bright cloud engulfed the summit, and God spoke: "This is my Son, whom I love; with him I am well pleased. Listen to him!" (Matthew 17:5 NIV). Terrified, the three disciples fell to the ground.

Later, as they climbed down, Jesus warned them not to talk about what they'd seen until after He was

Moses and Elijah appeared during the Transfiguration, speaking with Jesus about His

resurrected. Some thirty-five years later, Peter still marveled at the day that "we saw his majestic splendor with our own eyes" on the mountain (2 Peter 1:16 NLT).

Have you ever had even a small taste of the holiness and beauty of the Lord? If you have, you can never forget it.

253. A DEMONIAC BOY IS HEALED \\ MATTHEW 17:14–21; MARK 9:14–29

>> When they returned to the other disciples, they saw a large crowd. Then a man explained that he had brought his deaf and mute son, and that the disciples had tried to drive out the evil spirit, but they couldn't.

They brought the boy to Jesus, and the instant the spirit saw Him, it threw the boy into a convulsion and he rolled around, foaming at the mouth.

The father begged, "If you can do anything, take pity on us and help us."

"'If you can'?" Jesus repeated. "Everything is possible for one who believes."

The man cried out, "I do believe; help me overcome my unbelief!" (Mark 9:22–24 NIV).

Then Jesus commanded the evil spirit to leave the boy. The spirit shrieked, convulsed him violently, and fled.

When they were away from the crowds, Jesus' disciples asked why they couldn't cast it out. Jesus answered that only prayer and fasting could deliver people from that kind of evil spirit.

Many of us today pray for Jesus to help us *if He can*," but He can. He hasn't changed. "Jesus Christ is the same yesterday, today, and forever" (Hebrews 13:8 NKJV).

254. FISHING TO PAY THE TEMPLE TAX \\ MATTHEW 17:24–27

>> Jesus had avoided Galilee for six to eight months. Now He "passed through Galilee, and He did not want anyone to know it" (Mark 9:30 NKJV). It was still very dangerous there.

When Jesus and His disciples arrived in Capernaum, the officials stopped Peter and asked, "Does your Teacher not pay the temple tax?"

Peter blurted out, "Yes."

But when he entered the house, perhaps hoping to quietly ask Judas for money, Jesus asked him, "What do you think, Simon? From whom do the kings of the earth take customs or taxes, from their sons or from strangers?"

Peter knew where this conversation was going. He answered, "From strangers."

Jesus said, "Then the sons are free" (Matthew 17:24–26 NKJV). In other words, no, He *didn't* pay the temple tax.

But since Peter had stated that He did, Jesus instructed him to go to the lake, cast in a hook, and catch a fish. When he opened its mouth, he'd find

Peter paid the temple tax using a coin he had taken from a fish's mouth.

a coin, a Roman *stater*. That was the precise amount to pay the tax for both Jesus *and* Peter.

Often we too blurt out a response when we need to stop, pray, and think about the right answer.

255. DISCIPLES DISPUTE WHO IS GREATEST
\\ MATTHEW 18:1–5; MARK 9:33–37

» Jesus and His twelve disciples traveled unobtrusively through Galilee. He avoided attracting large crowds. After their trip, they returned to Peter's house in Capernaum.

But the disciples had been quietly arguing while traveling. When they were safely in the house, Jesus asked, "What was it you disputed among yourselves on the road?" (Mark 9:33 NKJV).

There was a long and embarrassed silence, because on the road a heated dispute had arisen among them as to who would be greatest in the kingdom they believed Jesus was soon to establish.

Jesus sat down, called the Twelve, and said, "If anyone desires to be first, he shall be last of all and servant of all" (Mark 9:35 NKJV). Blank looks.

Jesus decided to further illustrate His point. He called a little boy, took him in His arms, and told them that unless they had a change of heart and became as trusting as little children, they wouldn't enter God's kingdom. In addition, whoever took on such a childlike attitude would be the greatest in heaven.

Too often we also seek power and position. Jesus wants us to serve others and live with childlike faith.

256. JESUS' BROTHERS MOCK HIM \\ JOHN 7:2–10

» Jesus' brothers had never believed in Him. At the height of His public ministry, they thought that He was out of His mind and attempted to stage an intervention and take Him into custody (Mark 3:21, 31–32). They still doubted Him.

When the Feast of Booths approached, Jesus' brothers met Him and mocked how secretive He was being these days. They said, "Leave Galilee and go to Judea. . . . No one who wants to become a public figure acts in secret. Since you are doing these things, show yourself to the world" (John 7:3–4 NIV).

But Jesus had powerful enemies in both Galilee and Judea. If He showed Himself publicly, He'd be arrested and executed—and it wasn't His time to die yet. So He told them: "You go to the festival. I am not going up to this festival, because my time has not yet fully come" (John 7:8 NIV). After saying this, He stayed in Galilee. However, after His brothers left, the time *had* come, and Jesus then went to Jerusalem. He didn't go publicly, however, but in secret.

To this day, many Christians in nations hostile to the Gospel must be very cautious and secretive.

» In the middle of the Feast of Booths, Jesus went into the temple courts and began to teach openly. At first, the chief priests didn't interfere, so many people speculated that the authorities themselves must have concluded that He was the Messiah.

Multitudes of Jews believed in him. "After all," they said, "would you expect the Messiah to do more miraculous signs than this man has done?" (John 7:31 NLT).

Even the guards who were sent to arrest Jesus were awed by Him.

The Pharisees and chief priests heard the masses whispering these things and were alarmed. They immediately sent temple guards to arrest Him.

Jesus then proclaimed, "If anyone thirsts, let him come to Me and drink. He who believes in Me. . .out of his heart will flow rivers of living water" (John 7:37–38 NKJV).

The people responded, "Surely this man is the Prophet." Others said, "He is the Messiah" (John 7:40–41 NIV).

The temple guards returned to the chief priests and Pharisees. When asked why they hadn't arrested Jesus, the guards replied that they'd been awed by His words.

Jesus had powerful words and did miraculous signs, but we must respond to Him and believe in Him if we wish to have eternal life.

258. JESUS FORGIVES AN ADULTERESS \\ JOHN 8:1–11

» The next morning as Jesus was teaching, the scribes and Pharisees brought a woman who had been caught committing adultery. They first reminded Jesus that Moses, in the Law, commanded such people to be stoned. They then asked Jesus to give *His* ruling.

If Jesus had answered, "Stone her," He'd have been arrested for breaking Roman law—which didn't allow Jews to execute criminals. If He'd said, "Let her go," He'd be breaking Jewish law.

Jesus stooped and wrote on the stones with His finger. When they kept insisting He answer, He answered that whoever was without sin among them should throw the first stone.

Again He stooped and wrote. Then the scribes and Pharisees, overcome by their guilty consciences, left. Finally only the woman remained. Jesus looked up and asked, "Woman, where are they? Did no one condemn you?"

She answered, "No one, Lord."

So Jesus said, "I do not condemn you, either. Go. From now on sin no more" (John 8:10–11 NASB). He had gently but firmly told her to repent.

This story illustrates the point: "The law was given by Moses, but grace and truth came by Jesus Christ" (John 1:17 KJV).

259. JEWS ATTEMPT TO STONE JESUS \\ JOHN 8:31–59

» Later, Jesus' opponents found Him and began arguing with Him. Jesus told them, "Very truly I tell you, whoever obeys my word will never see death" (John 8:51 NIV).

His foes angrily pointed out that their father Abraham had died—as had all the prophets—so was Jesus claiming to be greater than Abraham? Who exactly did He think He was?

Jesus said, "Your father Abraham rejoiced at the thought of seeing my day; he saw it and was glad" (John 8:56 NIV).

Incredulous, they asked, "You are not yet fifty years old, and have You seen Abraham?"

Jesus answered, "Most assuredly, I say to you, before Abraham was, I AM" (John 8:57–58 NKJV). Jesus was boldly claiming to be the always-existing God, the great "I AM" who had appeared to Moses in the burning bush (Exodus 3:14).

At this point His opponents went berserk with rage, shouting, "Blasphemy!" They scrambled to find stones to hurl at Him. But Jesus hid Himself and left the temple area.

Jesus is not only the promised Prophet and Messiah, but He's the Son of God, equal to God the Father. We must understand this to truly know Him.

260. SEVENTY DISCIPLES ARE SENT OUT \\ LUKE 10:1–24

» Jesus had spent most of the first two years traveling around Galilee and the north, proclaiming the Gospel and doing great miracles. It was now time to reach Judea.

Jesus therefore gathered His crowd of disciples around Him, appointed seventy of them, and "sent them two by two before His face into every city and place where He Himself was about to go" (Luke 10:1 NKJV).

Just as He had done with the apostles six to eight months earlier, Jesus gave these disciples power to heal sicknesses and cast out demons and commanded them to preach the Gospel.

Several weeks later, they returned rejoicing, saying, "Lord, even the demons are subject to us in Your name."

Jesus replied, "Do not rejoice in this, that the spirits are subject to you, but rather rejoice because your names are written in heaven" (Luke 10:17, 20 NKJV).

Jesus gave many people the power to do miracles—even Judas—but they didn't all have His Spirit dwelling *inside* them (John

Jesus gave seventy disciples the ability to perform miracles—and told them their names would be written in heaven.

14:17). Jesus talked about this in Matthew 7:21–23 (NKJV), stating that He'd tell certain people, "I never knew you."

So let's rejoice that we *know* Jesus and that our names are written in the Book of Life!

261. SAMARITAN HELPS AN ENEMY \\ LUKE 10:25–37

» One day a scribe asked what Leviticus 19:18 (NKJV) meant when it said that "you shall love your neighbor as yourself." He wanted to know *exactly* who he was obligated to love, so he asked Jesus, "And who is my neighbor?" (Luke 10:29 NASB).

Jesus then told the story of a Jew traveling from Jerusalem to Jericho. The man was attacked by bandits and severely beaten, robbed of all his possessions—even his clothing—and left half-dead beside the road.

A Jewish priest passed by later, but walked around the wounded man and continued on. A Levite also walked by and saw him, but didn't stop to help either.

But a despised Samaritan saw him and had compassion. He cleaned and bandaged the man's wounds, then took him to an inn. The next day he had to leave, but he gave the innkeeper money to continue looking after him.

Jesus then asked, "Which of these three do you think proved to be a neighbor to the man. . . ?" The scribe answered, "The one who showed mercy toward him." Then Jesus said, "Go and do the same" (Luke 10:36–37 NASB).

Our neighbor is *any* human being who needs our help.

262. JESUS VISITS MARY AND MARTHA \\ LUKE 10:38–42

» One day Jesus and His disciples stopped at the village of Bethany (John 11:1). It was just two miles east of Jerusalem, at the foot of the Mount of Olives.

There, a wealthy woman named Martha opened her home to Jesus. She was delighted to do so, because, as she later told Him, she believed that He was the Messiah, the Son of God (John 11:27).

Martha had a brother named Lazarus whom Jesus loved (John 11:3). She also had a sister called Mary. Now, while Martha was overseeing meal preparations, Mary sat at Jesus' feet listening to Him.

Martha could have let her servants do their jobs, but she was very particular and wanted things done right. Frustrated, she asked, "Lord, do You not care that my sister has left me to serve alone? Therefore tell her to help me."

Martha was upset that her sister would not help take care of their guests. . .such as Jesus.

Jesus answered, "Martha, Martha, you are worried and troubled about many things. But one thing is needed, and Mary has chosen that good part, which will not be taken away from her" (Luke 10:40–42 NKJV).

Are you worried about many things? Take time to hear from Jesus and to receive His peace (Philippians 4:7).

263. HEALING A WOMAN ON THE SABBATH \\ LUKE 13:10–17

» One Sabbath Jesus was teaching in a synagogue in Judea and saw a woman bent over. He called her to Him and told her that she was now set free from her infirmity. He then placed His hands on her, and she instantly straightened up.

The synagogue leader indignantly announced, "There are six days in which work should be done; so come during them and get healed, and not on the Sabbath day" (Luke 13:14 NASB).

Very likely several people nodded their heads and mumbled their agreement.

Jesus said, "You hypocrites! Doesn't each of you on the Sabbath untie your ox or donkey from the stall and lead it out to give it water? Then should not this woman, a daughter of Abraham, whom Satan has kept bound for eighteen long years, be set free on the Sabbath day from what bound her?" (Luke 13:15–16 NIV).

Jesus' opponents knew He was right. They had probably done such things that very morning—and were completely humiliated. Most of the people, however, were delighted with all the wonderful things Jesus was doing.

We must obey God and not stray into sin, but we must also guard against loveless legalism.

264. HEALING A MAN BORN BLIND \\ JOHN 9:1–38

» One Sabbath, Jesus saw a man who had been born blind, so He made mud with His spit, applied it to his eyes, and sent him to wash. The

The Pharisees said Jesus was not the Son of God because He had healed a blind man on the Sabbath.

man immediately received his sight.

The astonished people took him to the Pharisees, who then indignantly declared that Jesus couldn't be of God, because He'd healed on the Sabbath. They asked the former blind man *his* opinion of Jesus, and he replied, "He is a prophet" (John 9:17 NASB).

After the Pharisees confirmed from the man's parents that he'd actually been born blind, they still insisted that Jesus was a sinner—miracles notwithstanding.

The man argued, "Whether he is a sinner or not, I don't know. One thing I do know. I was blind but now I see!" (John 9:25 NIV). He then gave a rousing defense of Jesus.

The Pharisees became so mad that they excommunicated him. Jesus later found the man and asked him, "Do you believe in the Son of God?" He said, "Lord, I believe!" (John 9:35, 38 NKJV). And he fell down and worshipped Jesus.

The former blind man had a continually greater revelation of who Jesus was. May we also receive the same.

265. THE GOOD SHEPHERD DESCRIBED \\ JOHN 10:1–18

» In fertile Galilee, Jesus had told many farming parables. Now in the drier south, He talked about shepherds and sheep—something people in Judea were very familiar with. (See also Luke 15:1–7.)

He described the tender care that a shepherd had for his flock and how he knew his sheep individually and called each one by name. When he took them out to pasture, he walked before them to show the way. The sheep recognized his voice and trusted him, so they followed only him—not a stranger.

Jesus described how a good shepherd would lay down his life defending his flock. He said: "I am the good shepherd. The good shepherd gives His life for the sheep. But a hireling. . .sees the wolf coming and leaves the sheep and flees" (John 10:11–12 NKJV).

Jesus then prophesied about coming events, saying, "I lay down My life that I may take it again. . . . I have power to lay it down, and I have power to take it again" (John 10:17–18 NKJV).

His crucifixion would seem like a total defeat, but things were never out of God's control. Jesus knew He would triumph in His resurrection.

Jesus is *still* the Good Shepherd, and He *still* has things under control.

>> Jesus was somewhere across the Jordan River in Perea when a messenger arrived from Mary and Martha, telling Him that their brother Lazarus was deathly sick and asking Jesus to come heal him. However, Jesus stayed where He was two more days before going to Judea.

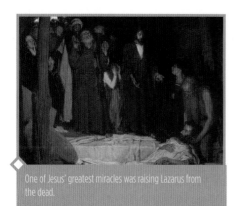

One of Jesus' greatest miracles was raising Lazarus from the dead.

When Jesus arrived, Lazarus was already dead and buried. Martha and Mary went out to meet Jesus. Now, Bethany was near Jerusalem, so many leading Jews had come to comfort the sisters. They now followed Mary, thinking she was going out to mourn.

When Jesus arrived at the tomb, He told them to move the stone. Martha replied, "Lord, by this time there will be a stench, for he has been dead four days" (John 11:39 NASB).

Jesus reminded her to believe. Then He shouted, "Lazarus, come out!" (John 11:43 NIV). And Lazarus, bound with grave wrappings, walked out. The entire shocked crowd witnessed this.

This was one of Jesus' greatest miracles, and it caused many to believe in Him. And "these are written that you may believe that Jesus is . . .the Son of God, and that by believing you may have life in his name" (John 20:31 NIV).

267. SANHEDRIN PASSES DEATH SENTENCE \\ JOHN 11:45–57; 12:9–11

>> After Jesus raised Lazarus, several stunned witnesses hurried to report it to the authorities.

Jesus' enemies called an emergency council and asked, "What shall we do? For this Man works many signs. If we let Him alone like this, everyone will believe in Him, and the Romans will come and take away both our place and nation" (John 11:47–48 NKJV).

Caiaphas, the high priest, observed that it was expedient for them that one man should die for the people, rather than that the whole nation perish. He was unwittingly prophesying that Jesus would die for the Jewish nation.

"Then, from that day on, they plotted to put Him to death." Jesus was no longer able to move publicly in Judea because they "had given a command, that if anyone knew where He was, he should report it, that they might seize Him" (John 11:53, 57 NKJV).

Jesus was now in danger in both Galilee and Judah, so He and His disciples withdrew quietly to a city in northern Judah, on the Samarian border, and stayed there.

With His enemies closing in, Jesus could have opted out at any time. Instead, He steadfastly headed toward the cross.

268. TEN LEPERS ARE HEALED \\ LUKE 13:31–33; 17:11–19

» After some time, Jesus crossed north through Samaria and entered Galilee. He wasn't there long before He was warned, "Get out and depart from here, for Herod wants to kill You" (Luke 13:31 NKJV). Knowing that He must die in Jerusalem, not Galilee, Jesus returned south.

At the Galilee-Samaria border, He passed ten lepers, Jews and Samaritans, standing a great distance away. Recognizing Jesus, they began yelling, "Jesus, Master, have pity on us!"

Jesus shouted back, "Go, show yourselves to the priests" (Luke 17:13–14 NIV). According to the law, those healed from leprosy were to do this (Leviticus 14:2–32).

And as they went, they were cleansed.

However, a Samaritan, realizing that his leprosy had been cured, ran back, loudly praising God. He flung himself at Jesus' feet and profusely thanked Him.

Jesus asked, "Were not all ten cleansed? Where are the other nine? Has no one returned to give praise to God except this foreigner?" (Luke 17:17–18 NIV).

Jesus hadn't commanded them to return and give thanks, but gratitude should have compelled them to do so. How often do we too receive blessings from God, then neglect to thank Him? (See Psalm 103:2.)

269. THE PRODIGAL SON DESCRIBED \\ LUKE 15:11–32

» Jesus told a parable about a wealthy man and his sons. The youngest son begged his father to give him his share of the estate early, so the father finally agreed. Not long after, the youngest son left for a far country where he wasted his money on parties and prostitutes.

After he had squandered everything, there was a famine in that country, and he was forced to take a job feeding pigs.

Just as the father rejoiced when the prodigal son returned home, God rejoices when a sinner repents.

Half starving, he finally came to his senses and repented of his wasteful lifestyle. He then set out for his father's estate, even if it meant working as his hired servant from then on.

But when his father saw his son returning, he rushed toward him, flung his arms around him, and kissed him. He then declared, "Let's have a feast and celebrate" (Luke 15:23 NIV).

The older brother was indignant about the lavish reception for such an "unworthy" son, but the father insisted, "We had to celebrate and be glad, because this brother of yours was dead and is alive again; he was lost and is found" (Luke 15:32 NIV).

To this very day, all heaven rejoices every time a wasteful, unworthy sinner repents (Luke 15:10).

❯❯ Jesus told a story about a rich man who dressed in fine clothing and feasted extravagantly every day. But a beggar named Lazarus, covered with sores, begged at his gate—and went hungry.

Eventually the beggar died, and angels took him to Abraham's bosom, where he was comforted. The rich man also died and went to Hades.

Seeing the beggar, the rich man wailed, "Father Abraham, have mercy on me, and send Lazarus that he may dip the tip of his finger in water and cool my tongue; for I am tormented in this flame" (Luke 16:24 NKJV). But Abraham replied that he now had to receive his just dues.

The rich man begged Abraham to send Lazarus to warn his brothers, so they didn't end up tormented in Hades. He argued that although they didn't obey God's Word, if someone rose from the dead, they'd repent.

Abraham replied, "If they do not hear Moses and the prophets, neither will they be persuaded though one rise from the dead" (Luke 16:31 NKJV).

Sure enough, although Jesus later rose from the dead, His enemies refused to repent. May we have tender hearts and believe and obey God's Word.

271. THE RICH YOUNG RULER MAKES A POOR CHOICE
\\ MATTHEW 19:16–30; LUKE 18:18–30

❯❯ Jesus and His disciples crossed the Jordan River then headed south into Perea. There, a young man from a wealthy family came running to Jesus, knelt, and asked, "Good Teacher, what good thing shall I do that I may have eternal life?" (Matthew 19:16 NKJV).

He was convinced that *he* had to do some great "good thing" to be saved, but when asked earlier, "What shall we do, so that we may work the works of God?" Jesus had explained, "This is the work of God, that you believe in Him whom He has sent" (John 6:28–29 NASB).

The young ruler claimed to have kept all God's commandments, but did he truly obey the two *greatest* commandments—to love God and his fellow man? Was he now willing to believe in and follow God's Son?

The rich ruler refused to follow Jesus when he was told to give up all his possessions.

He wasn't. When Jesus challenged him to give his money to the poor and follow Him, the young man refused. He was covetous, which is idol worship (Colossians 3:5).

Jesus then said how hard it was for a rich man to stop trusting riches and find eternal life. Is anything hindering *you* from entering the kingdom of heaven?

272. A TAX COLLECTOR MEETS THE MASTER \\ LUKE 19:1–10

» From Perea, Jesus and His disciples crossed the Jordan River and came to Jericho. A large crowd of Jews, mostly Galileans, arriving for the Passover, began traveling with them.

Many Galileans accepted Jesus as a great prophet. Surrounded by so many supporters, He was safe from being arrested. . .for now.

As Jesus walked through Jericho, a tax collector was eager to see Him. Being short, he couldn't see over the crowds, so he ran ahead, scaled a tree, and waited for Jesus to pass under.

Jesus looked up and said, "Zacchaeus, come down immediately. I must stay at your house today" (Luke 19:5 NIV).

The crowd grumbled that Jesus was consorting with a lowlife, but Zacchaeus announced that he'd give half his possessions to the poor, and if he'd cheated anybody, he'd pay back four times as much.

How different *his* attitude was from that of the rich young ruler! Therefore Jesus said, "Today salvation has come to this house" (Luke 19:9 NIV).

Now, if we give all we possess to the poor, but don't have love, we gain nothing. But if we *have* God's love, we will help the needy freely (1 Corinthians 13:3; 1 John 3:16–17).

273. BLIND BARTIMAEUS IS HEALED
\\ MATTHEW 20:29–34; MARK 10:46–52; LUKE 18:35–43

» As Jesus and His disciples left Jericho, a large crowd followed them. A blind man named Bartimaeus was sitting at the roadside, begging. Matthew 20:30 specifies that there were *two* men, but Bartimaeus was the outspoken one, so Luke and Mark's Gospels focus on him.

When Bartimaeus heard that Jesus was passing, he began shouting, "Jesus, Son of David, have mercy on me!" (*Son of David* meant "Messiah.") The crowd ordered Bartimaeus to be quiet, but he only shouted louder, "Son of David, have mercy on me!" (Mark 10:47–48 NLT).

Jesus heard him, so He stopped and said to call him. Moments later, he approached Jesus, followed by his friend. Jesus asked, "What do you want Me to do for you?" Bartimaeus answered, "I want to regain my sight!" (Mark 10:50–51 NASB).

Jesus responded, "Go, for your faith has healed you" (Mark 10:52 NLT). Instantly he and the other beggar could see. Bartimaeus then followed Jesus down the road.

Very often, we must persist in prayer and not give up asking for what we need. Jesus had just finished teaching on that very point (see Luke 18:1–8). Those are the kind of prayers that eventually get answers.

274. MARY ANOINTS JESUS AT BETHANY
\\ MATTHEW 26:6–13; MARK 14:3–9; JOHN 12:2–8

» When Jesus arrived at Bethany, a dinner was held in His honor, and Mary, Martha, and Lazarus were present. During the meal, Mary broke open a one-pint alabaster vase of nard, a rare, costly perfume, and poured it on Jesus' head and feet.

It was customary to anoint the heads of guests—but not to *this* extent!

Jesus' disciples grumbled, "Why this waste of perfume?" (Mark 14:4 NIV). Judas Iscariot rebuked Mary harshly: "Why wasn't this perfume sold and the money given to the poor? It was worth a year's wages" (John 12:5 NIV).

Jesus responded, "Why do you bother the woman? . . . For when she poured this perfume on My body, she did it to prepare Me for burial" (Matthew 26:10, 12 NASB).

Indeed, although Nicodemus placed spices (myrrh and aloes) in Jesus' burial linens, there wasn't time to anoint His body (John 19:39–40). This is what the women wanted to accomplish Sunday morning (Luke 23:56; 24:1–3).

Jesus said that Mary's good deed would be forever told in honor of her. And it has been.

In heaven, all *our* good deeds will be honored as well.

275. THE MESSIAH ENTERS JERUSALEM
\\ MATTHEW 21:1–11; LUKE 19:29–44; JOHN 12:12–18

» News of Jesus raising Lazarus had spread among the thousands of pilgrims camped on the Mount of Olives. So in the morning, when Jesus headed to Jerusalem, the crowds rushed out to meet Him.

Then Jesus sent two disciples to the village ahead and had them bring a donkey and her colt. This fulfilled an ancient prophecy: "See, your king comes to you, righteous and victorious, lowly and riding. . .on a colt, the foal of a donkey" (Zechariah 9:9 NIV).

As Jesus entered Jerusalem, He wept over the destruction that would befall the unrepentant city.

Then the multitudes spread their cloaks and branches from the trees on the road, for Jesus to ride over. They began jubilantly shouting,

"Hosanna to the Son of David!" (Matthew 21:9 NKJV). *Hosanna* means "God save us!"

As Jesus rode down the western slope and entered Jerusalem, the entire city was caught up in the excitement. Yet Jesus wept over unrepentant Jerusalem for the destruction that was coming upon her (Luke 19:41–44).

For years, Jesus had said, "Repent of your sins and believe the Good News!" (Mark 1:15 NLT). Most of the people *hadn't* repented—yet they now expected Jesus to save them. How often do we have a similar attitude?

276. JESUS CLEARS OUT THE TEMPLE AGAIN
\\ MATTHEW 21:12–17; MARK 11:15–18

» Jesus rode the donkey through the Eastern Gate and into the temple courts—surrounded by tumultuous crowds shouting that He was the Messiah. The Pharisees groaned, "Look how the whole world has gone after him!" (John 12:19 NIV).

Jesus then waded into the merchants buying and selling goods and violently overturned the tables of the money changers and the seats of those who sold doves.

He shouted, "It is written, 'My house shall be called a house of prayer,' but you have made it a 'den of thieves'" (Matthew 21:13 NKJV). An energized multitude cheered Him on.

Jesus took control of the entire temple courts while the temple guards stood by helplessly, unable to interfere—knowing that the crowd would attack them if they attempted to arrest Jesus.

It looked as if Jesus was about to sweep the corrupt priests from power and declare Himself king. Then, instead of riding the momentum, He began. . .healing the blind and the lame. The people waited, wondering when He'd take over. But He didn't.

Jesus *knew* they expected a militant Messiah, but He had come to die for their sins, and that's exactly what He would do.

» The next morning, as Jesus returned to Jerusalem, He was hungry. He saw a fig tree in the distance and went over. It wasn't fig season yet, but this particular tree was full of leaves—a sign that it *did* have fruit early.

However, when Jesus found nothing on it but leaves, He said, "May you never bear fruit again!" At once the leaves withered. The disciples were amazed and asked, "How did the fig tree wither so quickly?" (Matthew 21:19–20 NIV).

Jesus used a fig tree to show the disciples the importance of faith.

Jesus explained that if they had faith and didn't doubt, they could even tell this mountain, the Mount of Olives, to throw itself into the sea, and it would.

The next morning as they returned to the city, they saw the fig tree withered from the *roots*. Peter exclaimed, "Rabbi, look, the fig tree which You cursed has withered" (Mark 11:21 NASB).

Jesus repeated what He had explained the day before then added, "Therefore I tell you, whatever you ask for in prayer, believe that you have received it, and it will be yours" (Mark 11:24 NIV). It often takes time and persevering in prayer to receive answers, however.

» Jesus boldly entered the temple courts and taught, and multitudes gathered around Him. Now, Jesus' enemies "were trying to destroy Him, and they could not find anything that they might do, for all the people were hanging on to every word He said" (Luke 19:47–48 NASB).

They therefore tried to discredit Jesus. They first praised Him for teaching the truth without caring what people thought. Then they asked,

"Tell us, therefore, what do You think? Is it lawful to pay taxes to Caesar, or not?"

The people hated the Romans and would turn against Jesus if He said to pay. If He said *not* to pay, the religious leaders would accuse Him of rebelling against Caesar—which they later *did* (Luke 23:2).

Jesus responded, "Show Me the tax money." Someone held up a denarius, and He asked, "Whose image and inscription is this?"

The man answered, "Caesar's."

Jesus said, "Render therefore to Caesar the things that are Caesar's, and to God the things that are God's" (Matthew 22:17–21 NKJV).

His answer left his opponents speechless. Pray for God to give *you* answers to tricky and difficult questions (Matthew 10:19–20).

279. JESUS PROPHESIES ABOUT THE END TIME
\\ MATTHEW 24:1–31; MARK 13:1–27

» When Jesus told His disciples that the temple would be destroyed, they asked, "Tell us, when will all this happen? What sign will signal your return and the end of the world?" (Matthew 24:3 NLT). The temple was destroyed in AD 70, but the world would end much later.

Jesus said that there would be many false messiahs, wars, famines, and earthquakes—but these would be just the beginning of trouble.

He warned, "You will be hated all over the world. . . ." Despite intense persecution Christians would preach the Gospel in the entire world "and then the end will come" (Matthew 24:9, 14 NLT).

When the abomination of desolation is set up in God's temple, believers must flee—for then the Great Tribulation begins (Matthew 24:15–21), the greatest time of trouble the world has ever known.

Then, immediately after those days, "they will see the Son of Man coming on the clouds of the sky with power and great glory" (Matthew 24:30 NASB). He will gather all believers to Himself and, shortly after, set up His kingdom on the earth.

To this very day, Christians eagerly await the coming of Jesus.

» To avoid traveling to Bethany, Jesus and His disciples began spending nights on the nearby Mount of Olives. This allowed Him to go early every morning to the temple to teach. Also, being surrounded by the thousands of sympathetic Galilean pilgrims offered protection.

The chief priests and elders, meanwhile, assembled to discuss ways of secretly arresting and killing Jesus. But it had to be "when no crowd was present," or there would be "a riot among the people" (Luke 22:6; Matthew 26:5 NIV).

They couldn't come up with any plan. Jesus was *always* surrounded by crowds.

That's why they were delighted when Judas came asking, "What are you willing to give me if I deliver him over to you?" (Matthew 26:15 NIV). They paid him thirty pieces of silver. From that time on, Judas began watching for an opportunity to betray Jesus.

Then Satan gave Judas a devious plan. The crowd *could* be present, after all—surrounding Him on the Mount of Olives—as long as they were all asleep.

The devil thought he was defeating God's plan, but he played right into it. God still outsmarts the devil's schemes today.

281. EATING THE LAST SUPPER \\ MATTHEW 26:17–29; MARK 14:12–25; LUKE 22:7–20

» When Passover arrived, Jesus sent two disciples into Jerusalem to a certain man's house, to make preparations. That evening, Jesus and the other disciples arrived.

Judas was present for only the first portion of the meal. Immediately after Jesus dipped some bread into the dish and handed it to him, Judas hurried out to betray Him. Jesus and His remaining disciples then celebrated the full Passover.

After the meal, Jesus infused the bread and the cup of wine with new meaning.

Jeremiah had prophesied six hundred years earlier, "'Behold, days are coming,' declares the LORD, 'when I will make a new covenant with the house of Israel. . .and their sin I will remember no more" (Jeremiah 31:31, 34 NASB).

Jesus therefore broke the bread and gave it to His disciples, saying, "Take, eat; this is

Judas left during the Last Supper to betray Jesus. The room pictured is the traditional location where Jesus met His disciples for the meal.

My body." Then He passed the cup, saying, "Drink from it, all of you. For this is My blood of the new covenant, which is shed for many for the remission of sins" (Matthew 26:26–28 NKJV).

The following day, Jesus' body was broken with scourging, and His blood was poured out so that our sins could be forgiven.

282. JESUS TEACHES ABOUT GRAPEVINES \\ JOHN 15:1–17

» The land around Jerusalem was covered with grapevines, and Jesus stopped with His disciples to examine one and to bring out several truths. Jesus explained that He was the true vine and that His Father was the gardener.

His vine contains many branches. If a branch bears no fruit at all, God simply cuts it off. These people never actually knew Jesus. Such branches don't remain in Him but are tossed into a pile, where they wither. They are later cast into the fire and burned.

However, every branch in Jesus that is actually joined to Him *does* bear fruit. It is pruned of useless growth so that it can devote energy to the areas bearing fruit. As a result, they bear even *more* fruit.

Jesus then brought out a key point: "If you keep my commands, you will remain in my love." And what are His commands? "This is my command: Love each other" (John 15:10, 17 NIV). John later states: "And this is His commandment: that we should believe on the name of His Son Jesus Christ and love one another" (1 John 3:23 NKJV).

Let's bear fruit by letting Jesus' love flow through our lives.

283. JESUS PRAYS IN GETHSEMANE \\ MATTHEW 26:30–46; MARK 14:26–42

➤ Jesus and His disciples came to the Garden of Gethsemane on the Mount of Olives. He told them to wait in the lower garden then took Peter, James, and John higher up. After telling the three, "Stay here and watch" (Mark 14:34 NKJV), He went some distance further and began to pray fervently.

Jesus knew how greatly He would suffer, so He prayed that if possible the agony could be avoided. But He added, "Yet I want your will to be done, not mine" (Mark 14:36 NLT).

After praying, He went to the three disciples. They were asleep. He woke Peter up and asked if he was unable to watch with Him even one hour.

Again Jesus went away and prayed, repeating the same desperate words. Then He returned and found the three asleep once more. They were embarrassed and didn't know what to say. Heavy at heart, Jesus left to pray again.

Finally He came and woke them a third time, informing them that the hour had come—He was about to be arrested.

Jesus still asks us to watch and pray so that we'll have the strength to not fail in the hour of testing.

284. JESUS IS ARRESTED AND ABANDONED
\\ MATTHEW 26:47–56; MARK 14:43–52; JOHN 18:2–12

➤ Jesus' disciples were suddenly shocked awake. Judas had arrived, leading a large crowd armed with swords and clubs, and brandishing torches.

Heading straight to Jesus, "Judas said, 'Greetings, Rabbi!' and kissed Him" (Matthew 26:49 NIV). Judas anticipated that it would be difficult to identify Jesus in the dark, so this signaled who to arrest.

Turning to the mob, Jesus asked, "Who is it you want?" They replied, "Jesus of Nazareth." Jesus said, "I am he." The entire crowd suddenly surged backward and fell to the ground. When they arose, Jesus said, "If you are looking for me, then let these men go" (John 18:4–6, 8 NIV).

When Peter tried to interfere with the Lord's arrest, Jesus ordered him to stop.

The order was given to seize Jesus. Peter, realizing what was happening, drew his sword and swung at Malchus, the high priest's servant.

Jesus ordered Peter to stop. He had just demonstrated that if He didn't want to be arrested, He could prevent it. Plus, God could easily send seventy-two thosuand angels to defend Him. Peter's actions were well-meaning but futile.

Then all the disciples abandoned Jesus, and He was arrested.

May we be in tune with God's will and not try to implement weak human solutions.

285. JESUS IS FALSELY ACCUSED AND CONDEMNED
\\ MATTHEW 26:57–68; MARK 14:53–65

» The mob took Jesus to the palace of Caiaphas, the high priest, where many members of the ruling council, the Sanhedrin, were waiting.

After Jesus was brought in, false witnesses stepped forward and accused Him of crimes, to give the council a legal basis for passing a death sentence. But their statements conflicted. Finally, two men testified that Jesus had said that He was able to destroy the temple and rebuild it in three days. But Jesus said nothing.

Frustrated, Caiaphas asked, "Well, aren't you going to answer these charges?" (Matthew 26:62 NLT). Jesus remained silent. So Caiaphas demanded that Jesus tell them if He was the Messiah, the Son of God.

Jesus replied, "I am. And you will see the Son of Man sitting at the right hand of the Mighty One and coming on the clouds of heaven" (Mark 14:62 NIV).

Caiaphas cried, "Blasphemy!" He turned to the council. "What is your verdict?" They shouted, "Guilty! He deserves to die!" (Matthew 26:65–66 NLT).

Bitter, jealous men falsely accused the very Son of God, so we shouldn't be surprised if we're sometimes treated the same way (John 15:18–21).

286. PETER DENIES JESUS \\ MATTHEW 26:58, 69–75; MARK 14:54, 66–72

» Meanwhile, Peter had made his way into the high priest's courtyard. He was taking a huge risk. Some of the crowd might recognize him from the garden. But he had vowed he'd never desert Jesus.

Peter was sitting around the fire when a servant girl said, "You also were with Jesus of Galilee." One of the men took a closer look. "Didn't I see you with him in the garden?" (Matthew 26:69; John 18:26 NIV). But Peter denied it.

Peter retreated to the gateway, but there another woman announced that he was Jesus' follower. Peter swore an oath that he didn't know who she was talking about.

Soon, however, some men argued that he *must* be Jesus' disciple,

Peter denied Jesus three times before the rooster crowed.

because, after all, he was from Galilee. His accent gave him away.

Then Peter called down curses on himself if he knew Jesus—and immediately a rooster crowed. Peter had done what he'd boasted he would never do (Matthew 26:33–35).

Often we condemn those who stumble, look down at them, and insist that *we'd* never do such things. And perhaps we're strong and we wouldn't. But even Peter failed the Lord, and Jesus later restored him.

287. JESUS IS ACCUSED BEFORE PILATE \\ LUKE 23:1–5; JOHN 18:28–38

» The Sanhedrin had condemned Jesus but lacked the authority to execute Him. Only the Romans could do that. So early in the morning, they led Him to Pilate.

They had condemned Jesus for blasphemy but knew that Pilate wouldn't care about that. So they declared, "We found this fellow perverting the nation and forbidding to pay taxes to Caesar, saying that He Himself is Christ, a King" (Luke 23:2 NKJV).

When Pilate asked if He *was* the King of the Jews, Jesus replied, "My kingdom is not of this world." Pilate asked, "You are a king then!" (John 18:36–37 NIV). Jesus answered that the whole reason that He had been born was to bear witness to the truth.

At this point, Pilate knew that Jesus was no threat to Rome. He also knew that the chief priests were accusing Jesus out of envy (Mark 15:10 KJV).

He wanted to dismiss the case, but the chief priests repeated the charge of sedition: "He stirs up the people, teaching throughout all Judea, beginning from Galilee to this place" (Luke 23:5 NKJV).

May we never be guilty of trying to hurt or destroy someone out of envy.

288. PILATE GIVES IN TO THE RELIGIOUS LEADERS
\\ MATTHEW 27:15–26; LUKE 23:13–25

» Pilate had a custom: every Passover feast, to show his "mercy," he released a prisoner. At this time, he had a notorious prisoner called Barabbas who had committed murder in an armed insurrection.

Pilate reasoned that if the chief priests were concerned about Jesus stirring up rebellion, they wouldn't choose Barabbas. So he asked,

"Whom do you want me to release for you? Barabbas, or Jesus who is called Christ?" (Matthew 27:17 NASB).

Pilate agreed to release a criminal named Barabbas—and sentenced Jesus to be crucified.

To his dismay, they requested Barabbas. When Pilate asked what he should do with Jesus, the crowd shouted for Him to be crucified.

Pilate asked what evil Jesus had done, but this made the mob madder. When Pilate saw that he was getting nowhere and that a riot was starting, he released Barabbas. Although he'd repeatedly declared that Jesus was innocent, he sentenced Him to be crucified.

Pilate wasn't actually being merciful to release a prisoner every year. It was simply a PR move. Nor was he merciful in trying to get Jesus released. He probably just disliked the religious leaders coercing him into doing their dirty work.

When we do good deeds, let's act sincerely—not in pretense.

289. JESUS IS SAVAGELY SCOURGED
\\ MATTHEW 27:26; MARK 15:15; JOHN 19:1–16

» The Bible states, "Then Pilate took Jesus and had him flogged" (John 19:1 NIV). Flogging, also called scourging, was a brutal punishment. A person frequently didn't survive it. Roman authors called it "the half death."

Jesus was stripped naked and His hands were bound to a whipping post. Then two soldiers alternated in flogging. Forceful blows were delivered to His shoulders, His back, His buttocks, and His upper legs—down to His feet.

The Roman scourge had a wooden handle with leather thongs; lead balls and pieces of sheep bone were attached to each thong. These so deeply lacerated the muscles that Jesus' back was soon cut in ribbons.

Not only was the pain intense, but multiple arteries were sliced open. Blood loss was dramatic and Jesus' body went into hypovolemic shock, leaving Him so weak that He was unable to carry His crossbeam to Golgotha (Luke 23:26).

Pilate brought Jesus out afterward, hoping that the sight of a severely beaten man would satisfy them. But Jesus' enemies still demanded His crucifixion—so it was done.

Jesus suffered all this for us and shed His life's blood for our sins because He loved us.

290. JESUS IS NAILED TO A CROSS \\ MATTHEW 27:32–44; LUKE 23:32–43

» The Romans forced a passerby to carry Jesus' crossbeam to Golgotha. Once there, Jesus was crucified between two criminals.

The goal of crucifixion was to bring about death in the most painful way possible. Iron nails were driven between Christ's wrist bones, causing excruciating pain as they severed the median nerve. After that, a nail was driven through His feet.

For the next six hours, Jesus could inhale while hanging in a slumped position, but to exhale He had to raise himself up. To do so, He had to push against the nail in His feet and pull against the nails through His wrists, causing unbelievable agony.

Not only did Jesus suffer severe muscle cramps, but His back, laid wide open by scourging, constantly scraped against the rough wood of the cross as He repeatedly pulled Himself up, then slumped down. Jesus was wracked with torment at every moment.

On top of all of this, His enemies mocked Him as He suffered.

The cross was the ultimate symbol of shame and defeat, but Jesus transformed it. As Paul said, "The message of the cross is. . .the power of God" (1 Corinthians 1:18 NKJV).

» Jesus was crucified at nine in the morning, and at noon, a terrifying darkness came over the whole land until three in the afternoon. The historian Thallus, writing some twenty years after the crucifixion, referred to this darkness, though he tried to explain it naturally.

When Jesus had finished paying the price for our sins, He gasped, "It is finished" (John 19:30 NIV). Then He gave up His spirit.

On the day Jesus was crucified, the land was covered in darkness from noon until three.

Heavy blood loss and asphyxiation were the chief causes of His death. But doctors point out that the fact that "Jesus cried out with a loud voice, and breathed His last" (Mark 15:37 NKJV) suggests that He suffered a sudden cardiac rupture, induced by the severe physical and emotional trauma He had suffered.

Jesus suffered the agony of heartbreak because He had taken the sin of the world upon Himself and was, for the first time, separated from His Father. This is why, earlier, He had groaned, "My God, my God, why have you forsaken me?" (Matthew 27:46 NIV).

Jesus paid the full price for the sins that we committed. We must now put our faith in Him and accept His gift of salvation.

292. THE SON OF GOD IS BURIED \\ MATTHEW 27:57–66; MARK 15:42–47

» Sundown was approaching and the Sabbath about to begin, so to avoid having bodies on crosses on the Sabbath, the Jewish leaders requested that Pilate have them killed and taken down (John 19:31). So Pilate gave the order.

Moments later, Joseph of Arimathea, a secret disciple of Jesus, arrived at Pilate's fortress, asking for Jesus' body. He had just seen Him die. Pilate was surprised to hear that Jesus was already dead, as he'd barely given the order to end His life. So he sent a second messenger to summon the centurion and ascertain Jesus' death (Mark 15:42–45).

In the meantime, Pilate's first messenger arrived at Golgotha and gave his order, so the criminals' legs were broken and a spear was thrust through Jesus' heart (John 19:32–37).

Then when the centurion came and confirmed that Jesus was dead, Pilate gave Joseph permission to bury the corpse. So Joseph took down Jesus' body, wrapped it in linen cloth, and placed it in his own nearby tomb. Then he rolled a great stone in front of it, sealing the entrance.

Jesus was most definitely dead—which is what makes the following events so amazing!

293. JESUS RISES FROM THE DEAD
\\ MATTHEW 28:1–8; MARK 16:1–8; LUKE 24:1–8

» Glimmers of predawn light tinged the skies early Sunday morning. Suddenly there was a jarring earthquake and a mighty angel descended and rolled the stone away from Jesus' tomb. Seeing this supernatural being, the guards collapsed in terror.

Then the Spirit of God raised Jesus' corpse to life, transforming it into a glorious eternal body. And Jesus walked out of the tomb alive!

Meanwhile, as it was still dark, two groups of women set out, intent on anointing Jesus' body. The first group was led by Mary Magdalene and came from a house close to the tomb, just inside the city gate (Mark 16:1–2).

The second group was likely led by Joanna, the wife of

Women were the first to learn that Jesus' tomb was empty.

Herod's steward, and came from Herod's palace, farther away from the tomb (Luke 8:2–3; 23:7; 24:10).

Both groups, arriving at different times, saw the angels in the tomb. They announced, "Do not be afraid, for I know that you are looking for Jesus, who was crucified. He is not here; he has risen, just as he said" (Matthew 28:5–6 NIV).

The women then ran to share the news. This is still our job today.

294. WOMEN BRING STARTLING NEWS \\ LUKE 24:9–12; JOHN 20:2–10

❯❯ Mary Magdalene and the women with her ran back to the house. There they told Peter and John the shocking news—Jesus' body was missing!

At this same time, Joanna and her group arrived at the tomb and saw the angels. They immediately fled to tell the main group of disciples. The disciples had all been staying at Bethany a few days previously and were apparently hiding there now (Matthew 21:17; 26:6).

Meanwhile, Peter and John raced to the garden tomb, entered it, and confirmed that Jesus' body was gone. But they didn't see any angels.

Sometime later, the other group of women arrived at Bethany and told the disciples that angels had told them that Jesus was alive. "But they did not believe the women, because their words seemed to them like nonsense" (Luke 24:11 NIV).

Mary Magdalene soon saw Jesus Himself—but when she told the disciples, they didn't believe her either (Mark 16:9–11). Later, when Jesus appeared, "He rebuked their unbelief and hardness of heart" for not believing the women (Mark 16:14 NKJV).

May God forgive us for the times that *we* have unbelief and hard hearts.

» Now, Mary Magdalene had followed Peter and John back to the tomb, and after they left, she stayed to mourn. As she was standing there, weeping, she turned and saw a man, and didn't realize that it was Jesus.

Jesus asked, "Woman, why are you weeping? Whom are you seeking?"

Mary assumed that he was the gardener, so she said, "Sir, if you have carried Him away, tell me where you have laid Him, and I will take Him away."

Jesus simply said, "Mary!" Crying out in joy, she raced over and threw her arms around Jesus, but He said, "Stop clinging to Me, for I have not yet ascended to the Father" (John 20:15–17 NASB).

Mary ran back to the house to tell Peter and John, but they'd left for Bethany to discuss events with the other disciples.

As she was weeping at Jesus' tomb, Mary Magdalene saw the Lord.

Mary Magdalene then returned with the other Mary, and *both* women saw Jesus (Matthew 28:1, 5–10). Then they hurried out to Bethany and told the gathered disciples.

Mary had a dark past, but Jesus delivered her and made her one of His dearest, closest followers (Mark 16:9). He does the same with us today.

» That afternoon a disciple named Cleopas and a companion left Jerusalem and headed to Emmaus, seven miles to the northwest.

Meanwhile, Simon Peter, stirred by Mary Magdalene's claim to have seen Jesus *twice*, returned to the garden tomb. There he became the first man to see Jesus (1 Corinthians 15:5).

While Cleopas and friend walked, they talked about Jesus' death and the women's cryptic visions. Then a stranger walked up and asked why they were sad. This man was Jesus, but they were prevented from recognizing Him. He talked with them all the way to Emmaus.

As they sat down to eat, they suddenly recognized Jesus! Then He vanished. The two men immediately ran back to Jerusalem in the dark. They told some disciples that they'd seen Jesus, but the men didn't believe them (Mark 16:12–13).

Cleopas and companion then headed to Bethany to tell the apostles. To their surprise, the apostles replied, "It is true! The Lord has risen and has appeared to Simon!" (Luke 24:34 NIV).

The apostles didn't believe the women (Mark 16:14), but they *did* believe Peter. May God help us not to allow prejudices to affect us.

297. JESUS APPEARS TO HIS DISCIPLES
\\ MARK 16:14; LUKE 24:36–43; JOHN 20:19–23

» The disciples were afraid that their enemies might try to kill them too, so after they let Cleopas and companion in, they closed and locked the door tightly.

Then, as Peter and Cleopas were sharing their stories, Jesus appeared in their midst, saying, "Peace to you." The apostles were terrified, thinking it was Jesus' ghost. He *had* come right through a locked door, after all.

Jesus asked, "Why are you troubled? And why do doubts arise in your hearts? Behold My hands and My feet, that it is I Myself. Handle Me and see, for a spirit does not have flesh and bones as you see I have" (Luke 24:38–39 NKJV).

Then He showed them His nail-pierced hands and His feet and let them touch Him. They were still unsure whether they should believe their senses, so He asked them for some food. Then while they watched, He ate a piece of broiled fish.

They were finally convinced that He wasn't a ghost—and had tremendous joy. It should give *us* great joy as well. Jesus said, "Because I live, you will live also" (John 14:19 NKJV).

298. DOUBTING THOMAS IS CHALLENGED \\ JOHN 20:24–31

» Thomas hadn't been there when Jesus appeared. When the apostles told him that they'd seen Jesus, even touched Him, Thomas demanded *more* proof: "Unless I. . .put my finger where the nails were, and put my hand into his side, I will not believe" (John 20:25 NIV).

Now, Jesus had instructed His disciples to go to Galilee (Matthew 28:7, 16), so the apostles told everyone, and they all headed north. Thomas went too, even though he didn't believe.

One week later—probably in Peter's house at Capernaum— the apostles were together, and the doors were locked. Once again, Jesus appeared among them and announced, "Peace be with you!"

Thomas had to see and touch Jesus before he could believe that the Messiah had risen.

Turning to Thomas, Jesus held out a nail-pierced hand. He opened His tunic and showed the spear wound above His heart. Then He said, "Put your finger here; see my hands. Reach out your hand and put it into my side. Stop doubting and believe."

Thomas blurted out, "My Lord and my God!" (John 20:26–28 NIV).

It took some convincing for Thomas to believe, but when he did, he had a deep revelation of who Jesus was—not only the risen Messiah, but God himself. Have you had that revelation?

» Many people think that Peter and other disciples went fishing because they were discouraged and were drifting back to their old jobs. This is improbable. Jesus was alive! They were extremely excited and motivated.

Very likely, a crowd was gathering to meet with Jesus (Matthew 28:16), and the apostles wanted some fish to take there.

So they fished all night and caught nothing. In the morning, they saw a man on the shore who asked them if they had any fish. When they answered no, He said, "Cast the net on the right-hand side of the boat and you will find a catch" (John 21:6 NASB).

They did, and enclosed a multitude of large fish. At once they realized that the man was Jesus. They remembered Cleopas's account of how the Lord had disguised Himself to travel publicly around Israel.

When they got to shore, they saw that Jesus already had a charcoal fire going, had provided some bread, and was cooking fish for their breakfast.

Jesus did great miracles that showed His power. But He also did thoughtful, kind acts that showed His love. If we can't do miracles, we can still follow Jesus' example.

300. JESUS APPEARS TO A MULTITUDE
\\ MATTHEW 28:16–20; 1 CORINTHIANS 15:6

» This is one of Jesus' least-known appearances, but it's almost the most important because of the many people it affected.

Jesus had told His disciples to meet Him on a mountain in Galilee (Matthew 28:16). But He had already appeared to His apostles on *three* separate occasions. So why did He wish to meet on a mountain?

Very likely this was when He was seen by over five hundred disciples at once (1 Corinthians 15:6). Most of Jesus' followers hadn't yet seen Him after His resurrection, and this was an opportunity to encourage many disciples' faith at once.

It wasn't God's will for Jesus to be seen by the public (Acts 10:41), so they had to meet at an isolated location. Often even going to deserted regions didn't work, as the crowds found out (Matthew 14:13).

So they went "to the mountain which Jesus had designated. When they saw Him, they worshipped Him; but some were doubtful" (Matthew 28:16–17 NASB). Jesus then proved to them that He was risen from the dead, just as he had done for doubting Thomas.

Thank God that He still takes the time to encourage our faith today.

301. JESUS ASCENDS TO HEAVEN \\ MARK 16:19–20; LUKE 24:50–53; ACTS 1:4–12

❯❯ Jesus then instructed His disciples to return to Jerusalem. Most of the five hundred couldn't go. They had jobs and obligations in their home villages. But the Eleven, the Seventy, and Jesus' closest female disciples made the journey.

Then as they ate together, Jesus commanded them, "Do not leave Jerusalem until the Father sends you the gift he promised. . .in just a few days you will be baptized with the Holy Spirit" (Acts 1:4–5 NLT).

Before He ascended into heaven, Jesus told His disciples they would be baptized with the Holy Spirit.

Finally, Jesus led His disciples out to Bethany, lifted up His hands, and blessed them. In that moment He was carried up into heaven and vanished into a cloud. From there "He was received up into heaven, and sat down at the right hand of God" (Mark 16:19 NKJV).

While the disciples continued looking, two angels appeared and said, "Men of Galilee. . .why are you standing here staring into heaven? Jesus has been taken from you into heaven, but someday he will return from heaven in the same way you saw him go!" (Acts 1:11 NLT).

Then the disciples worshipped Jesus and went to Jerusalem with great joy. We should also have great joy as we serve Jesus until He returns.

302. THE DISCIPLES PRAY IN JERUSALEM
\\ ACTS 1:4–8, 12–15; LUKE 24:52–53

» The Son of God had risen from the dead! The Messiah had made a way for people to be saved from their sins! This was such terrific news that the apostles had "great joy" (Luke 24:52 NKJV). They could hardly wait to share it.

But they would also face terrific opposition, so Jesus instructed them to wait in Jerusalem until He sent His Spirit to empower them (Acts 1:4–5, 8). They simply couldn't do this great task in their own wisdom and power.

While they waited, they prayed. "They all met together and were constantly united in prayer" (Acts 1:14 NLT). For ten days, day after day, they prayed.

The apostles met daily with Jesus' brothers (who now believed), His mother, and several other women in the upper room of the place where they were staying. But there were 120 disciples in all, so this large crowd was "continually in the temple praising and blessing God" (Luke 24:53 NKJV).

Instead of rushing out to do God's work, spend time with Him first. Start each day with prayer, and God will give you power to do what He wants done.

303. THE HOLY SPIRIT DESCENDS \\ ACTS 2:1–41

» It was the Feast of Pentecost, fifty days after Passover, and all 120 disciples were crowded into the large house of a wealthy disciple—when suddenly the sound of a mighty rushing wind filled the place where they were sitting.

"They saw what seemed to be tongues of fire that separated and came to rest on each of them" (Acts 2:3 NIV). Everyone was filled to overflowing with the Holy Spirit and began to praise God in unknown languages.

Multitudes of Jews had come from foreign lands to attend the Feast of Pentecost, and as the disciples rushed out of the house praising God, the pilgrims were astonished. They could see that these were Galileans, yet they were speaking the foreign languages the pilgrims spoke.

Peter then declared that this miracle was the fulfillment of a prophecy (Joel 2:28–32)—and that, according to the prophecy, it was time to call on the name of the Lord and be saved. As a result, about three thousand people received salvation.

When the Holy Spirit descended upon them, the disciples could speak in unknown languages.

Paul urges us to "be filled with the Spirit" (Ephesians 5:18 NASB). We may not speak in foreign languages, but we can still praise God and tell of His goodness.

304. A LAME MAN IS HEALED \\ ACTS 3:1–16; 4:1–14

» The apostles had healed in Galilee over a year earlier, when Jesus "gave them power and authority to. . .cure diseases" (Luke 9:1 NIV). But they hadn't done miracles since then—at least none that are recorded. That was about to change.

One day Peter and John were going to the temple when they saw a lame man. He begged for money, but Peter replied, "Silver and gold I do not have, but what I do have I give you: In the name of Jesus Christ of Nazareth, rise up and walk" (Acts 3:6 NKJV).

Immediately the man was healed. He ran, leaped in the air, and praised God with a loud voice. The crowds, recognizing the formerly lame man, were astonished.

Peter then declared that the man had been healed by the power of Jesus Christ. He preached a powerful sermon, and many people were saved. The religious rulers arrested Peter and John, but when they appeared before them, Peter boldly witnessed that Jesus was the only way to salvation.

God still does miracles today to encourage faith. He doesn't always move *this* dramatically, but He still heals and answers prayer. That's why we pray.

305. DISCIPLES COMMANDED NOT TO PREACH \\ ACTS 4:14–31

» The people of Jerusalem were praising God for the lame man's healing, and the religious rulers themselves couldn't deny that it had happened. After all, the formerly lame man was standing there with Peter and John.

The rulers also realized that no one would believe the argument that such a wonderful miracle had been done by the power of the devil.

Sending Peter and John out of the chamber, the Sanhedrin discussed what they could do. Unable to think of any way to punish them, they called Peter and John back in and ordered them not to speak anymore in the name of Jesus Christ.

However, Jesus had commanded His disciples, "Go into all the world and preach the Good News to everyone" (Mark 16:15 NLT).

So Peter and John responded, "Which is right in God's eyes: to listen to you, or to him? You be the judges! As for us, we cannot help speaking about what we have seen and heard" (Acts 4:19–20 NIV). The chief priests threatened them again then released them.

As Christians, we must obey the laws of the land (1 Peter 2:13), but we can't obey any law that forbids us to preach the Gospel.

306. ANANIAS AND SAPPHIRA LIE AND DIE \\ ACTS 4:32–37; 5:1–11

» The temple ran a relief program for widows, orphans, and the destitute. However, when these people became disciples of Jesus, they found themselves excommunicated and desperate.

The believers quickly took action: wealthy disciples with extra houses and lands sold them and brought the money to the apostles— who distributed to those in need (Acts 2:44–45; 4:34).

These generous donors were highly esteemed, though that *wasn't* why they gave.

A couple named Ananias and Sapphira wanted praise and prestige, so they sold their land and gave a sum to the apostles, claiming it was the full price. But they were lying, keeping back a portion for their personal use.

Ananias and Sapphira died after they lied about how much they were giving.

As Peter pointed out, the land was *theirs*, and after they'd sold it the money was *still* theirs to do with as they wished. Their sin was to lie that they'd sacrificially given everything. So God judged them—and they both fell down dead.

Paul later wrote, "Each of you should give what you have decided in your heart to give" (2 Corinthians 9:7 NIV). There's no compulsion. But the point is: we should be honest and not claim to be giving more than we actually are.

307. MIRACULOUS JAILBREAK AND MERCILESS BEATING
\\ ACTS 5:17–42

》 The rulers and elders finally had enough. They arrested the apostles and locked them in prison. That night, however, an angel opened the prison doors and released them. Early the next morning, the apostles returned to the temple courts and boldly began teaching.

When the rulers sent guards to the prison to bring the prisoners, they returned with astonishing news: although the prison was locked and the guards standing at duty outside, the cells were. . .empty!

When the chief priest heard that the apostles were teaching at the temple, he had guards arrest them and bring them. When the apostles arrived, Caiaphas angrily reminded them that they'd been strictly commanded to *stop* teaching in Jesus' name.

Peter replied, "We must obey God rather than human beings!" (Acts 5:29 NIV).

The rulers and elders became furious and ordered the apostles flogged. The pain was intense, and the wounds many and deep. How did they react? "The apostles left the Sanhedrin, rejoicing because they had been counted worthy of suffering disgrace for the Name" (Acts 5:41 NIV).

Jesus said that we also should rejoice when we're maligned or persecuted for His sake (Luke 6:22–23).

308. SEVEN GOOD MEN GET NEW JOBS \\ ACTS 6:1-7

» The number of disciples was steadily increasing, and even "a great many of the priests were obedient to the faith" (Acts 6:7 NKJV). It was wonderful that there were so many thousands of believers, but this rapid growth also created problems.

The majority of Christians were local Hebrews, but a significant number of Greek-speaking Jews (from foreign nations) were living in Jerusalem and had become believers. But through an oversight, their widows were being overlooked in the daily distribution of necessities.

So they complained to the apostles and asked them to rectify the situation.

Rather than getting involved, the Twelve replied, "It is not desirable that we should leave the word of God and serve tables" (Acts 6:2 NKJV). Instead, they told the disciples to select seven honest, wise men, full of the Holy Spirit, whom they could appoint over this matter.

And so the first deacons came into existence. This allowed the apostles to continue devoting their time to prayer and preaching the Gospel.

The church today still needs good men and women to handle the practical, day-to-day business and ministries. Never think that these things are unspiritual or unimportant.

》 The apostles had specified that deacons be full of the Holy Spirit, and a man named Stephen was so "full of God's grace and power" that he "performed amazing miracles and signs" (Acts 6:8 NLT).

Stephen was Greek speaking, so he witnessed his faith to other Greek-speaking Jews. One day, several of them began to debate with him. They soon realized that they couldn't stand against his wisdom and power.

Bitter, they dragged him before the Sanhedrin and had men lie that he had blasphemed both God and Moses.

Suddenly, everyone stopped talking and stared at Stephen, because his face was glowing as brightly as the face of an angel. Stunned, they listened as he gave an impassioned sermon about God's history of dealing with His disobedient people (Acts 6:15).

Stephen's face glowed as he gave a sermon about the history of God's judgment.

But when Stephen ended by telling them that they themselves disobeyed the law and resisted God's Spirit, they became enraged. They dragged him outside the city and stoned him. He became the church's first martyr.

Persecution is still happening. Christians around the world today are suffering greatly for Jesus' name. We can support them in prayer and in practical ways (Hebrews 13:3).

310. SAUL PERSECUTES THE CHURCH \\ ACTS 8:1–4; 26:9–11

» When the mob stoned Stephen, they took off their cloaks and gave them to a young man named Saul to watch (Acts 7:58). Saul was in full agreement with killing Stephen.

That day, a great persecution broke out against the disciples in Jerusalem. Saul quickly became a leader in the inquisition. He went from one synagogue to another to find secret believers. He had them savagely beaten in the synagogues "to get them to curse Jesus" (Acts 26:11 NLT).

People reported on Christians, and soon Saul raided home after home. He dragged off both men and women and cast them in prison. If they refused to blaspheme Jesus, Saul voted to kill them.

The believers in Jerusalem fled for their lives and were soon scattered throughout Judea and Samaria, but Saul, "being furiously enraged at them. . .kept pursuing them even to foreign cities" (Acts 26:11 NASB).

Having received authority from the chief priests, Saul went far afield, arresting Christians and bringing them back to Jerusalem.

Jesus had warned that such persecution would come—and now it had (Matthew 10:16–23; 23:34–36). Persecution will come in the end times as well (Matthew 24:9–10).

311. THE GOSPEL IS PREACHED IN SAMARIA \\ ACTS 1:8; 8:4–8

» Saul's persecution, devastating as it was, had one immediate good effect: it resulted in the Gospel finally being preached to the Samaritans.

In AD 27, Jesus and His disciples had stayed two days in the Samaritan village of Sychar, and many people there believed that He was the Messiah (John 4:39–42).

Later, in AD 30, Jesus specifically commanded His disciples to preach the Gospel in Samaria (Acts 1:8). But five years had passed, and they were still witnessing only to fellow Jews. They knew what Jesus had said, but nobody really *wanted* the job.

But during Saul's persecution, many disciples fled to Samaria—where they preached the Gospel. And the Samaritans, who believed in Moses, were receptive.

Philip, one of the seven deacons, went to the city of Samaria and preached that Jesus was the Messiah. "When the crowds heard Philip and saw the signs he performed. . .there was great joy in that city," and "they believed Philip as he proclaimed the good news" (Acts 8:6, 8, 12 NIV).

God can bring good even out of our troubles. "God causes everything to work together for the good of those who love God" (Romans 8:28 NLT).

312. A SORCERER SEEKS POWER \\ ACTS 8:9–24

» A man named Simon had practiced sorcery in Samaria for many years, claiming to be someone great. Everyone in the city had been amazed by his magic and said, "This man is the great power of God" (Acts 8:10 NKJV).

And that *was* what Simon wanted more than anything—*power.*

But when the Samaritans believed the Gospel and were baptized, Simon also believed. He followed Philip around, in awe of the powerful miracles he performed.

The apostles heard that the people of Samaria had received the Gospel, so they sent Peter and John. When they arrived, the two apostles laid their hands upon the new believers and prayed for them, and they received the Holy Spirit.

When Simon saw this, he offered them money. "'Let me have this power, too,' he exclaimed, 'so that when I lay my hands on people, they will receive the Holy Spirit!'" (Acts 8:19 NLT).

But Peter rebuked him, warning that he was full of bitter jealousy and that he needed to repent of his wickedness.

When we have deeply entrenched sinful habits, we need to make sure that we thoroughly repent of them, lest they choke out our new life in Christ.

» Afterward, an angel told Philip to go south to the road that ran between Jerusalem and Gaza. So Philip went and met the treasurer for Candace, queen of the Ethiopians.

The treasurer was returning from Jerusalem, and as he rode in his chariot, he was reading aloud from Isaiah. He was at Isaiah 53:7 (NIV), which says, "He was led like a lamb to the slaughter, and as a sheep before its shearers is silent, so he did not open his mouth."

After he explained the passage in Isaiah, Philip baptized the treasurer from Ethiopia.

Philip ran up to him and asked if he understood what he was reading. The man admitted that he didn't, so he invited Philip to ride with him and explain it.

Philip then told him how Jesus had fulfilled these prophecies by refusing to defend Himself from accusations at His trial. Philip then explained that Isaiah 53 went on to describe how Jesus died for our sins.

They came to some water, stopped the chariot, and Philip baptized him. Then the Spirit suddenly transported Philip away, and he reappeared at Azotus, miles to the north. Meanwhile, the treasurer returned to Ethiopia rejoicing.

When God puts it on your heart to speak to someone about Jesus, obey Him!

» Saul, meanwhile, was on the road to Damascus, intending to enter all the synagogues there, arrest Jesus' followers, and bring them back to Jerusalem.

As he and his escort approached the city, a light blazed around him. Saul fell to the ground and a voice said, "Saul, Saul, why are you persecuting Me?" He asked, "Who are You, Lord?" The voice answered, "I am Jesus whom you are persecuting, but get up and enter the city, and it will be told you what you must do" (Acts 9:4–6 NASB).

Trembling, Saul rose. Then he realized. . .he was *blind*!

Saul's guards had no idea what had just happened, but they took him into Damascus, where for three days he ate and drank nothing. The news of this baffling event apparently swept through all the synagogues.

Then the Lord told a disciple named Ananias to go to the house where Saul was staying. So Ananias went, laid his hands on Saul, and prayed for him. Instantly scales fell from Saul's eyes. He regained his sight and was filled with the Holy Spirit. Then Ananias baptized him.

God is still piercing the darkness in people's lives today with His marvelous light.

» Saul spent several days learning from the disciples at Damascus. He then began going from synagogue to synagogue, describing how he had persecuted believers in Jerusalem and had come to Damascus to arrest them but now knew that Jesus was the Son of God.

Saul was knowledgeable in the scriptures, and as the Holy Spirit showed him the prophecies Jesus had fulfilled, Saul astonished the Jews, proving that Jesus was their promised Messiah.

Eventually they plotted to kill him. By the time Saul learned about it, it was too late to escape. His enemies had enlisted the help of the city governor, and guards watched the gates both day and night.

Then the disciples came up with a daring plan. Placing Saul in a large basket, they lowered him down the city walls by rope—and he escaped. He lay low in Arabia for two or three years before finally returning to Damascus (Galatians 1:15–24).

From the city walls of Damascus, the disciples lowered Saul in a basket so he could escape angry Jews.

The Christians then heard, "He who formerly persecuted us now preaches the faith which he once tried to destroy" (Galatians 1:23 NKJV). And they praised God.

We today can also praise God for the many incorrigible lives He is changing.

316. PETER RAISES TABITHA TO LIFE \\ ACTS 9:31–43

» After Saul's persecution, things quieted down; the church had a time of peace, and the number of believers increased.

As Peter traveled about, he visited the disciples in Lydda. A man named Aeneas had been paralyzed for eight years, so Peter told him, "Aeneas, Jesus Christ heals you" (Acts 9:34 NIV). Immediately Aeneas got up! As a result, *everyone* in Lydda became believers.

Nearby in Joppa was a disciple named Tabitha who always made clothing for other believers and helped the poor. Then she fell sick and died. Two men rushed to Lydda, urging Peter to come.

When Peter arrived, he was taken to the upper room where her body lay. All the widows stood around, weeping and showing him the clothing that Tabitha had sewn.

After sending them all from the room, Peter knelt and prayed. Then looking at the unmoving corpse, he said, "Tabitha, get up" (Acts 9:40 NIV). Tabitha opened her eyes and sat up. Peter then called the disciples back into the room.

News of this great miracle filled Joppa, and many people believed in Jesus.

God may not often raise the dead, but He still does miracles today to inspire faith.

317. PETER HAS A ROOFTOP VISION \\ ACTS 10:1–23

» Caesarea, the Roman administrative center of Israel, was thirty miles up the coast from Joppa. A centurion named Cornelius was stationed there, and he and all his family believed in God.

One afternoon while Cornelius was praying, an angel appeared and told him to send men to Joppa to bring back a man called Peter, who was staying with Simon, a tanner. Cornelius obeyed.

The next day, while the noon meal was cooking, Peter went up on Simon's roof to pray. Then he had a vision of a large sheet filled with "unclean" animals, reptiles, and birds that Jews were forbidden to eat (Leviticus 11).

A voice commanded, "Get up, Peter. Kill and eat." Peter protested that he'd never eaten anything impure, but the voice said, "Do not call anything impure that God has made clean" (Acts 10:13, 15 NIV). This vision was repeated three times.

While Peter was wondering what it meant, the three men Cornelius sent arrived at the door. God told Peter to go with them, even though Jews were forbidden to keep company with Gentiles (Acts 10:28).

God loves *every* person on earth, even the strange birds we'd rather not associate with. We must love them too.

318. PETER PREACHES TO GENTILES \\ ACTS 10:24–48; 11:1–18

» The next day Peter broke a major Jewish taboo when he and several other Jews entered the house of a Gentile (non-Jew). It was packed with Gentiles. Cornelius had invited all of his relatives and close friends.

The centurion then explained that an angel had appeared to him, telling him to send for Peter. They had therefore all gathered to listen to what he had to say.

Peter then gave a brief history of how Jesus had gone throughout Galilee and Judea, doing good and healing the sick—and though the religious rulers had crucified their Messiah, three days later God raised Him from the dead.

Peter had no sooner finished saying, "Everyone who believes in him will have their sins forgiven" (Acts 10:43 NLT), than the Holy Spirit entered everyone's receptive hearts. Peter then baptized the first Gentile believers.

When Peter explained all these things to the church in Jerusa-

Peter baptized the first Gentile believers after the Holy Spirit had entered their hearts.

lem, they said, "We can see that God has also given the Gentiles the privilege of. . . receiving eternal life" (Acts 11:18 NLT).

Since that day, Christians have obeyed Christ's command to go into the entire world and preach the Gospel to all people (Mark 16:15).

319. PREACHING TO GREEKS IN ANTIOCH \\ ACTS 11:19–26

» Some of the Jewish Christians scattered by Saul's persecution had fled to distant places such as Phoenicia, Cyprus, and Antioch. There were seven million Jews living throughout the Roman Empire, so they were busy telling only Jews about Jesus.

However, they'd heard that Peter had witnessed to Gentiles, so some believers in Antioch began to preach the Gospel to Greeks. God mightily blessed their efforts, and multitudes of Greeks believed in Jesus and were baptized.

Antioch was famous for making up nicknames, and "the disciples were called Christians first in Antioch" (Acts 11:26 KJV).

The leaders in Jerusalem heard about the many new Gentile converts, so they sent Barnabas to Antioch. When he saw the many enthusiastic Greek believers, he encouraged them to continue following the Lord with all their hearts.

Saul was nearby, in his hometown of Tarsus, so Barnabas went there and brought him to Antioch. Then for an entire year Barnabas and Saul taught great numbers of new Christians. Antioch would soon become a missionary base for reaching the rest of the Roman Empire.

Sometimes it takes only a few people pioneering, and that's enough to get a major new outreach going.

320. HEROD PERSECUTES THE CHURCH. . .AND DIES
\\ ACTS 12:1–4, 19–23

» In AD 44, nearly ten years after Saul's persecution had ended, Herod Agrippa (grandson of Herod the Great) was king of Judea. The Romans normally had governors rule Judea, but were allowing Jewish self-rule for a time.

Now, Herod arrested James the brother of John and had him executed with a sword. When he realized how much this pleased their enemies, he arrested Peter also. But Peter escaped, and Herod returned to Caesarea in a very bad mood.

Herod had a dispute with the people of Tyre and Sidon, and this was bad news for those cities, since Israel supplied most of their food. So their citizens, wishing for peace, arranged a meeting.

On the appointed day Herod put on a shimmering silver robe and delivered an oration. The crowd exclaimed, "The voice of a god and not of a man!" (Acts 12:22 NASB).

Herod claimed to believe in God but didn't rebuke the people. So an angel immediately afflicted him with a terrible infestation of worms that killed him.

God doesn't always act swiftly to judge evil, but He does act eventually. That's why we must leave judgment in His hands (Romans 12:19).

321. AN ANGEL FREES PETER FROM PRISON \\ ACTS 12:1–17

» Before his death, Herod had arrested Peter during Passover but decided to wait until after the festivities to bring him out for a public trial. So he locked him in prison, commanding "four squads of four soldiers each" to guard him (Acts 12:4 NIV).

But many Christians prayed unceasingly for God to do a miracle.

The night before his trial, Peter was sleeping between two soldiers. Suddenly a brilliant light filled the dungeon, and an angel ordered, "Quick! Get up!" (Acts 12:7 NLT). At once his chains snapped open. Then the angel commanded Peter to get dressed and follow.

As an angel was freeing him from prison, Peter first thought he was having a vision.

They left the cell, passed the first and second set of guards, and came to the outer gate, which opened of its own accord.

All the time Peter thought this was a vision. But as they walked down the street, the angel vanished. Then Peter realized that this was *really* happening. He quickly informed the believers then went into hiding.

At daybreak, the guards were in an uproar, unable to find Peter. Herod was so upset that he had them all executed.

God can still do miracles in answer to fervent prayers. Christians down through the ages have experienced God's deliverance.

322. PAUL CONFRONTS PETER IN ANTIOCH \\ GALATIANS 2:11–21

» Peter was on top of the wanted list in Judea, so it was a good time for him to visit distant cities.

When he came to Antioch, he accepted the Gentile believers and ate with them, although it was against Jewish customs. He *had*, after all, eaten with Cornelius.

But when disciples came from James, the Lord's brother, Peter began to separate himself from the Greeks. These Jews were zealous for the law, and Peter feared upsetting them.

Unfortunately, the other Jewish Christians followed Peter's example; even Barnabas withdrew from the Greeks' company. This was hypocrisy, so Paul opposed Peter to his face, saying in front of everyone: "You are a Jew, yet you live like a Gentile and not like a Jew. How is it, then, that you force Gentiles to follow Jewish customs?" (Galatians 2:14 NIV).

Paul reminded him that they all knew that they weren't made righteous by keeping the law, but by faith in Jesus Christ. He argued that "if righteousness could be gained through the law, Christ died for nothing!" (Galatians 2:21 NIV).

Now that we've been saved and set free by grace, let's not get sidetracked into legalism.

323. BARNABAS AND SAUL BECOME MISSIONARIES
\\ ACTS 11:27–30; 12:25; 13:1–5

» Sometime earlier, a prophet named Agabus had warned that a great famine was coming. The poor disciples in Judea would be especially hard hit, so the disciples in Antioch sent Barnabas and Saul to Jerusalem with relief money.

God called Barnabas and Saul to a special missionary work.

When the pair returned to Antioch, they brought a young man named John Mark (commonly called Mark) back with them. Mark was Barnabas's cousin (Colossians 4:10), so Barnabas had a special affection for him.

Christians had been evangelizing Antioch since AD 35 and it was now AD 46. After eleven years, the church had grown large and was strong in the faith—yet the rest of the Roman world had never even *heard* the Gospel.

So a group of prophets and teachers—Barnabas, Saul, Simeon, Lucius, and Manaen—fasted and prayed for guidance. Then God said, "Dedicate Barnabas and Saul for the special work to which I have called them" (Acts 13:2 NLT).

So Simeon, Lucius, and Manaen prayed over them and sent them off. "They also had John [Mark] as their assistant" (Acts 13:5 NKJV).

Once we've finished one job for God, we need to pray about what He wants us to do next.

324. STRIKING A SORCERER BLIND \\ ACTS 13:4–12

» The first place Barnabas and Saul traveled to was Cyprus. The island had been briefly evangelized eleven years earlier, but Barnabas was from there and had a strong desire to see his countrymen saved (Acts 4:36; 11:19).

Saul's Greek name was Paul, and he now began using this name.

They began proclaiming the Gospel in the synagogues and traveled throughout the entire island to the capitol, Paphos. The governor, Sergius Paulus, was an intelligent, inquisitive man, so he summoned Barnabas and Paul to share the word of God.

Previously the governor had consulted a Jewish magician named Elymas, and Elymas now began contradicting Barnabas and Paul to keep the governor from the faith.

Filled with the Holy Spirit, Paul stared at Elymas and said, "You who are full of all deceit and fraud, you son of the devil. . .behold, the hand of the Lord is upon you, and you will be blind and not see the sun for a time" (Acts 13:10–11 NASB).

Instantly darkness descended on Elymas, and he had to be led out of the chamber. Astonished, Sergius Paulus believed.

God opens the eyes of the spiritually blind and can blind seeing eyes (John 9:39–41).

» Paul and companions then sailed to Perga. But Mark, finding the missionary life too hard, left them and returned home to Jerusalem.

Undaunted, Paul and Barnabas continued on to Pisidian Antioch. On the Sabbath they entered the synagogue. The Jewish leaders, delighted to have guests, requested them to speak. Paul then told them about their Messiah, Jesus.

He declared, "I want you to know that through Jesus the forgiveness of sins is proclaimed to you. Through him everyone who believes is set free from every sin" (Acts 13:38–39 NIV). As a result, several Jews and God-fearing Greeks became believers.

The next Sabbath nearly the entire city showed up. But when some Jews saw the huge crowds, they jealously began contradicting Paul and insulting him.

Paul and Barnabas then began witnessing to Greeks throughout the entire region. But their opponents persuaded powerful contacts to persecute the apostles and drive them out. The church was thriving, however, and the new believers "were filled with joy and with the Holy Spirit" (Acts 13:52 NIV).

Jesus is the Jewish Messiah, so the Gospel must be preached to them—"to the Jew first, and also to the Greek" (Romans 1:16 KJV).

» Paul and Barnabas went to Iconium, spent a long time there witnessing, then went to Lystra.

In Lystra, Paul saw a man who had never walked, so he commanded, "Stand up straight on your feet!" (Acts 14:10 NKJV). Immediately the man leaped up and walked.

The astonished crowds cried out, "The gods have come down to us in human form!" (Acts 14:11 NIV). They named Barnabas "Zeus," and since Paul was the chief speaker, they called him "Hermes," Zeus's messenger.

The priest of Zeus, swept up in the excitement, quickly brought oxen, intending to sacrifice them to Barnabas and Paul.

Shocked, the apostles shouted not to do this, because they were only men, and in fact were preaching that people should *turn* from these false gods to worship the one true God.

Later, enemies arrived from Antioch and Iconium and turned the crowds against them. They stoned Paul and, thinking him dead, dragged his body out of the city. When the disciples gathered around Paul, however, he got up, still alive.

Paul later told these disciples that "we must through much tribulation enter into the kingdom of God" (Acts 14:22 KJV). This is still true today.

327. CHRISTIANS ARGUE OVER THE LAW \\ ACTS 15:1–32

» Sometime after Paul and Barnabas returned to Antioch, some Jewish Christians arrived from Judea and taught the Greeks that believing in Jesus wasn't enough, that unless they became circumcised and kept the law of Moses, they couldn't be saved.

Paul and Barnabas strongly disputed this, but the issue wouldn't die. So the church sent Paul and Barnabas to the apostles and elders in Jerusalem to discuss this.

Once there, some Pharisees who believed in Jesus insisted, "It is necessary to. . .command them to keep the law of Moses" (Acts 15:5 NKJV).

Peter, however, reminded them that when he'd preached to Cornelius and the other Romans, God had purified their hearts by faith alone. In fact, he added, even *Jews* weren't saved by keeping the law. "But we believe that through the grace of the Lord Jesus Christ we shall be saved in the same manner as they" (Acts 15:11 NKJV).

James, the Lord's brother, agreed, and had an official letter written and sent to all the churches. When they read it, the disciples in Antioch rejoiced.

Even today, we must guard against the teaching that we're saved by God's grace *plus* our own good works (Romans 11:6).

328. PAUL WRITES A REBUKE TO GALATIA
\\ GALATIANS 1:1–9; 2:15–16; 4:17; 5:6–12

❱❱ That official letter from Jerusalem settled the dispute for most disciples—but certain Jewish Christians weren't convinced.

Many thousands of believers in Judea were "zealous for the law" (Acts 21:20 NKJV). Even those who knew they were saved by grace still felt it was *beneficial* for Jews to observe the law. But the Judaizers maintained that *all* Christians needed to keep the law to be saved.

They then taught their doctrine in Galatia, north of Antioch. When Paul learned of this, he wrote to the Galatians, telling them that "some people are throwing you into confusion and are trying to pervert the gospel of Christ." He called their doctrine "a different gospel—which is really no gospel at all" (Galatians 1:7 NIV).

Paul wrote the church in Galatia to warn believers against following a false gospel.

Paul said that those people were persuading the Galatians, not to help them, but to make them into their disciples. But Paul declared that the law brought people under a curse, and that people who preached salvation by keeping the Law were cursed (Galatians 1:8–9; 3:10–13).

For two thousand years since then, Paul's epistle to the Galatians has been known as the freedom charter of the Christian faith.

329. PAUL AND BARNABAS DISAGREE SHARPLY
\\ ACTS 13:13; 15:36–41

❱❱ In AD 46, on Paul and Barnabas's first missionary journey, Mark had deserted them. And this was before any trouble had begun! Then in AD 50, Paul said to Barnabas that they should visit every city where they'd preached the Gospel, to see how the disciples were doing.

Barnabas agreed and suggested they take Mark. Paul was adamant that they *not* take him, since he'd deserted them four years earlier.

They got into such a sharp disagreement over this that they couldn't work with each other anymore. So Barnabas took Mark and sailed to Cyprus. Paul chose a believer named Silas and together they traveled "through Syria and Cilicia, strengthening the churches" (Acts 15:41 NIV).

The good news is that within five years, Paul and Barnabas were working together again (1 Corinthians 9:5–6). Paul even eventually respected Mark. He hadn't been of any use in AD 50, but in AD 67 Paul wrote Timothy, "Get Mark and bring him with you, for he is useful to me for ministry" (2 Timothy 4:11 NKJV).

Even good people can have strong opinions and have serious disagreements, but God wants us to forgive one another and work together.

330. TIMOTHY JOINS THE APOSTLES \\ ACTS 16:1–5; 2 TIMOTHY 1:5

» When Paul was in Lystra in AD 47, an older Jewish lady named Lois became a Christian, and her daughter Eunice—together with Eunice's son Timothy—believed as well.

Timothy's father was a Greek, so Timothy had never been circumcised. This was a nonissue when it came to faith in Jesus, but it became a problem later.

When Paul visited the church in Lystra four years later, he and Silas needed a strong young helper to take care of practical matters while they taught and preached. (That had previously been Mark's job.) So Paul wanted to take Timothy along.

Timothy was very interested, and the believers recommended him. But the problem was that they'd often witness to Jews, who would judge Timothy over his lack of circumcision. Paul therefore circumcised him. They then traveled from city to city witnessing and encouraging the disciples.

Paul said, "When I was with the Jews, I lived like a Jew to bring the Jews to Christ." Timothy needed to make this concession to witness effectively to Jews. We too need to "try to find common ground with everyone" to whom we witness (1 Corinthians 9:20, 22 NLT).

» After strengthening the churches, Paul, Silas, and Timothy headed into new territory. They prayed and asked God to lead them.

The Roman province of Asia seemed like a logical choice, but the Holy Spirit forbade them to preach the Gospel there. They then tried to go into Bithynia, but the Spirit didn't permit that either. Wondering what to do, they came to the port city of Troas.

Around this time, they were joined by a Greek believer named Luke, who was a doctor.

Then one night Paul had a vision. A man appeared and pled: "Come over to Macedonia and help us" (Acts 16:9 NIV). The four men then sailed to Philippi, a leading city of Macedonia (northern Greece).

There was no synagogue in

Ruins of Philippi, where a woman named Lydia invited the missionaries to stay at her house.

Philippi and the Jews there met beside the river, so Paul spoke to the women who gathered there to pray. A well-to-do woman named Lydia believed the Gospel and invited Paul and his companions to stay at her house. And so the adventure began.

It can be frustrating when God hems us in and blocks our plans, but He often does this to lead us to where *He* wants us to go—and He knows best.

332. CASTING A DEMON OUT OF A PSYCHIC \\ ACTS 16:16–24

» Every Greek city had an *agora*, a market square, where merchants sold goods and people met to talk, and Paul and his companions often witnessed there.

Philippi's market had a fortune-teller, a demon-possessed slave girl who earned a great deal of money for her masters because of her predictions. One day she began following Paul and Silas around, shouting, "These men are servants of the Most High God, and they have come to tell you how to be saved" (Acts 16:17 NLT).

She continued doing this for several days until Paul, exasperated, turned and commanded the spirit to come out of her. She was instantly delivered.

When her masters realized that she could no longer predict fortunes and their livelihood was gone, they dragged Paul and Silas before the authorities, saying, "They are teaching customs that are illegal for us Romans to practice" (Acts 16:21 NLT).

The mob began shouting in anger, so the officials ordered the apostles stripped and beaten with wooden rods. Afterward they were thrown into prison.

Our battle isn't against people, but "against the spiritual forces of evil" (Ephesians 6:12 NIV). However, this frequently brings people into conflict with us as well.

333. EARTHQUAKE SHAKES UP A PRISON \\ ACTS 16:25–40

» Paul and Silas were in terrible pain, but about midnight they were praying and singing praises to God. The other prisoners were impressed.

Then a great earthquake struck, violently shaking the prison. Every jail door broke open and all the prisoners' manacles snapped open. The jailer awoke and, seeing the prison doors open, feared that all the prisoners had escaped. This would cost him his life, so he drew his sword to kill himself. But Paul cried out for him to stop, that all the prisoners were still here.

Trembling with fear, knowing that God had revealed His power, the jailer fell down before Paul and Silas and asked, "Sirs, what must I do to be saved?" They answered, "Believe in the Lord Jesus, and you will be saved" (Acts 16:30–31 NASB).

The jailer took them to his nearby house and washed their wounds. There Paul and Silas witnessed to him and he and his entire household believed. The next morning, the officials personally escorted them from the prison, realizing that they had made a serious mistake.

If we still praise God when we're experiencing misfortune and hardship, it's a powerful testimony to others.

>> Paul and his companions went to Thessalonica and witnessed in the synagogue that Jesus was the Messiah, and many Jews and Greeks became believers. But the unbelieving Jews gathered some lowlifes from the market and started a riot.

The mob stormed the house where Paul and Silas were staying, but when they didn't find them, they dragged their converts before the officials, shouting, "These who have turned the world upside down have come here too" (Acts 17:6 NKJV).

They accused them of defying Caesar's decrees. This alarmed the officials. But since Paul and Silas couldn't be found, the officials made their friends post bond and let them go.

The believers then sent the apostles to the next city, Berea, under cover of night. There they went to the synagogue and began witnessing, and the Berean Jews "received the message with great eagerness" (Acts 17:11 NIV).

Thessalonica today, where unbelievers once started a riot as Paul and Silas witnessed.

But when enemies in Thessalonica learned of it, they showed up and stirred up a riot in Berea. The believers again quickly sent Paul away—this time to Athens.

Paul was constantly in trouble and forced to flee for preaching the Gospel. What are we willing to endure for Jesus?

335. PREACHING ON MARS HILL \\ ACTS 17:16–34

>> In Athens, Paul was struck by how many idols and pagan temples there were. Towering over Athens was the Acropolis, filled with temples to the Greek gods.

Paul was preaching in the marketplace when some philosophers heard him. He taught how Jesus had risen from the dead, and this was a strange idea to Greeks. So they brought him to Mars Hill to speak to the Areopagus, Athens's ruling religious council.

Paul established common ground by pointing out that there was an altar in their city with the inscription "To the Unknown God." He said, "Therefore, the One whom you worship without knowing, Him I proclaim to you" (Acts 17:23 NKJV).

Paul was familiar with Greek poets and quoted the verse where Epimenides said, "For in Him we live and move and have our being" (Acts 17:28 NKJV). He then went on to declare that the true God wasn't worshipped by idols, or in temples, but had revealed Himself in Jesus Christ.

Paul was not only able to witness to commoners, but to intellectuals. We too are advised: "If someone asks about your Christian hope, always be ready to explain it" (1 Peter 3:15 NLT).

336. A RIOT BREAKS OUT IN CORINTH \\ ACTS 18:1–17

» From Athens, Paul went on to Corinth, a leading commercial center. He had great success there preaching to both Jews and Greeks. The synagogue leader and his entire household believed in Jesus, as did many Corinthians.

After his previous troubles, Paul wondered if trouble would arise here, but God told him, "Do not be afraid; keep on speaking, do not be silent. For I am with you, and no one is going to attack and harm you, because I have many people in this city" (Acts 18:9–10 NIV).

So Paul preached and taught for a year and a half. Then one day the Jews who had rejected the Gospel made an attack on Paul and brought him to the judgment seat of Governor Gallio. They accused him of teaching people to worship God contrary to the law.

Before Paul could speak to defend himself, Gallio impatiently dismissed them, saying, "I will not be a judge of such things" (Acts 18:15 NIV). And he sent them away.

They attacked Paul, yes, but as God had promised, they were unable to "attack and harm" him. God is able to protect us today as well and to defuse trouble.

337. APOLLOS PREACHES AND DISPUTES \\ ACTS 18:18–28

» Paul met a Jewish couple in Corinth, Aquila and his wife, Priscilla, and during the year and a half he stayed in Corinth, he instructed them in the faith. They became leaders and coworkers, and when he sailed for Jerusalem, they went with him.

They stopped at the great port city of Ephesus, and Paul briefly witnessed in the synagogue there. Then he continued on, leaving Aquila and Priscilla to teach about Jesus.

Some time later, a Jew named Apollos arrived from Alexandria, the world-renowned center of learning in Egypt. Apollos was well versed in the scriptures and was a powerful, eloquent speaker who taught clearly about Jesus. But there were gaps in his education.

"When Priscilla and Aquila heard him preaching boldly in the synagogue, they took him aside and explained the way of God even more accurately" (Acts 18:26 NLT).

Apollos then went on to Achaia, where he defeated critics of Christianity in public debates. Quoting the scriptures, he gave powerful proofs that Jesus was the Messiah.

As Paul said, "The things which you have heard from me. . .entrust these to faithful men who will be able to teach others also" (2 Timothy 2:2 NASB). We are still to do this today.

338. THE APOSTLES LEAVE JERUSALEM \\ MARK 16:15; ACTS 1:8; 15:2; 21:18

» In AD 30, Jesus had commanded the apostles, "Go into all the world and preach the gospel to every creature." He had specified that "you shall be witnesses to Me in Jerusalem, and in all Judea and Samaria, and to the end of the earth" (Mark 16:15; Acts 1:8 NKJV).

However, twenty-three years had passed, and they were still concentrating on Jerusalem, Judea, Galilee, and Samaria. Peter had made one brief trip to Antioch. . .but that was *it.*

Meanwhile, the apostle Paul was boldly taking the Gospel through-

The apostles left Jerusalem—and its familiar temple—in order to spread the Gospel to other nations.

out the Roman Empire, and every time he visited Jerusalem—as he did now in AD 53 (Acts 18:22 NIV)—he had exciting testimonies to tell the apostles.

They finally realized that their job was finished in Israel, so they went out. When Paul had gone to Jerusalem for the council in AD 50, he met with the apostles and elders. But when he visited Jerusalem in AD 57, he only saw James and the elders (Acts 15:2; 21:18 NIV).

Where were the apostles? They had gone into all the world to preach the Gospel. And it's up to *us* to finish this task before Jesus comes (Matthew 24:14).

339. PAUL DOES WONDERS IN EPHESUS \\ ACTS 19:1–20

» After returning to Ephesus, Paul spoke in the synagogue for three months, but when the opposition became too much, he took the disciples and taught them daily in a lecture hall.

Paul continued teaching there for two years, and everyone living in the province of Asia heard the Gospel.

Paul said, "My speech and my preaching were not with persuasive words of human wisdom, but in demonstration of the Spirit and of power" (1 Corinthians 2:4 NKJV), and sure enough, "God did extraordinary miracles through Paul" (Acts 19:11 NIV).

Paul was a tentmaker by profession (Acts 18:3), and when his workman's handkerchiefs and aprons were carried to the sick, their diseases were cured, and demons left them.

Some exorcists tried to imitate Paul by invoking Jesus' name over a demon-possessed man, but they lacked the power and suffered a terrible beating. As a result, the name of Jesus was held in high esteem in Ephesus.

Not all Christians were miracle workers, even in New Testament times (Acts 9:36–41; 1 Corinthians 12:29). But *any* answered prayers are proof of God's existence—and God still answers prayer today. But whether He does miracles or not, we must share our faith.

340. EPHESUS ERUPTS IN AN UPROAR \\ ACTS 19:21–41

» The goddess Diana (Artemis) was worshipped in a renowned temple in Ephesus, and the silversmiths there earned a lucrative income making silver shrines and idols.

Then a man named Demetrius called the silversmiths together, alarmed by Paul's success in convincing people that idols weren't real gods. Not only were they losing money, but Diana and her temple were being discredited.

The tradesmen in Ephesus accused Paul and his companions of blaspheming the goddess Diana.

When they heard this, the tradesmen cried out, "Great is Diana of the Ephesians!" (Acts 19:28 NKJV). Soon the entire city was in a confused uproar. Seizing Paul's travel companions, the mob rushed into the amphitheater and shouted for about two hours, "Great is Diana of the Ephesians!"

Paul wanted to try to speak to the crowd, but the disciples wouldn't let him.

Finally, the city clerk calmed the people down by assuring them that yes, Diana was great, but the Christians hadn't robbed temples or blasphemed her—and if Demetrius had a legitimate grievance, he should bring it to court, not start a riot. Then he dismissed them.

We may not feel we're having such a great effect in our city as Paul did in Ephesus, but we must remain faithful nevertheless.

341. PAUL WRITES TO THE ROMANS \\ ACTS 19:21–22; ROMANS 1:11–15

» For over a year, Paul instructed churches to gather donations for the poor believers in Jerusalem and Judea (2 Corinthians 9:1–5). He now decided to go to Jerusalem with those who would be carrying the donations.

It took three months to finish visiting the churches in Macedonia and Achaia (Greece) and gather the money. In the port city of Cenchrea, or in nearby Corinth, Paul sat down and wrote the Christians in Rome, promising to visit them after he'd been to Jerusalem.

What seems to have spurred him to write was that a woman named Phoebe, a deaconess of the church in Cenchrea, was heading to Rome on business. Since there was no postal system, Paul took the opportunity to send a letter with her (Romans 16:1–2).

Paul may have intended to write just a brief epistle, but God inspired him to share profound thoughts that have benefited millions of Christians for the last two thousand years. Repeatedly, Paul described faith in Jesus Christ and the grace and mercy of God that save us.

As we attempt to inspire and encourage others, God can use our efforts in far greater ways than we could ever imagine.

342. PAUL HEADS INTO DANGER \\ ACTS 20:1–6, 22–23; 21:1–14

» Paul and seven companions, carrying the relief money, finally set sail for Jerusalem. Paul had originally planned to send the money with others, but said that he'd go *also* "if it seems advisable" (1 Corinthians 16:3–4 NIV).

It was actually *not* advisable. As Paul later admitted, "I go bound in the spirit to Jerusalem" even though "the Holy Spirit testifies in every city, saying that chains and tribulations await me" (Acts 20:22–23 NKJV). But he still went.

They sailed south to Tyre. While staying with the disciples there, "through the Spirit they urged Paul not to go on to Jerusalem" (Acts 21:4 NIV). But he wouldn't be deterred.

From Tyre they sailed to Caesarea. There, the prophet Agabus warned Paul that the Jewish leaders in Jerusalem would hand him over to the Romans. After hearing this warning, everyone begged him *not* to go to Jerusalem. But Paul insisted that he was ready to die for Jesus. He couldn't be talked out of it.

Why did Paul insist on going to Jerusalem? Perhaps he wanted to be present when the money was given. We simply don't know. May we always examine *our* own motives.

343. PAUL IS ARRESTED AT THE TEMPLE \\ ACTS 21:17–36

» When Paul and company arrived in Jerusalem, James and the church leaders told him that there were many thousands of believers "and all of them are zealous for the law" (Acts 21:20 NIV).

These believers had heard that Paul taught Jews not to follow the law. So the leaders advised Paul to go through a purification ceremony so that "everyone will know there is no truth in these reports about you, but that you yourself are living in obedience to the law" (Acts 21:24 NIV).

God had warned Paul that he would face danger in Jerusalem.

Now, Paul *had* just gone through such a Jewish ceremony in Cenchrea (Acts 18:18). But he didn't *usually* follow the law (1 Corinthians 9:19–21).

Nevertheless, he went along with their advice. But when the ceremony was nearly over, some unbelieving Jews recognized him and stirred up the crowd.

They dragged Paul away and tried to kill him, but news reached the commander of the Roman troops, and he immediately took soldiers into the crowd. He then arrested Paul and bound him with chains.

This was the situation God had repeatedly warned Paul about. When God warns you of danger, He desires to spare you needless trouble—so listen to Him.

344. FLEEING JERUSALEM BY NIGHT \\ ACTS 23:11-33

» While the Romans held Paul prisoner, over forty Jews formed a conspiracy. They had the chief priests and elders ask the Romans to bring Paul to a meeting, pretending that they wanted to question him. The conspirators planned to ambush Paul on the way.

But Paul's nephew heard of it, hurried to the fortress, and told his uncle. Paul then had a Roman officer take him to the commander.

When the commander heard the plot, he acted swiftly. Not only did he wish to avoid an attack, but Paul had been born a Roman citizen and under Roman law had unalienable rights, including the right of protection (Acts 22:24–29).

The commander ordered two officers, "Gct 200 soldiers ready to leave for Caesarea at nine o'clock tonight. Also take 200 spearmen and 70 mounted troops. Provide horses for Paul to ride, and get him safely to Governor Felix" (Acts 23:23–24 NLT).

The heavily armed contingent left Jerusalem under cover of darkness and marched to Antipatris. The next morning the horsemen took Paul on to Caesarea, where they delivered him to the governor.

As a citizen of your country, you too have rights, and sometimes you must insist on them.

» Governor Felix ordered Paul kept in the prison, and for the next five years, from AD 57 to AD 62, Paul would be under Roman arrest.

Five days after Paul's arrival, the Jewish high priest Ananias, together with elders and an attorney named Tertullus, came, bringing charges against Paul. Tertullus stated: "We have found this man a real pest and a fellow who stirs up dissension among all the Jews through-out the world, and a ringleader of the sect of the Nazarenes. And he even tried to desecrate the temple" (Acts 24:5–6 NASB).

Paul refused to pay bribes for release from prison.

Paul, however, denied that he had been causing any trouble.

Felix realized that Paul had committed no crimes, but that this was only a religious quarrel. He nevertheless kept Paul in prison. He wanted a large bribe to set him free. But Paul refused. He had, after all, been preaching to Felix about living righteously.

After two years passed, Festus became the new governor, and desiring to do the Jews a favor, Felix left Paul imprisoned.

When our cause is just, we need to depend on God to deliver us, not grease the wheels to obtain man's favors.

» When Paul had sailed to Jerusalem, Luke accompanied him. We know this because Luke, who wrote the book of Acts, said, "But we sailed away from Philippi" (Acts 20:6 NKJV).

Luke went along for a special purpose. Matthew and Mark had already written Gospels, but Luke saw the need for a Gospel written specifically for Greeks. So he set out to do that.

Luke hadn't seen or heard Jesus, so he decided to travel to Israel to interview eyewitnesses who had. And there were *hundreds* of living witnesses (1 Corinthians 15:6). So for two years, while Paul was imprisoned in Caesarea, Luke traveled Judea and Galilee, interviewing, researching, and writing his Gospel.

His purpose was to write a "careful account. . .so you can be certain of the truth of everything you were taught" (Luke 1:3–4 NLT). He definitely succeeded!

When that was finished, Luke began researching a history of the early church called the book of Acts. He had plenty of opportunity to interview Paul in prison about his adventures (Acts 24:23).

Because of the efforts of men like Luke, we today can be certain of the truth of the Gospels and what the early Christians believed.

347. PAUL APPEALS TO CAESAR \\ ACTS 25:1–12

» Three days after arriving at Caesarea, the new governor went to Jerusalem. There the priests and elders requested him to transfer Paul to Jerusalem. They planned to ambush him on the way.

Festus, however, told them to come to Caesarea and to press charges there. After returning, he had Paul brought in.

Once again the religious rulers brought accusations against him, and once again Paul declared that he hadn't done anything against the Jewish law, the temple, or Caesar.

Festus, eager to establish good relations with the Jews, asked Paul if he was willing to go to Jerusalem and stand trial before him there. Paul, however, knew his rights. He answered: "I have not done any wrong to the Jews, as you yourself know very well. . .no one has the right to hand me over to them. I appeal to Caesar!"

Roman citizens had the right to be tried by Caesar himself, so Festus said: "You have appealed to Caesar. To Caesar you will go!" (Acts 25:11–12 NIV).

This was a wise decision, since Caesar would later dismiss the charges and set Paul free. We too must sometimes exercise our rights to maintain our freedom.

348. FESTUS AND HEROD JUDGE PAUL \\ ACTS 25:13–27; 26:1–32

» King Herod Agrippa came to Caesarea to greet the new governor, and Festus told him about Paul. He was being sent to Rome, but Festus thought it unreasonable to send a prisoner to Caesar and not to specify the charges against him.

Herod desired to hear Paul, so Festus arranged an audience.

Paul was glad to present his case before Agrippa, since the king was well versed in Jewish customs. Paul told his life story, and as he was discussing the resurrection, Festus said loudly, "Paul, you are beside yourself! Much learning is driving you mad!" (Acts 26:24 NKJV).

God fulfilled His promise that Paul would witness to Gentiles and their kings.

Paul assured Festus that he wasn't insane but was speaking reasonable things that Agrippa was familiar with. He then asked Agrippa if he believed the prophets. Agrippa answered, "Do you think that in such a short time you can persuade me to be a Christian?" (Acts 26:28 NIV).

The two rulers then ended the audience and agreed that Paul was innocent.

God had promised long ago that Paul would witness "to the Gentiles and their kings" (Acts 9:15 NIV). Paul was now doing so—and would soon witness to Caesar himself. God knows the future well in advance.

349. A SAVAGE STORM GROUNDS PAUL \\ ACTS 27:1–26

» The time came to depart. Julius, a centurion of the Imperial Regiment, escorted Paul and other prisoners. Sailing north to Myra, they found an Egyptian grain ship bound for Rome. So they boarded and set sail.

When they reached Fair Havens in Crete, Paul warned them to winter there—that it was too dangerous to continue sailing. But the captain insisted they head for a more sheltered port.

No sooner were they out in the open than a powerful wind swept down on them and drove them out to sea. "The terrible storm raged for many days, blotting out the sun and the stars, until at last all hope was gone" (Acts 27:20 NLT). Literally, all hope was *gone*!

The crew was so physically sick and terrified that they didn't eat anything for two weeks (Acts 27:33). Then an angel appeared to Paul and told him, "Don't be afraid," that he and all 276 passengers on the ship would survive (Acts 27:24 NLT).

Paul then ate some food and told everyone to do the same. And they were encouraged.

God has not abandoned us, even in our most desperate times—even when all hope seems to be gone.

350. SURVIVING A TERRIFYING SHIPWRECK \\ ACTS 27:27–44

» The sailors did some soundings and discovered that they were approaching land. So they let down anchors to hold the ship in place.

The sailors then lowered the lifeboat to escape, "pretending" that "they were going to loose some anchors from the bow" (Acts 27:30 NIV). But Paul warned Julius that unless they stayed, no one would survive. So Julius had the ropes cut and the lifeboat drifted away. *Now* they listened to Paul!

In the morning they saw a sandy beach ahead, so they threw all the ship's grain overboard to lighten the vessel so it would ride higher in the water. They then cut the anchor ropes and hoisted the foresail, hoping to be driven up on the beach.

But they got stuck on a sandbar some ways out, and the stern began breaking to pieces in the heavy surf. The soldiers wanted to kill the prisoners lest they swim away, but Julius determined to spare Paul—so they didn't.

Instead, Julius ordered everyone who could swim to make it to the beach. Those who couldn't swim hung onto planks and were washed ashore. And everyone made it to land safely.

Everyone on Paul's ship—276 people—made it to land safely because they followed Julius's orders.

If you consistently speak sound, good advice, even unbelievers will eventually listen.

351. PAUL DOES MIRACLES ON MALTA \\ ACTS 28:1–11

» The land turned out to be the island of Malta. And the hospitable islanders hurried to the beach and built a great bonfire to warm the survivors.

As Paul was helping put wood on the fire, a viper, hiding in the brushwood, bit him. The Maltese saw it and exclaimed, "This man must be a murderer; for though he escaped from the sea, the goddess Justice has not allowed him to live" (Acts 28:4 NIV).

Paul, however, simply shook the viper into the fire. The people waited and waited, expecting him to fall down dead. But Paul trusted God and suffered no ill effects.

Publius, the leading Roman official of the island, invited Julius and company into his home for several days. Now, Publius's father was bedridden with dysentery and fever. Paul therefore went into his room, prayed over him, and healed him.

Word of this miracle quickly spread. Soon every sick person on the island came and was healed. Then, for three months, Paul most likely preached the Gospel.

Paul suffered a terrible storm and shipwreck, but God allowed it because, as a result, Malta was evangelized. God still brings good out of our setbacks and difficulties today.

352. WITNESSING IN ROME \\ ACTS 28:11–31

» When they finally arrived at Rome, Julius delivered the prisoners to the imperial prison. But Paul was permitted to dwell in his own rented house with a soldier guarding him.

After he'd been there only three days, Paul invited the Jewish leaders to visit him. They would soon hear that he'd arrived, so he wanted to share the Gospel with them before they were influenced by negative reports.

They *had* heard bad reports—though not about him personally. They had heard negative opinions about the Christian faith in general. Nevertheless, they took a very open-minded approach, saying, "But we desire to hear from you what you think; for concerning this sect, we know that it is spoken against everywhere" (Acts 28:22 NKJV).

So for one entire day, Paul taught from the scriptures that Jesus was the Jewish Messiah. Several people believed.

Paul then continued living two years in his own house, freely sharing the Gospel with everyone who came to visit him, and strengthening believers. Paul had long dreamed of evangelizing in Rome (Romans 1:9–15), and now he was doing it!

God puts dreams in our hearts, and though they take time to come to pass, they will be fulfilled.

353. JAMES IS MARTYRED \\ JAMES 1:1; ACTS 15:13–29

» "James, the Lord's brother" (Galatians 1:19 NKJV), didn't originally believe in Jesus. But Jesus appeared to James after His resurrection, and he became an ardent follower.

James eventually rose to become the first bishop of Jerusalem. After Peter escaped from prison, he made a point of telling his disciples to notify James (Acts 12:17).

James was one of the key authors of the Jerusalem Decree in AD 50, and at some point—we don't know exactly when—he wrote the epistle of James to Jewish believers scattered throughout the Roman Empire.

The Jewish historian Josephus tells us that James was martyred in the summer of AD 62. This was while Paul was still under house arrest. Porcius Festus, the governor of Judea, had died, and while the new governor Albinus was on his way, the high priest, Ananus (a son of Annas), incited a mob to seize James.

They tried to force him to deny Jesus, but James refused and was martyred. The common people were so outraged by this act that they persuaded Albinus to depose Ananus.

Jesus said that those who obeyed God were His true brothers (Matthew 12:48–50). James was a true brother.

James was martyred when he refused to deny Jesus.

354. PAUL MEETS A RUNAWAY SLAVE \\ PHILEMON 1–24; COLOSSIANS 4:7–9

» Paul had many visitors in Rome, but one of his most unusual was a runaway slave.

Onesimus belonged to a wealthy Christian master named Philemon, a leader of the church of Colossae. The believers met in Philemon's home.

One day Onesimus fled Colossae, taking some of his master's money, and sailed for Rome. He intended to start a new life as a free man but soon ran out of money and realized his mistake. So he apparently went to Paul and confessed what he'd done.

Paul led him to faith in Jesus, and Onesimus was a huge help to the aged apostle. Paul wanted to keep Onesimus with him, but decided to send him back to Colossae with Tychicus, bearing the letter to Philemon *and* an epistle to the church.

Paul called Onesimus "our faithful and dear brother" (Colossians 4:9 NIV) and urged Philemon to treat him "no longer as a slave, but better than a slave, as a dear brother" (Philemon 16 NIV). As for the money, Paul offered to personally repay it.

Many years later this epistle inspired British and American Christians to free the slaves. God used this incident to accomplish very large purposes.

355. PAUL JOURNEYS TO SPAIN \\ ROMANS 15:23–28; PHILEMON 22

» When Paul finally appeared before Emperor Nero in AD 62, Nero was still under the influence of wise counselors. It appeared that he would release Paul. So Paul asked Philemon to prepare a guest room for him when he visited Colossae.

The church historian Eusebius wrote in *Ecclesiastical History* 2.22 that Paul was indeed released.

If Paul went to Colossae, he didn't stay there. He had finished his work in the east and had already written back in AD 57 that "from Jerusalem all the way around to Illyricum [Albania], I have fully proclaimed the gospel of Christ. . .there is no more place for me to work in these regions" (Romans 15:19, 23 NIV).

Paul had clearly stated that he was planning to evangelize the Roman province of Spain. The Muratorian Canon (an early church document) says, "Paul went from the city of Rome to Spain." So it appears likely that he *did* spend time preaching the Gospel there.

Are you finished with your work in a certain area? Do you feel like it's time to move on to new horizons? Pray for God to show you *when* and *how* to step out.

356. PAUL STANDS AGAINST FALSE TEACHING
\\ 1 TIMOTHY 1:3–4 ; TITUS 1:5, 10–11; 3:9–11

» After evangelizing in Spain, Paul returned to the eastern Mediterranean. He stopped in Crete, where he strengthened the churches. He had earlier stated that "there is no more place for me to work in these regions" (Romans 15:23 NIV). But there *was* unfinished work, after all.

He wrote Titus, "I left you on the island of Crete so you could complete our work there" (Titus 1:5 NLT). He urged Titus not only to appoint elders in the churches, but to stop false teachers (Titus 3:9–11).

Paul referred to "idle talkers and deceivers. . .whose mouths must be stopped," people who went around "teaching things which they ought not" (Titus 1:10–11 NKJV).

From Crete, Paul traveled to Ephesus. Years earlier he had warned the elders that false teachers would arise (Acts 20:29–31). Now they had. So Paul wrote Timothy, "When I left for Macedonia, I urged you to stay there in Ephesus and stop those whose teaching is contrary to the truth" (1 Timothy 1:3 NLT).

Paul encouraged Titus and Timothy to stop false teachers.

Paul not only preached the Gospel but completed his work by refuting false teaching. We also must "contend earnestly for the faith" (Jude 3 NKJV).

357. PAUL IS MARTYRED \\ 2 TIMOTHY 4:6–18

» While traveling through the province of Asia, Paul was arrested—apparently in Troas (2 Timothy 4:13). He was then taken to Rome in chains.

Nero had released Paul in AD 62 when he was still tolerant of Christians—but two years later, that had all changed. Rome burned in July,

AD 64, and it was commonly believed that Nero had started the devastating fires to make room for a major building project.

To deflect blame from himself, Nero accused the Christians of starting the fire. Christians were burned at the stake and fed to wild beasts.

Now when Paul was brought before Nero, an old enemy from Ephesus, Alexander the metalworker, testified against him. To Paul's dismay, not a single person dared come to his defense. Even many of his closest coworkers fled (2 Timothy 4:10, 14, 16).

Paul was sitting in the Mamertime Dungeon in AD 67, facing the end, when he wrote his final epistle to Timothy. Not long after, Paul was beheaded.

As he wrote, "I have fought the good fight, I have finished the race, I have kept the faith" (2 Timothy 4:7 NIV). May we be able to say the same.

358. PETER IS CRUCIFIED \\ JOHN 21:18–19; 1 PETER 1:1–9; 2:11–17

» After leaving Jerusalem, Peter preached in the provinces of Asia, Galatia, Pontus, Cappadocia, and Bithynia. He apparently visited Corinth as well (1 Peter 1:1; 1 Corinthians 1:12).

Before his death, Peter reminded Christians to live godly lives.

By AD 68, Peter was in Rome—called "Babylon" by Christians (1 Peter 5:13). At this time, there was great trouble. The Jews had revolted against Rome in AD 66 but were being crushed. Roman armies now surrounded Jerusalem. Peter warned, "The end of the world is coming soon" (1 Peter 4:7 NLT).

Even though Nero had gone insane, Peter reminded Christians to obey the law: "Submit yourselves for the Lord's sake

. . .to the emperor, as the supreme authority, or to governors, who are sent by him" (1 Peter 2:13–14 NIV). He also reminded Christians to live godly lives.

Peter knew that he would die soon (2 Peter 1:13–14), and he did. According to tradition, he was arrested shortly after Paul's execution and crucified upside down.

Even though it looked as if the world was ending and Christians were persecuted, this was no excuse for them to break the law or live dishonorably. They had to remain steadfast in the faith, now more than ever. The same holds true for us today.

359. JERUSALEM IS DESTROYED \\ LUKE 19:41–44; 21:5–24

» In AD 30, Jesus prophesied over Jerusalem: "The days will come upon you when your enemies will build an embankment against you and encircle you and hem you in on every side" (Luke 19:43 NIV).

In AD 66, the Jews revolted against Rome, but the Romans struck back and were soon besieging Jerusalem itself. They dug a trench around the city and built a high wall around that. The city was captured in AD 70.

Jesus had also prophesied: "They will be killed by the sword or sent away as captives to all the nations of the world" (Luke 21:24 NLT). Some 1.1 million Jews were killed during the siege, and 97,000 were sold as slaves throughout the Roman Empire.

Jesus predicted that the temple would be utterly destroyed: "Assuredly, I say to you, not one stone shall be left here upon another, that shall not be thrown down" (Matthew 24:2 NKJV). And it was so. The cedar paneling in the temple was set ablaze, and the heat melted the gold covering the temple. The Romans then took apart the temple to get at the gold.

God fulfilled Jesus' prophecies in great detail—proof that He is the Messiah.

360. JOHN WRITES HIS GOSPEL \\ JOHN 1:1–3, 14; 19:35; 21:24

❯❯ The Gospels of Matthew, Mark, and Luke were written between AD 50 and AD 60, but the fourth Gospel was not written till AD 85–90.

According to the church fathers, John was living in Ephesus when he was old. Then the bishops of the province of Asia asked him to compose a Gospel that would oppose the heresies of Cerinthus (an early Gnostic) and the Ebionites (Hebrews who believed that Jesus was the Messiah but not the divine Son of God).

Therefore John, more than any other Gospel writer, related stories that stressed the deity of Christ. His opening words, in fact, declare clearly that Jesus is God (John 1:1–3, 14).

The Gospel of John is written in correct, polished Greek, even though Greek wasn't John's mother tongue. The reason for this is that, as the Muratorian Canon states, John had help composing his Gospel. Internal evidence supports this. (See John 19:35; 21:24.)

John also told many stories that the other three Gospels never mentioned.

Sometimes it may seem that a particular task has already been accomplished, but God may still inspire us to present new facts in new ways to get out His message.

361. JOHN HAS A VISION ON PATMOS \\ REVELATION 1:9–19

When John was imprisoned, he had visions of the future.

❯❯ In AD 95, Emperor Domitian violently persecuted Christians, and thousands died. Others were banished. The apostle John was imprisoned on the island of Patmos.

One day John heard a loud voice. He turned to see who was speaking, and there, in all His glory, was Jesus Christ, the Son of God.

"His head and hair were white like wool, as white as snow, and His eyes like a flame of fire; His feet were like fine brass, as if refined in a furnace, and His voice as the sound of many waters. . .and His countenance was like the sun shining in its strength" (Revelation 1:14–16 NKJV).

When John saw Him, he collapsed at His feet like a dead man. But Jesus placed His hand on him and said, "Do not be afraid. I am the First and the Last. I am the Living One; I was dead, and now look, I am alive for ever and ever!" (Revelation 1:17–18 NIV).

He then gave John tremendous visions of the future, to encourage generations of believers in their sufferings—from John's day to the present.

Jesus is *with* us today, too, even in our most difficult experiences (Hebrews 13:8).

362. JOHN SEES GOD'S THRONE ROOM \\ REVELATION 4:1–11; 5:1–7

❯❯ After John received messages for the churches, he heard a voice say, "Come up here, and I will show you things which must take place after this" (Revelation 4:1 NKJV).

Immediately John saw a throne in heaven, and God sat on it. There was an emerald rainbow glowing around Him. Seven lamps were blazing, reflecting off a sea of crystal glass.

John saw fearsome cherubim, full of eyes. The first one was like a lion, the second like a calf, the third like a man, and the fourth like an eagle. They praised God continually. Sitting on thrones around God were twenty-four elders, clothed in white robes and wearing golden crowns.

John saw God holding a scroll. Then Jesus, "the Lion of the tribe of Judah" (Revelation 5:5 NKJV), opened the scroll. Jesus appeared as a lamb with seven horns and seven eyes.

This was the beginning of a series of fantastic, mysterious visions of heaven, which show us not only the future, but the glory and the power of God.

We can get lost trying to interpret some of Revelation's symbols. But this much we know: God is powerful, knows the future, and is in control.

» One of the greatest messages of the book of Revelation is that Jesus is coming back. It states in the opening chapter, "Behold, He is coming with clouds, and every eye will see Him, even they who pierced Him" (Revelation 1:7 NKJV).

Christians have different opinions about exactly when Jesus will return. But one thing is very clear: Jesus *is* coming back! And "they see the Son of Man coming on the clouds of heaven, with power and great glory." Then the angels "will gather his elect from the four winds, from one end of the heavens to the other" (Matthew 24:30–31 NIV).

Later, John had a vision of Jesus sitting on a cloud, holding a great sickle. He then reaped the harvest of the earth—all those who believe in Him (Revelation 14:14–16). Jesus then took the believers to heaven. As the Gospels say, He will "gather his wheat into the garner; but he will burn up the chaff with unquenchable fire" (Matthew 3:12 KJV).

We can be comforted knowing that despite the trials and tribulations we suffer here, Jesus cares deeply for us and will one day take us to heaven to be with Him.

364. THE BATTLE OF ARMAGEDDON
\\ REVELATION 14:18–20; 16:12–16; 19:11–21

» After the rapture, an angel will swing his sickle, harvest the clusters from the grapevine of the earth, and throw them into the winepress of the wrath of God—the Valley of Megiddo in Israel.

The judgments of God will be poured out on the wicked who persecuted His children—and will culminate in a conflict called the Battle of Armageddon. Here's how it will happen:

The Euphrates River will be dried up so that an army of 200 million men (Revelation 9:16), led by "the kings from the East," can cross over. "Then they gathered the kings together to the place that in Hebrew is called Armageddon" (Revelation 16:12, 16 NIV).

The battle will stretch south to the walls of Jerusalem, "and blood came out from the wine press, up to the horses' bridles, for a distance of two hundred miles" (Revelation 14:20 NASB).

Jesus and the armies of heaven will then decisively defeat these armies. After the Battle of Armageddon, the Lord will set up His kingdom on earth.

Fearful things are coming in the future, but Jesus will defeat all His enemies—and then there will be peace at last.

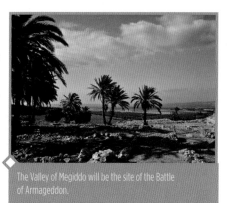
The Valley of Megiddo will be the site of the Battle of Armageddon.

365. HEAVEN COMES TO EARTH \\ REVELATION 20:1–9; 21:1–11, 22–27

» It will be wonderful after Jesus sets up His kingdom on the earth—but the unregenerate humans who survive the Battle of Armageddon won't be satisfied or live peaceably even with Jesus Christ ruling in justice and love over them.

At the end of the thousand-year period called the millennium, the nations of the world will rebel and attack Christ's capital, Jerusalem. God will then wipe out the entire earth with fire.

He will then remold the surface of the earth and create new heavens (atmosphere). There will be "no more sea" (Revelation 21:1 NJKV). This likely means that there will be plenty of land for people to live in (Revelation 21:1 NJKV).

Then the resplendent city of light, the New Jerusalem, will come down out of the heavenly dimension and will be on earth. God Himself lives in that city, so He will then be personally living on this beautiful new planet with us.

This will be the final, glorious ending to the long history of God's interaction with mankind. And it will be the beginning of His wonderful eternal plan!

God says, "I am making everything new!" (Revelation 21:5 NIV). And to think! He's doing all this for us!

SCRIPTURE INDEX